D1251528

HAUSA FOLK-LORE

II

Plate I

CHIEF, WIVES, AND RETINUE

[*Fro*

HAUSA FOLK-LORE
CUSTOMS, PROVERBS, ETC.

COLLECTED AND TRANSLITERATED WITH ENGLISH TRANSLATION AND NOTES

BY

R. SUTHERLAND RATTRAY

IN TWO VOLUMES: VOL. II

OXFORD
AT THE CLARENDON PRESS

Oxford University Press, Ely House, London W. 1

GLASGOW NEW YORK TORONTO MELBOURNE WELLINGTON
CAPE TOWN SALISBURY IBADAN NAIROBI LUSAKA ADDIS ABABA
BOMBAY CALCUTTA MADRAS KARACHI LAHORE DACCA
KUALA LUMPUR SINGAPORE HONG KONG TOKYO

FIRST PUBLISHED 1913

REPRINTED LITHOGRAPHICALLY IN GREAT BRITAIN
AT THE UNIVERSITY PRESS, OXFORD
BY VIVIAN RIDLER
PRINTER TO THE UNIVERSITY
1969

CONTENTS OF VOL. II

PART III

PAGE

ANIMAL STORIES:

22. The lion and the leopard 10
23. The water of Lādi and how the hyena was made to disgorge the maiden he had eaten 14
24. The lizard and the hyena, and how the latter came to leave the home and live in the bush 26
25. The he-goat and how he came to be a domestic animal, while the lion, the leopard, and the hyena, live in the bush 34
26. The beetle and how he got his thatching done for him . 58
27. The spider and the lion 74
28. The spider and the crows 88
29. The spider and the Dōdō 106
30. The spider, and the hippo, and the elephant . . . 124

PART IV

CUSTOMS AND ARTS:

31. Marriage, the bride, and naming of a child . . . 150
32. Marriage, the bridegroom, and telling the age a girl has her menses 170
33. Marriage of a widow or divorced person 174
34. The actual marriage ceremony 178
35. The birth of a child 186
36. The naming of a child 188
37. Circumcision 192
38. Removal of the clitoris of a girl 200
39. Burial customs, preparing the body (general) . . . 204

PAGE

40. Burial customs, the digging of the grave 214
41. Burial customs, washing of the corpse 218
42. Trading 222
43. Buying of 'cloths' 230

ARTS:

44. How 'Benin' figures are made 234
45. Tanning, and dyeing of leather 244
46. How 'kuloko' is made 248

PART V

PROVERBS. 133 Proverbs 251

PART VI

NOTES 281

ILLUSTRATIONS

PLATE I. Chief, wives, and retinue . . . . *Frontispiece*

PLATE II. Heads, showing *cire perdue* method of casting, front view . . . . *to face page* 240

PLATE III. Heads, showing *cire perdue* method of casting, side view . . . . . *to face page* 242

PART III

ANIMAL STORIES

WANAN BĀBI NE NA GĀTANAR NĀMUN DĀJI

THIS IS THE BEGINNING OF TALES ABOUT WILD ANIMALS

وَنْزِيَايِينْ نَفَدَتِزْ
تَامُنْحَاجْ

No. 22.

Wanan tātsunīar zāki che
da dāmisa.

[1] Gātanan, gātanan, ta je, ta kōmō. Zāki,
da shi, da dāmisa, su-ka-gamu wurin farauta. Zāki
[2] ya kashe nāma, ya aje, ya tafi shi-na-bidan wani.
Sai dāmisa ya tafō, ya ishe nāma, bābu kōwa.
Shi kūa yā ji yunwa, sai ya tsuguna, shi-na-chi. Sai
zāki ya tarda shi, shi-na-chi. Sai zāki ya kāma
shi. Da kōkūa, su-na-kōkūa, sai kūra
ta zō. Ta-na-wuchewa da hamzari. Ba ta che masu
kōmi ba. Ashe fakara ta-na bisa itāche, [3] ta-na
-ganin kūra, sai ta che, 'Ke kūra ki-na-gani
mainya su-na-fada, ki-na-wuchewa, ba ki raba su.'

This story is about a lion and a leopard. A story, a story. Let it go. Let it come. A lion and a leopard met (when) out hunting. The lion killed some game, put it away, (and) went off to look for some more. And the leopard came (and) found the meat, with no one near it. Now he felt hungry, so he squatted down and was eating (it). And the lion came across him as he was eating; and the lion seized him. They were struggling and wrestling, when a hyena came up. He was scuttling past, and did not say anything to them; but a bush fowl was up above on a tree, (and) she saw the hyena, (and) she said, 'You, hyena, you see the great ones quarrelling, (and) you pass on (and) do not separate them.'

وَقَّنْ تَامْلُوقِينْ ذَ ايكيذ

دَدَ آمِسْنْ

غَامَقَّنْ غَامَقَّنْ تِيمِكْنْ تْكُومُولْ ذَاكِي ::
دْشِمْ :: دْدَ امِسْنْ تْسَكْغُمْ : وُرْنْبَرُّوتْ : ذَاكِي :
يَكْشْبْنْ نَامْ : يَا آمِكْنْ يْتَّقِ : شْنَا بِمْقُونْ ::
تْسْ دَ امِسْنْ يَتَّبْجُوا : يَمِلْشْبْنْ نَامْ : بَابْ كُووَا ::
شِيكُوّ : يَامِ يُقْنْو : تْسْ يَمْظْغُمْ : شْنَاقِ : تْسْ
ذَاكِي : يَقْنَرْ دْشِمْ : شْنَاقِيهْ : تْسْ ذَاكِ : يْكَامَا
شِنْ دْكُوكُوّ شْنَا كُوكُوّ : تْسْ كُوّرَا ::
تْنَرُوا : تْنَا وُقْبُوا : دْقَمْرُوي بْتَمْبْقِسْ
كُوحِيبْ : ابْشْبْكَرَا : تْنَا بِمْسْ اِتَاقْ تْنَا
غْمْنْ كُوّرَا : تْسْ قْتْبْ : بْكُوّرَا : كْنَا غْنِمْ
تْقْبَا اسْنَا قْبَعْ : كِنَا وُقْبُوا : بَا يكْمْ قْبَاشْ

Sai ta [4] kyale, ta-na-[5] tafia tata. Sai zāki ya daka mata tsāwa, ya che, 'Ke, kūra, kōmō.' Sai ta kō-mō, ta che,

'Zāki bari, dāmisa bari, fadanku na mainya, wa shi ke shiga,
sai wāwa, sai mahaukachi?'

Sai zāki ya ji dādi, sai ya [6] kwāshi rawa, ya tafi da nīsa. Dāmisa shi kuma ya ji dādi, ya kwā-shi rawa, ya tafi da nīsa. Ba su kōmō maza ba. Sai [7] kūra ta gudu. Shi ke nan. [8] Kungurus kan kūsu.

But she paid no attention, (and) was going off her own way. But the lion roared out at her (and) said, 'You, hyena, come back.' So she returned and said, (sang)

'Lion, leave off! leopard, leave off!
Your fighting is the quarrelling of the mighty ones,
Who is going to mix himself up in it
Except a fool, except a madman?'

Now the lion felt tickled (by the tune) and danced off to it and went far away. The leopard too was pleased (with the song) (and) he commenced to dance, (and) went far away. They did not soon return. And the hyena ran off. That is all. Off with the rat's head.

سن تكبل ۞ قند تبيا قت ۞ لسن داك ۞ يجكم

مت طاوا ۞ يتبكورا ۞ كومو ۞ سن تكو

فو ۞ قتب

داك بجه دامسربر ۞ فدنك نهند ۞ واشكشغل

سن واوا ۞ سن معوكشم ۞

سن داك ۞ يج داد ۞ سن يكوا شروا ۞ يتف

دفيسن ۞ دامسر شيكم ۞ يج داد ۞ يكوا

ش ورا ۞ يتف دفيسن ۞ بسكو موا ۞ مدب

سن كورا تغد ۞ شيكن فنغرس

كرفوس ۞

No. 23.

Wanan tātsuniar ruan Lādi.
che.

Wani mahalbi [1] ya yi gida tsakar dāji. Ya haifi diansa bīū. Ya mutu, ya bar su, da mache da namiji. Su-na nan, kulum namiji shi tafi farauta, shi bar kanwa tasa a-gida, shi dauki kaia, shi [2] tōshe bākin kōfa. Idan ya tafō daka dāji sai shi che, 'Fātsimatan, Fātsimatan, Māgira, būde mani kōfa in shiga Māgira, būde mani kofa in shiga, in fita, gīwar gari.' Kulum idan ya fitō daka dāji, hakanan shi ke yi. Ashe kūra ta ji. Ranan ya tafi dāji. Sai [3] kūra ta zō, ta che, '[4] Fājimata, Fājimata, Majia, būje mani kōfa in shiga Mājia, būde mani kōfa in shiga, gīwa gai.' Sai yārinya ta che, 'Ai [5] nā san ki

---

This story is about the water of Ladi. A certain hunter made a hut in the middle of the bush. He begat two children. He died and left them, a girl and a boy. And so they lived; and always the man (when) he went to hunt (and) left his sister in the house, took thorns, (and) shut up the entrance to the door. If he returned from the bush then he said, 'Fatsimata, Fatsimata, Magira, open the door for me to enter, Magira. Open the door for me to enter, to come out, the elephant of the town.' Always if he came from the bush he used to do this. Now of a truth the hyena overheard (him). One day he went to the bush. Then the hyena came and said, 'Fajimata, Fajimata, Majia, open je door for me that I may enter, Majia. Open de door for me to enter, the elephant of je town.' But the girl said, 'No, I have known you,

وَقَنْ تَاصُو فِيرْ ∴ رُوَنْدَاجِ

ثْ ∴

وَنْمَعَلِيمْ ∴ بِيغِدَا ∴ تَطَكَرْ دَاجِ ∴ بِحَنْبِي ∴ دِيَفُسْ

بِيُو ∴ يَفَنْ بِيَبَرْسَ ∴ كَمَثْ دَ نِيمِجِ ∴ اَسَلَ فَمْ ∴ كُلُمْ

نِمِجِ ∴ اِشْتُفِ جَرْوَتْ ∴ اِشْبَرْ فَنُوا اشْمَسْ اَغِدَا ∴

يِنْدَوْكِ عَتِي ∴ شُنْوْشِي بَاكُنْكُوفَ ∴ اِدَنْ ∴ بِيَا

تَبُوَا ∴ دَكَدَاجِ ∴ تَسَنْ شَبْ ∴ فَاطِمَةَ ∴ فَاطِمَةَ

مَاغِمَرَا ∴ بُودُ نَمَنْ كُوفَ ∴ اِنْشِغَوْ مَاغِمَرَا ∴

بُودُ نَمَنْ كُوفَ اِنْشِغَوْ ∴ اِنْجِنَا غِيُوزَغِمِي

كُلُمْ ∴ اِدَنْ يِدَا بِثُوَا ∴ دَكَدَاجِ ∴ تَكَنْ شَبْكَمِي

اَبْشِي عُوَرَ اقَاجِ ∴ وَقَنْ بِتَقِ دَاجِ ∴ تَسَنْ كُوَرَا

تَغُو ∴ تَبْ فَاطِمَةَ فَاطِمَةَ ∴ مَاغِمَيَا ∴ بُودُ بِجِمَنْ

كُوفَ اِنْشِغَلِي ∴ مَاغِمَيَا ∴ بُودُ نَمَنْ كُوفَ اِنْشِغَلِي

غِمِيُو غِمِيَّ ∴ تَسَنْ بِيَدَا وَقُمْ تَبْ ∴ اَغْمَ اَسَنْكِ ∴

ke che kūra,' Sai kūra ta kōma, ta tafi
wurin zāki, ta karbō māgani wurin zāki,
na [6] yāmin bāki, ta zō, ta che, 'Fātsimatan, Fā-
-tsimatan, Māgira, būde mani kōfa in shiga
Māgira, būde mani kōfa in shiga, in fita,
gīwar gari.'
Sai yārinya ta būde kōfa, sai kūra
ta kāme ta, ta hadie. Sai wan yārinya
ya kōmō daka dāji, ya che,
'Fātsimatan, Fātsimatan, Māgira, būde mani kōfa
Māgira, būde mani kōfa in shiga, in fita,
gīwar gari.'
Sai ya ji shirū; ya kāra, bai ji ta amsa ba,

---

you are the hyena.' Then the hyena went off, (and) went to the lion. She received from the lion medicine for curing a lisp, and came back, (and) said, 'Fatsimata, Fatsimata, Magira, open the door that I may enter, Magira, open the door that I may enter, that I may come out, the elephant of the town.' So the maiden opened the door, and the hyena seized her, (and) swallowed her. And the elder brother of the girl returned from the bush and said, 'Fatsimata, Fatsimata, Magira, open the door for me, Magira, open the door for me to enter, to come out, the elephant of the town.' Then he was silent; he repeated it again; he did not hear her answer,

بِسْ كُورَا : آسِنْ كُورَا : تَكُومَ : قَتِّي ءِ

وُرِفْدَاكِ : تَكَمْ بُوَامَا غَنِمْ : وُرِفْدَاكِ :

فَيَا مِنْ بَاكِمْ : تَمْدُورِ : تَشْ فَاطِمَةَ بَا

طِمَةَ مَاغِمْرَا : بُوبْ مَحَمْشْ كُوفْ إِنْشَنْكَشْ

مَاغِمْرَا : بُوبْ مَحَمْ كُوفْ : إِنْشِنْكِي إِنْ بِنَا

غِيُوزْغَمِي

سِنْ يِيَارِفِّي : تَبُوبْ كُوفْ : آسِنْ كُورَا :

تَكَابِسْتَ : تَمْحِي بِيكِ : آسِنْ أَفِيَارِفِي :

يَكُومُوَا : دِكَدَامِ : يِيشْ

فَاطِمَةَ فَاطِمَةَ مَاغِمْرَا : بُوبْ مَحَمْ كُوفْ

مَاغِمْرَا : بُوبْ مَحَمْ كُوفْ : إِنْشِنْكِي إِنْ بِنَا

غِيُوزْغَمِي

سِنْ يِجْ شِرْوَا : يَكَادِ : بِيمِجْ تَدَا أَمْسَابْ

har sau uku, sai ya yi kōkari, ya būde kōfa.
Ya shiga, bai gani yārinya ba. Sai ya fita, ya dauki
gōransa, shi-na-tafia har ya kai bākin rāmen
kūra, ya gani [7] alāgidigūa dā zanen yārinya,
shi-na-kwanche bākin rāme. Sai ya che, 'Abin nan kūra
ta yi shi.' Sai ya wuche. Akwai wani tabki da nā-
-mun dāji duka nan [8] su-ke-shan rua. Sai ya je nan, bābu
wani rua kuma, ya dauki gōransa na māgani,
ya kwālfe rua nan duka. Ya je, ya hau bisa itāche,
shi-na-zamne. Sai garken gīwa ya zō, [9] zaa su
shan rua. Sai ya che, 'Ke giwa ina zaa ki?' Ta che,
'Zaa ni ruan Lādi.' Sai ya che, 'Ruan Lādi [10] yā kafe.

---

till (he repeated the words) three times, then he tried hard (and) opened the door. He entered, he did not see the maiden. Then he came out, lifted his calabash, and travelled until he reached the mouth of the hyena's den. He saw the girl's waist-beads and cloth lying at the mouth of the hole. And he said, 'This thing the hyena did,' and he passed on. Now there was a certain pool where all the wild animals of the place were wont to drink water. And he went there, there was no other water but this. He lifted up his magic calabash and scooped up all the water there, (and) went and climbed up a tree and was sitting there. Then a herd of elephants came, (and) were going to drink the water, when he said (to one), 'You there, elephant, where are you going to?' She replied, 'I am going to the water of Ladi.' And he said, 'The water of Ladi has dried up.

كَمَرْ لَسُوْاُكَ ∴ سَنْ يَنْ كُوكَمِي ∴ يَجُوبَ سِي كُوقِ

يَمَّوْكِ ∴ اسَنْ يَجِمْتَ ∴ رِفْبَابِ يَدْ بِنْغَنِمْ ∴ يَشْغَ

غُورَفْسَنْ شِنَا قَبِوْنَ ∴ حَمْ بَكَنْ ∴ بَا كِمْرَا أَمَّنْ ∴

كُورَا ∴ يَغَنِمْ الَاغِدِ غُوَا ∴ دَمْ كَبُنْ يَدْ رِفْسَ ∴

شِنَا كُوفُبْ ∴ بَا كِنْمَرَا امُوَ ∴ اسَنْ يَبَبْ آمِنَّسْ ∴ مْ كُورَا

قَيِّمِشْ ∴ سَنْ يَوْفُبْ ∴ آكُومْرْ ∴ وَفِتَنْبِكِ ∴ دَمْ نَمَ

مُرْ دَامِ دُكَ ∴ قَنَّرْ سُكَ شَفْرَا ∴ اسَنْ يَجِيَ قَنَّرْ ∴ مَدَابَ

وَفِمْرَا اغُمَّ ∴ يَدَّوْكِ ∴ غُورَفْسَنْ فَمَا غَفِمْ ∴

يَكُو لِبِجِنْ ∴ وُوَقَنَّمْ دُكَ ∴ يَجِيَ ∴ يَمُوْ بِسَرْ اِقَّتَابْ ∴

فِنَا دَمْفِبُنْ ∴ اسَنْ غَمْ بَكُمْ ∴ غَيِمُوَا ∴ يَدُرَا أدَاسُ

شُنْمُرَوَا ∴ اسَنْ يَجِبْ ∴ بَكِيِوَا ∴ اِقَمَادَاكِ ∴ قَبَ

دَأنُرْوَنْفِلَادِ ∴ اسَنْ يَجِبْ ∴ زَوْقِلَادِ ∴ يَدَا كَجِنْ ∴

11 Daa kin ba ni ma-chi kanwana, daa nā ba ki ruan Lādi.'
Sai gīwa ta yi amai chīawa da ta chi, 'Hab! kā gā abinda
na chi, hab! abin chiki sai tunbi.' Sai gīwa
ta wuche, ta je, ta kwanta, ta na hāki.
Garken bauna ya tafō, sai yārō ya che,
'Ke bauna ina zaa ki?' Ta che, 'Zaa ni ruan Lādi.' Ya che,
'Ruan Lādi yā kafē, daa kin ba ni ma-chi kanwana, daa nā ba
ki ruan Lādi.' Sai bauna ta che, 'Hab! kā gā abinda
na chi, abin chiki sai tunbi.' Kōwane garken
nāmun dāji ya zō, hakanan shi ke tanbaya su, su
kuma hakanan su ke amsa masa, saanan
su wuche, su je bākin rāfi, su kwanta, su-na-
-hāki, har nāmun dāji duka su-ka-wuche. Sauran

When you have given up to me the one who ate my sister, then I have given you back the water of Ladi.' So the elephant brought up the grass she had eaten, saying, 'Hab! you have seen what I ate, what is inside me now is only my stomach.' And the elephant passed on and went, (and) lay down, she was panting. A herd of bush-cows came up, and the boy said (to one), 'You, bush-cow, where are you going?' And she said, 'I am going to the water of Ladi.' He said, 'The water of Ladi has dried. When you have given me him who has eaten my sister, then I have given you the water of Ladi.' Then the bush-cow said, 'Hab! you have seen what I ate, what is inside is only my stomach.' Whatever herd of wild animals came it was so; he used to ask them, (and) they too made answer so, and then passed on, (and) went to the edge of the pool, and lay down (and) were panting, until all the wild animals in the bush had passed. There remained

دأكنبار : ميثم فنوار : دأمّا ملك : روّفتادم ::

سن غيبوا : متّو أمن شيبار ومتثم : قبنكاغم دابنم

متثم : قبا أمنشك : اسن قتنبم : اسن غيبوا ::

تمو ثبن : تجن تكوفت : قنا قاداكم ::

غمر بجن بوقمن : يتّفوا : سن ميدار : يمث

بجبوقمن : إقادا أك : متث دأر روفتادم : يمث

روفتادم : يا تجن : دأكنبار : متثفنوار : دأماما

ك روفتادم : سن بوقمن متث قبن كاغم ابنم

متثم : أمنشك : سن قتنبم : كوفن غمر كس

قا منداام : يخوا : قكمن : لشبكتنبين : سو

كتم : قكمن : لسبكما أفسا قمش : سغمن

سوثب : سجن باكمر أبم : لسكونتا : لسنا

قداكم : قمر قا مندام دك : سكوبن : سوون

garken kūra. Sai su-ka-tafō, kūra wada ta chi kanwa tasa ta-na-gaba, ta-na-hamzari, ta je, ta sha rua. Sai ya che, 'Ke kūra ina zaa ki?' Ta che, 'Zaa ni yuan Yādi.' Ya che, 'Ruan Lādi yā kafē, daa kin ba ni ma chi kanwata daa nā ba ki ruan Lādi.' Shirū! har sau uku, ba ta tanka ba. Sai zāki ya ji haushi, sai ya zaabura, ya kāma ta, ya tsāga ta bīū, sai yārinya ta fitō. Sai zāki ya che, 'Gā kanwarka.' Shi kua ya [12] bulbule masu rua, dōmin da ya gani kanwa tasa da rai. Sai nāmun dāji su-ka-rika [13] ribibi shan rua, mainya mainya su ka tākē kankanāna, su-ka-mutu dayawa. Sai yā- -rō ya sabkō daka bisa, da su-ka-wātse;

---

the house of the hyena. Then they came up; the hyena which had eaten his sister was in front; she was in great haste to come (and) drink water. And he said, 'You, hyena, where are you going?' And she said, 'I am going to the yater of Yadi.' He said, 'The water of Ladi is dried up. If you have given me the one who ate my sister then I have given you the water of Ladi.' Silence reigned until (he had repeated it) three times. She did not answer. But the lion got angry, and he sprang, (and) caught her, (and) tore her in two, and the maiden came forth. And the lion said, 'Behold your sister.' So he (the hunter) poured out the water for them because he had found his sister alive. Thereupon the wild beasts began to rush to the water to drink, the great ones trampled on the little ones, many died. And the boy got down from up above when they had dispersed;

عمر بجن كوورا ∴ اسن سكتبوا ∴ كوورا ∴ وع متي

فنوا قسن تعنا غب ∴ قنا قعدرى ∴ تجو تشا

زوا ∴ اسن يبث ∴ بكوورا ∴ اقا دا اكي ∴ تبث دا ان

يومبادي ∴ يبث زو فلادي يا كبو ∴ دا اكنبان ∴ مشم

فنوات ∴ دا اقا يا اكي رنو ملادي ∴ شرو ∴ قرسو

أك ∴ بث تنكاب ∴ اسن دا اكي يجم موشم

اسن يرابر ∴ يكا قات ∴ يطا غما ت ميبو ∴ اسن

يا دو فم تو يتوا ∴ اسن دا اكي يبث ∴ غما فنو زك ∴

شيكو ∴ يبلم قسر روا ∴ دو من م يغنم ∴ فنوا يملبلبر

تسن ∴ دو رن ∴ اسن نا منداجي ∴ سكرك ∴ زوبيبي ∴

شنروا ∴ منسر منن ∴ سكتا بكسن ∴

فنفنار ∴ سكحث ∴ دا يبو ∴ اسن يا

زوا ∴ متسنكو ∴ دكبسن دسكوابطي

ya yi [14] ta kwāsa nāma, har ya gaji. Ya tafi wani gari ya yi [15] gayā. Su ma su-ka-kwāche nāma, har su-ka-bar shi nan. Shi ke nan. [16] Kungurus kan kūsu.

---

he collected meat, till he was weary. He went to another town and summoned help. They too collected meat till they even left some there (there was so much). That is it. Off with the rat's head.

تيو تكواس قام ∴ قريغي ∴ ميتف ونغي ∴

بيو غيبا ∴ سومد سككواش قام ∴ قر ∴

سكبرش قرن ∴ شيبعشن ∴ فنغرسن ∴

كرفوسن ∴

No. 24.

Wanan tātsunīar damō che.

[1] Gātanan, gātanan, ta je, ta kōmō. [2] Maatar [3] kūra [4] ta tafi wurin dība wuta, zaa ta yi dafūa. Sai ta taras ana-kōkūa, kōwa ya yi kāye, sai shi dauki wanda ya kayas, shi je, shi chi. Sai maatar kūra ta che, gada ta zō su yi kōkūa. Sai gada ta fitō, su-ka-kāma kōkūa, sai kūra ta kāda gada, sai ta dunkule, ta damre, ta kai gida. Sai mijinta ya che, 'Ina ki-ka-sāmu?' Ta che, '[5] Nā je nā taras ana-wāsan kōkūa ne, kōwa ya kayas shi dauki wanda ya kayas, shi chi, sai ni kūa na che shi zō mu yi kōkūa, sai ya fitō mu-ka-yi kōkūa da shi. Na [6] kāshe shi.

This is a story about a lizard. A story, a story. Let it go. Let it come. The wife of the hyena went to a place for getting fire, in order to cook, and she came across people who were wrestling; whoever won a fall took up him whom he had thrown (and) came (and) ate him. And the wife of the hyena said the antelope was to come forward and they would wrestle. So one came out and they wrestled, and the hyena threw the antelope, and she rolled him up, (and) tied him, (and) brought him home. And her husband said, 'Where did you get (him)?' She said, 'I have gone and found people playing at wrestling; whoever threw (another) was to lift up the one thrown down and eat him. So I too said he was to come forward and we should wrestle, and he came out and we (I) wrestled with him. I threw him.

ونر تا طو نيير د موف

غما تنن : غما تنن تجي تكو موا : ما تنز كورا :

تنتفي : ورندي بب : وتن : د امن : د فوا : تسن :

تنرسن أما كوكوا : كورا : يي كدا يمن : تسن

شد ورك : ورفد يكا يسن شجي شث : اسر ما تم

كورا : فنث غمدا : فقو : سر كوكوا : تسن

غمدا تبفتوا : سككام : كوكوا : سن كورا

تكاد غما : اسن قد مكلبن تدمر كن تكس

غدا : سر مجنت : يث إمد ككسا موا :

فنث مديكن : مد ترسن أمدوا اسر كوكوابك :

كورا : يكا يسن : شد ورك : ورفد يكا يسن

شث : سر نيكو : مث شدوا : مر كوكوا :

سر يفتوا : مكر كوكوا : دشم : نكا بشش

Sai su-ka-che in dauki, sai na dauki, na zō da shi.'
Sai mijinta ya che, 'Ba ni kadan.' Ta ba shi. Sai ya che, 'Kāra mar
Ta kāra masa, ya chainye. Da ya ji dādi, sai ya che,
'Dauki duka ki ba ni in chainye, idan [7] nā je, nī ma
naa kayar naa kāwō mu chi.' Da ya gani kamar zaa ta kia,
sai ya che, 'Ba ni, ke ma da ki ke mache, kin kayar,
bale ni namiji!' Sai ta dauki duka, ta ba shi, ya chi.
Sai ya tāshi, ya tuma, ya buga katara, ya che, 'Idan nā
je, naa kāshe su, su duka, in kāwō
mu chi.' Sai ya tafi. Maatar tasa ta-na-yi masa
[8] adaa, ta-na-che, 'Ala shi sa shi kāshe su duka.'
Shi kūa da zuansa, sai ya gani damō
shi na zamne bisa itāche, sai ya che,

And they told me to take him away. And I lifted him up (and) broug
him (here).' And her husband said, 'Give me a small piece.' She ga
him. And he said, 'Give me some more.' She gave him some mo
he ate it up. When he found it good then he said, 'Lift it all and gi
me to eat. When I have gone (there) I shall easily throw some o
and bring back and we shall eat.' When he saw she was apparent
going to refuse then he said, 'Give me. As for you who are a woma
you have thrown (some one); how much more I who am a man!' S
she took all and gave him. He ate. Then he rose up, jumped and h
(his) thigh, (and) he said, 'When I have come (to the place) I sh
throw them, all of them, (and) bring (and) we shall eat.' So he set o
His wife wished him good luck. She said, 'May Allah cause him
throw them all.' As for him, on his arrival, he saw a lizard sitti
on a tree; and he said,

'Kai [9] sabkō, mu yi da kai.' Sai aka-che, 'Kai bākō ne, ba ka sani ba ne, ai sarkin gari ke nan?' Sai kūra ya che, 'Shi sabko naa yi da shi.' Aka-che, 'Ke kūra kar ki rūdi kainke.' Ya che, 'Shi dai, shi sabkō, naa yi da shi.' Yau damō ya sabkō, Su-ka-kāma kōkūa. Sai damō ya dauki wutsīa tasa, ya nade kafāfun kūrē, sai ya kāshe shi. Sai ana-shiri, a-damre kūrē, sai ya zaabura, ya tāshi, ya shēka, su-ka-bi shi, zaa su kāma shi. Ya tserē, ya je, ya tarda maatārsa, tā fūra wuta, ta-na-jiran nāma. Sai ya zamna. Shi na fuchi, jikinsa na-makarkata. Sai ta che, 'Me ya fāru?' Sai ya che, 'Nā je, nā gamu

---

'You get down. Let us try conclusions with you.' And they (the people assembled there) said, 'You are evidently a stranger. Do not you know that is the chief of the town?' But the hyena said, 'Let him come down; I would (wrestle) with him.' They said, 'You, hyena, do not deceive yourself.' He said, 'As for him, let him come down, I intend to wrestle with him.' So the lizard descended. They wrestled. But the lizard lifted his tail, and twined (it) round the hyena's legs, and threw him. And they were preparing to tie up the hyena, but he sprang (and) got up (and) ran off. They followed him to catch him. He escaped, and went and came across his wife, she has kindled a fire; she was waiting for meat. And he sat down. He was panting; his body was quivering. And she (his wife) said, 'What is the matter?' And he said, 'I have gone (and) closed

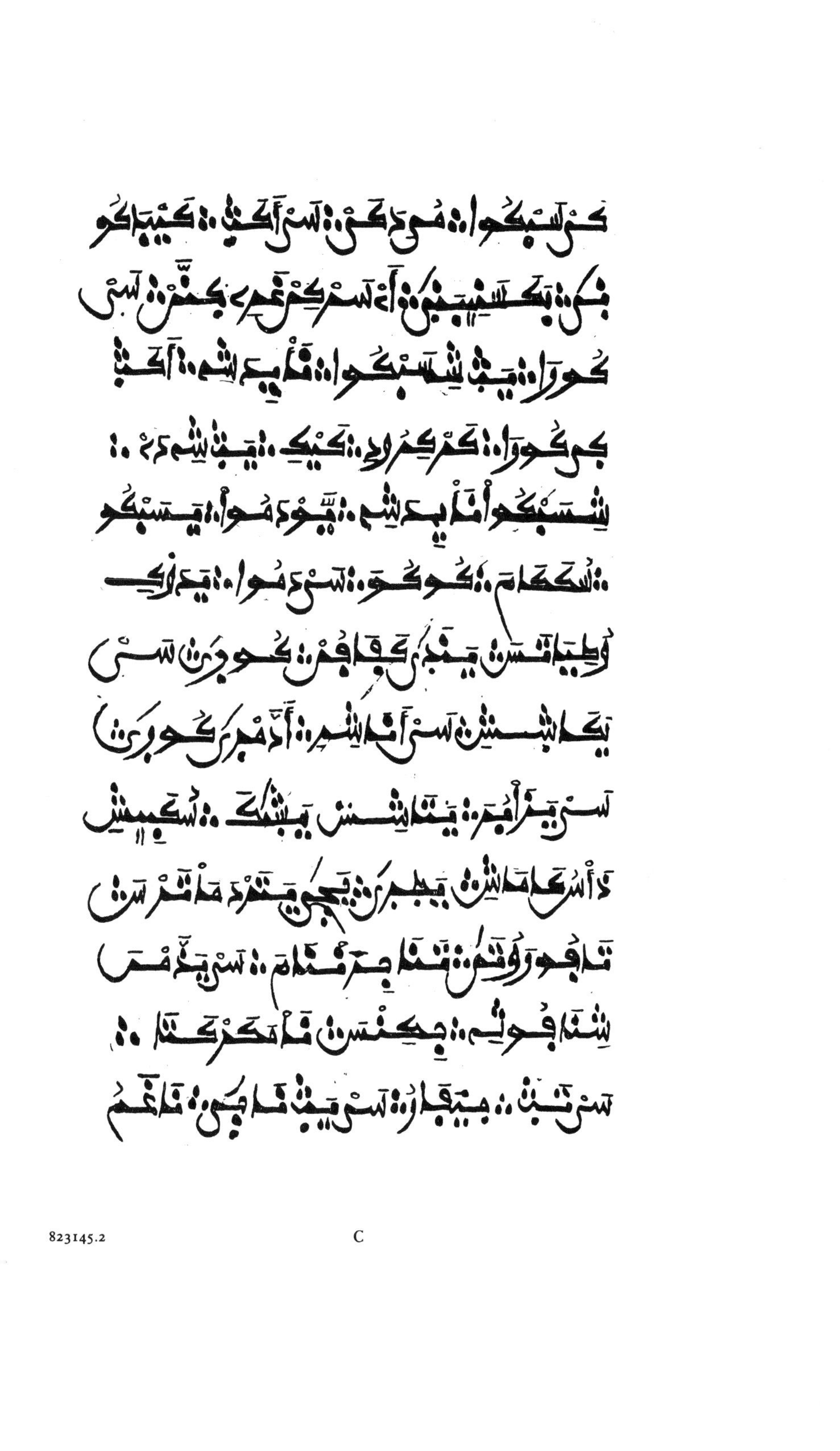

da wani kātō. Ya kāshe ni. Zaa su yanka ni, na [10] gudānō.' Sai maata ta bar fūra wuta kuma, su-na-zamne. Aka-jima sai gwamki ya zō. [11] Maatar ta che, 'Wanan ya kāshe ka?' Ya che, 'Aa wanan ba shi iya kāshe ni.' Aka-jima sai bauna ta zō, sai ta che, 'Wanan ya kāshe ka?' Sai ya che, 'Kai, wanan ba shi iya kāshe ni.' Sai zāki ya zō, shi-na--wuchewa. Ta che, 'Wanan ya kāshe ka?' Sai ya che, 'Kai, ba shi ba Aka-jima sai kadangare ya zō, shi na bin jikin dāki kar! kar! Sai ya che, 'Tō gā shi nan.' Sai ya tāshi, ya shēka, maatarsa ta bi shi. Mafāri ke nan, da wuri kūra gida shi ke. Kadangare ya kōre shi. Ya shiga dāji. Shi ke nan. [12] Kungurus kan kūsu.

---

with a certain huge creature. He threw me down. When they w about to cut (my throat), I ran here.' Thereupon the wife left off blowi the fire again. They are sitting there. So after a short time a hartebe came along. The wife said, 'Was that the one who threw you?' said, 'No, that could not throw me.' In a little while a bush-cow ca along, and she said, 'Did this one not throw you?' And he said, 'Tut! t thing could not throw me.' And a lion came along; he is passing She said, 'Did this one throw you?' And he said, 'Tut! it was he.' A little later a lizard came along; he was following along the wall the hut, scuttling. And he said, 'Yes, there he is.' And he got up (and) r off; his wife followed him. That was in the beginning. Long ago hyena was in the home, the lizard drove him out. He entered the bu That is it. Off with the rat's head.

دارنكا ثوا :: يكا بشمن :: دأسن ينكا ني :: قغدا نو

تسن ما قنا :: قتبر فوور قاكم :: سنا د قبن :: أكجم ::

تسن غمكم :: يذوا :: ما قتر قب :: وقر بكا بشك ::

يب :: عاعم :: وقر با بشعن كا بشر :: اكجم :: تسن

بحو قن :: تغوا :: تسن قب رقن :: بكا بشك :: تسن يب

بكن وقن :: با بشعن كا بشسن :: تسن داك يذوا :: بشما

وبجوا :: تب وقر بكا بشك :: تسن بكن با بشببن =

أكجم :: تسن كد قغبرن يذوا :: بشا بم وكن :: داك

بكم كم :: تسن يب ثوغا بشقن :: تسن قتا بين :: يبنبك

ما قترسن تيبيشن مقاري :: بكف

دور كووا :: غدا بشكم ::

كدن قغبرن :: بكو بكش

بشغ داج :: بشكبش

فنقغرسن :: عمن

قوسن ::

No. 25.

Wanan tātsunīar bunsurū che.

[1] Gātanan, gātanan. Bunsurū [2] ya je dāji, ya nemi
sābō wuri, ya nōmē, zaa shi yin sābō gida.
Da ya nōmē, sai ya kōmō gida. Gari ya wāye,
ya je shi sa gūtsun dāki. Sai ya taras wani
ya yi nōma kusa da shi, bai san kōwānene ba,
sai ya [3] kyale. Ya aza gūtsun dāki, ya tafō gida.
Da gari ya wāye, ya kōma, ya taras nōman nan
na kusa da shi, anyi gini, wani kuma ya yi nōma
kusa da wanchan. Ashe nafārin [4] kūra ne,
na bāyan kua dāmisa ne. Yau, ya yi gini, ya kōma
gida. Gari ya wāye, sai ya kōma wurin gini.
Ya taras wani ya yi nōma, ya kāra kusa da wadanchan.

This is a story about the he-goat. A story, a story. The he-goat went to the bush; he sought a new place to clear (as) he was about to make a new home. When he had cleared (a place) then he returned home. At dawn he went to put in the posts for his house. Then he found that some one had cleared the ground near him; he did not know whom, but he paid no attention. He set up the foundations of the house and went home. At dawn he returned, and found that a clearing was (now) near his, and (foundations) had been dug (in readiness to put in sticks for a house); and moreover some one else had cleared close to that again. Of a truth, the first (clearing) was the hyena's; the next again was the leopard's. And he dug and returned home. At dawn then he returned to the place where he was digging. He found some one else had cleared still nearer the other (clearings).

وَفَّنْ تَنَا طُو فِيَّنْ ∴ بُنْسَمُ وُبْ

غَدَ مَثَّنْ ∴ غَدَ مَثَّنْ بُنْسَمُ وَا ∴ يَجُّ وَعَ ام ∴ يَنِم

تَسَا مُبُو وُرِ ∴ يَنُو مِّكَ ∴ دَ أَشِيِّرْ تَسَا مُبُو غِدَا ∴

دَ مِينُو بِّي ∴ تَسْ يَكُو مُوَا غِدَا ∴ غَمِرِ يَبَوا اِيِّكِ

∴ يَا جِكُ ∴ لِنْسَ غُو طُرْ ∴ دَ اكِ ∴ تَسْ مِيَتَمْ سَنْ ∴ وُو

يَا اِيِّنُو مَدَ ∴ كُسَدِ لِشِم ∴ بِمِسَنْ كُو وَابُنْبَ

∴ تَسْ يَكْبُو ∴ يَا آدُ غُو طُرْ ∴ دَ اكِ ∴ مِيتَفَّبُو اُغِدَا

∴ دَ غَمِرِ يَبَوا اِيِّكِ ∴ يَكُومُ ∴ مِيَتَمْ سَنْ ∴ فُو مَشَّنْ ∴

تَكُسَرِ دَشِمِ ∴ أَنْمِ غَمِرْ ∴ وَ فِكُمَ يَا اِرِّ فُو مَدَ

كُسَنْ ∴ دَ وَفْشَنْ ∴ أَشِّ مَجَارِ ∴ كُو رَاايِّكَ ∴

فَبَا اِيَّنْ كُو وَّ ∴ دَ اِمْسَا بُكَ ∴ يَوُ بِّي غِمِرْ ∴ يَكُومَ

غِدَا ∴ غَمِرِ يَبَوا اِيِّكِ ∴ تَسْ يَكُومَ ∴ وُو نِغِمِرْ ∴

يَتَمْ سَنْ ∴ وَ فَيَا اِرِّ فُو مَ ∴ يَكَا وَا ∴ كُسَدِ وَ دَ فَشَنْ

Sai ya kyale, ya yi gininsa ya tafi gida. Da gari ya wā-
-ye, sai ya kōma, ya taras su duka sun yi gini, sai
shi kuma ya karkare gini, ya kōma gida, ya nemō
chiāwa, zaa shi baibaya. Sai ya taras, su ma sun kā-
-re nāsu gini. Sai ya baibaiye, ya kōma gida. Ranan
ya yi shiri, zaa shi kōmo sābo gidansa, ashe su ma,
sun gama nāsu aiki, ranan zaa su kōmāwa. Shi kūa,
bai san kō suwānene ba. Bunsurū ya kwāche
dīansa, da [5] maatarsa, da tarkachensa, ya kai [6] gidan.
Shi-na-zamne. Sai kūra ta zō, da kāyanta, da tar-
-kachenta, ta shiga dākinta. Aka-jima, sai dāmisa
ya zō, shi kuma da dīansa, da maatarsa, da tarkachensa.

But he said nothing, did his building (and) went home. At dawn then he returned and found that all have built (houses); and he too finished building, (and) returned home, and looked for grass to thatch. And he found that they too have completed their building. So he thatched (his roof) and went home. On the day he made ready to go to his new home, truly they too have completed their work, and on that day were about to come. As for him, he had not the least idea who they were. The he-goat carried off his children and wives and furniture, and brought them to the home. He was living (there). And the hyena came with his belongings, and household goods, (and) entered the house. Soon after the leopard came, he too had his children, and wife, and household goods.

لس يكجن ∴ ييي غمننسن يتجم غدا ∴ دغمر يجوا

پم ∴ لس يكوتم ∴ يتمرسن ∴ سودك ∴ سني غمر ∴ لسي

شبيكم ∴ يكم كجري غمن يكوتم ∴ غدا ∴ يبفوا ∴

شيا ∴ دا أشن ببيبن ∴ لسي يتمرن ∴ سوهكي ∴ سنكا

وري ∴ قداس غمن ∴ لس ييبنبين ∴ يكوتم غدا ∴ رقم ∴

يادي شمر ∴ دا أشي كوتم ∴ لسا بوغد فسن ∴ أشي سوما

سنكم ∴ قداسن ∴ أيكي رقمر دا اس كومدا ∴ شيكو ∴

بملسن كوسوا فنبب ∴ بفسروا ∴ يا كوا شت

ديفسن ∴ دما تمرسن ∴ دتمر كبتلسن يكن غدن ∴

شدا دمبن ∴ لسر كورا ∴ تدوا ∴ دكايفت ∴ دتمر

كبثت ∴ تشغ ∴ داكفت ∴ أكجم ∴ لسر دا امس

يغوا ∴ شبكم ∴ دديفسن ∴ دما تمرسن ∴ دتمر كبثس

Sai aka-jima zāki ya zō. Sai kūra ya che, 'Ina lālā-
-tachen nan ya fitō?' Sai zāki bai tanka ba. Da gari
ya wāye, sai kūra ya che, 'Mu chainye lālātache nan.'
Sai zāki ya che, 'Kai ka na gani mutun, ba ka san
wurinda ya fitō ba, ka che, mu chainye shi, [7] kā sani,
kō idan kā je garin kāmunsa, shi rinjā-
-ye ka?' Sai kūra ya che, 'Na san wada zaa mu yi
mu chi shi.' Sai zāki ya che. 'Kāka zaa mu yi mu chi shi?'
Kūra ya che, 'Zāki kirāwō shi, ka che masa
wurin nan, da mu-ka-zamna, sābō wuri ne,
ba azama banza. Kōwa shi tafi dāji,
shi sāmu nāman dāji, [8] mu giyāra wuri,
dōmin mu zamna lāfia. Idan ya che, Tō,

And soon after the lion came. And the hyena said, 'where did that worthless fellow come from (meaning the he-goat)?' But the lion did not answer him. Next morning the hyena said, 'Let us eat this worthless person.' But the lion said, 'You, you are seeing a man (for the first time), you do not know whence he came, and you say, Let us eat him up. Have you known if you have come to catch him he might get the better of you?' But the hyena said, 'I have known what I am going to do that we may eat him.' And the lion said, 'What are we going to do that we may eat him?' The hyena said, 'Lion, call him here. Say to him, The place where we live is a new place, people do not stay here without doing something. Let each go to the bush and find a wild animal, that we may propitiate the spot, (and) live in health. If he says, It is well,

سن أكيم ؞ دراك ؞ يخراه سن كوراه ؞ يب إمد الا ا
مبشن ؞ ميبيقوا ؞ سن دراك ؞ ميتفكاب ؞ دعمر
يوابيمن ؞ سن كوراييب ؞ متفبكن ؞ لالا أمبشن
سن داكم ميب ؞ كن فكنا غنم ؞ مشن ؞ بحكسن
ورفد ميقوب ؞ كحب متفيشن كدا سنم ؞
كوادرن كدابن ؞ غمرنكا مفسن شرفجد
بك ؞ سن كوراه ؞ ميب فدا سن ؞ وردا أمتن
يبب ميبشن سن داكم ؞ كداك ؞ دا أمن ؞ مبشن
كوراه ؞ يب داك ؞ كرا ورشن عبفسن ؞
ورفنن ؞ د مكع مرش سدا بوه ؞ وريبنى
بدا غد ندا ؞ بندا ؞ كوراه ؞ شنقم داجم ؞
شسدا موا ؞ قدا مندا اجم ؞ مغيا ؞ ورى ؞
دو مرن ؞ مخ مرن ؞ لاقمن ؞ إدرن ؞ يب مثو ؞

saanan kai zāki ka tafi, ka sāmū, saanan dāmissa shi tafi, shi sāmū, saanan ni kuma in tafi, in sāmū. Saanan mu che, shi kuma shi tafi dāji, shi sāmū. Idan bai sāmū ba, mu kāma shi, mu chainye.' Sai zāki ya che, 'Tō. Ku kirāwō shi.' Aka-kirāwō bunsurū. Zāki ya che, 'Dan uwa lāfia, mu-ka-kirāwō ka, mu-na-sō mu giyāra wurin zama nan nāmu, kā san sābo wuri, idan bābu giyāra, ba ajin dādin zama.' Bunsurū ya che, 'Gaskīa ne.' Sai zāki ya che, 'Gōbe ni ke fāra zūa, idan nā kōmō dāmisa shi tafi, idan yā kōmō kūra

---

then do you, lion, go and find (some game); then the leopard goes and gets some; then I too go and get some. Then we say, he too must go to the bush and get. If he does not get any, we seize him, (and) devour him.' And the lion said, 'It is well. Call him to us.' The he-goat was called. The lion said, 'Brother, greetings; we called you. We are wishing to propitiate this place. We have come to settle. You have known it is a new place; if we do not propitiate it, it will not be a good place to reside.' And the he-goat said, 'That is true.' (And) the lion said, 'To-morrow I am the first to go; when I have returned the leopard goes; when he has come back the hyena

سَعَفَّنْ ∴ كَسَامُوا ∴ كَتِي ∴ دَالِكِ مُهَنْ سَعَفَّنْ

دَامِسَنْ شِتَجِ ∴ شِسَامُوا ∴ سَعَفَّنْ زَيْكَمَّ

إِنَتِي ∴ إِنْسَامُوا ∴ سَعَفَّنْ مُبْ شِيكَمَّ

شِتَفِ دَاجِ ∴ شِسَامُوا ∴ إِدَّرْ ∴ مَمْ سَامُوبَ ∴

مُكَامَاشْ ∴ مُتَشِيمْ ∴ سَرْدَاكِ ∴ يَبْ ∴ شُو

كُكَمْ اوُوشْ ∴ أَكِكَمْ اوُرْ ∴ بُفْسُمْرُ ∴ دَاكِ

∴ يَبْ ∴ مُغْوَا ∴ لَابِجَ مُكَكَمْ اوُرْكِ ∴ مُنَا

سُوا ∴ مُغِيَارْ ∴ وُرِنْعَ مَنَمْ ∴ قَامُ ∴ كَدَاسَنْ

سَامُبْجُو ∴ اُورِي ∴ إِدَّرْ ∴ مَدَابُ غِيَارْ ∴ بَاعَجْمِ دَادِنْدْ قَدْ

∴ بُنْسُرُوا ∴ يَبْ ∴ غَسِكِيَا بُمْ ∴ سَرْدَاكِ يَبْ

∴ غُمُوبُمْ نِيكْجَاوُ دُوا ∴ إِدَّرْ ∴ قَدَاكُومُوا ∴

دَامِسَنْ شِتَفِ ∴ إِدَّرْ يَاغُومُوا ∴ كُورَا ∴

ta tafi; idan tā kōmō, kai kuma ka tafi.'
Bunsurū ya che, 'Nā ji.' Da gari ya wāye zāki
ya je, ya kasō gumki. Ya kira su. Su-ka-je,
su-ka-kwāsō nāma, su-ka-kāwō. Gari ya wāye
dāmisa ya je dāji, ya kasō māraya. Da gari
ya wāye, sai kūra ta tafi, ta kasō gada.
Dada sauran bunsurū. Gari ya wāye su-ka-che,
'Bunsurū sauran kai.' Ya che, 'Tō.' Sai bunsurū
ya tafi dāji. Tun da sāfe shi na yāwō, har
mareche, bai sāmu kōmi ba. Yunwa ta kā-
m̄a shi; ya kwanta gūtsun kūka, kamar
ya mutu. Sai maiki ya gane shi. Shi na zatō

---

will go; when she has come back you also will go.' The he-goat said, 'I have heard.' When it was dawn the lion went (and) killed a hartebeest. He called them. They came (and) gathered up the meat (and) brought (it) back. Next morning the leopard went to the bush. He killed a bush-buck. Next morning then the hyena went and killed an antelope. Then there remained the he-goat. At dawn they said, 'He-goat, there remains you.' He said, 'All right.' So the he-goat went to the bush. From early morning he was roaming till evening; he did not find anything. Hunger seized him (and) he lay down at the foot of a baobab-tree as if dead. And an eagle saw him. He thought

تتقم ؛ إدن ؛ قدكوموا ؛ كيكم ؛ كتقم

بنسرو ؛ ميبنامج ؛ دغمر ميواپي ؛ داكـ ؛

يجي ؛ يكسوا ؛ غمكم ؛ يكمراس ؛ سكجي ؛

سكهكواسوقدام ؛ سككداوو ؛ غمر ميواپي

دامسن يجي حاج ؛ يكسوا ؛ مداوبيا ؛ دغمر ؛

ميواپي ؛ اسن كورا ؛ متقم ؛ تكسوا غمر ؛

دد ؛ اسوق بنسروا ؛ غمر ميواپي ؛ سكث ؛

بنسرو ؛ اسونكن ؛ ميث ثو ؛ اسن بنسرا ؛

يتقم داج ؛ ثند صاوفي ؛ شنايداوو ؛ جمر ؛

مر مكث ؛ بنيسام ؛ كوميب ؛ يلونكا

مداش يكوفتا ؛ غموطمن كوك ؛ ككم

يدمث ؛ اسن قنبكي ؛ يكجلش ؛ شناهتو ؛

matache ne. Sai maiki ya sabka bisansa,
dōmin shi chi. Sai bunsurū ya kāma shi,
ya rike, zaa shi kashēwa, sai maiki ya che,
'Bar ni dōmin Ala, bunsurū.' Ya che, 'Ba ni bari-
-nka. Idan na bar ka, ni, ba abari na.' Sai
maiki ya che, 'Wānene ba shi barinka?' Ya che,
'Kā ji kā ji wada mu ka yi da makwabta na,
ni kūa, idan ban kai kōmi gida ba,
da ni, da yāyana da maatata, baa su barin mu.'
Sai maiki ya che, 'Sake ni, [9] naa ba ka māgani,
kulum kaa kashe nāma da shi.' Bunsurū
ya che, 'Rūdī na ka ke yi.' Maiki ya che, 'Aa,

---

he was dead. Then the eagle alighted on him in order to eat (him). But the he-goat seized him (and) held (him), (and) was about to kill him, when the eagle said, 'Release me, for the sake of Allah, O he-goat.' He said, 'I shall not release you. If I let you go, as for me, they will not let me go.' And the eagle said, 'Who will not let you go?' He said, 'Such and such is the state of affairs between me and my neighbours, and as for me, if I do not bring something home, myself, and children, and wife, they will not allow us (to live).' Then the eagle said, 'Let me go. I shall give you a charm, always you will kill game by means of it.' The he-goat said, 'You are deceiving me.' The eagle said, 'No,

مَتَبْجَنْ وُ سَنْ مَيْكِ ؞ يَبْجَكْ ؞ وسَنْفَلِينْ

دُومِنْ ؞ يشِ ؞ سَنْ مُنْسُرُوا ؞ يَكَدْ قَدَا يِشْ ؞

يَمْرِبَكَنْ ؞ أَشِ كَبْشُكُوا ؞ سَنْ مَنْبِجِ ؞ يَبْ

بَمْرِ ؞ دُمْرِ وُقَيْمَرْ ؞ آلْ ؞ بُمْسُرُوا ؞ يَبْشْ بَا يِقْبَرْ

نَكْ ؞ إِكَّرْ قَبَمْرِكْ ؞ فِيبَا عَمْبَرِ بِنَا ؞ سَنْ

مَنْبِكِ ؞ يَبْشْ وَاقَّمْبَنْ ؞ مَا شَبِرْ فَكْ ؞ يَبْ

كَامِ كَامِ ؞ وُرْدَ مُكَّوْ ؞ دَ مَكُبْتَا قَدْ ؞ ـ

فِيكُوَّ ؞ إِكَّرْ ؞ مَنْكَرْ كُومِ ؞ غِدَامَ ؞

دَفِمْ دَيَا أَمِيدَا فَنْ ؞ دَمَا قَدَا قَدَا ؞ مَا أُسْبِرْ فَمْ

سَنْ مَنْبِكِ ؞ يَبْشْ سَبْكُمْ ؞ فَا أُمْبَاكْ ؞ قَدْ غَنِمْ

؞ كُلُّمْ ؞ كَا أُكَبْشَنْدَامْ ؞ دَيشِمْ ؞ بُمْسُرَا ؞

يَبْشْ زَوْدِ بِينَا كَجْكُلّنْ ؞ مَنْبِكِ يَبْشْ عَمَا عَمْ ؞

ba rūdin ka ni ke yi ba, daidai sake ni.' Bunsurū ya sake maiki. Sai maiki ya yi amai kara guntāye farfarū guda uku, ya che, ' Gā su, amshi, idan ka tafi, ka gani kōwane iri nāma, kōmi girmansa, ka dauki karanga, ka sainya, tsakānin kafa baban yan yāsanka, kai yi lākātō, sai ka bari, ya wuche tukuna, saanan ka yi lākātō.' Bunsurū ya che, ' Nā ji.' Maiki ya tuma, ya yi bisa, ya bar bunsurū, shi-na-zamne. Sai ya gani gumake sun tafō, sai ya bari sai da su-ka-wuche. Saanan ya yi māgani, ya yi lākātō, sai gumki ya fādi, ya būshe. Bunsurū

---

it is not to deceive you I say so, but do you let me go.' The he-goat let the eagle off. Then the eagle vomited up small white straws, three in number, (and) said, ' Behold them. Take them, if you are going along and see any species of game whatever, whatever its size, take these straws and place them between your big toes, turn head over heels, then let (the animal) go on a little way, then turn head over heels.' The he-goat said, ' I have heard.' The eagle jumped and went aloft, and left the he-goat sitting. Then he saw (some) hartebeest have come and he let them pass. Then he brought the charm into use, turned head over heels, and a hartebeest fell, (and) stiffened. The he-goat

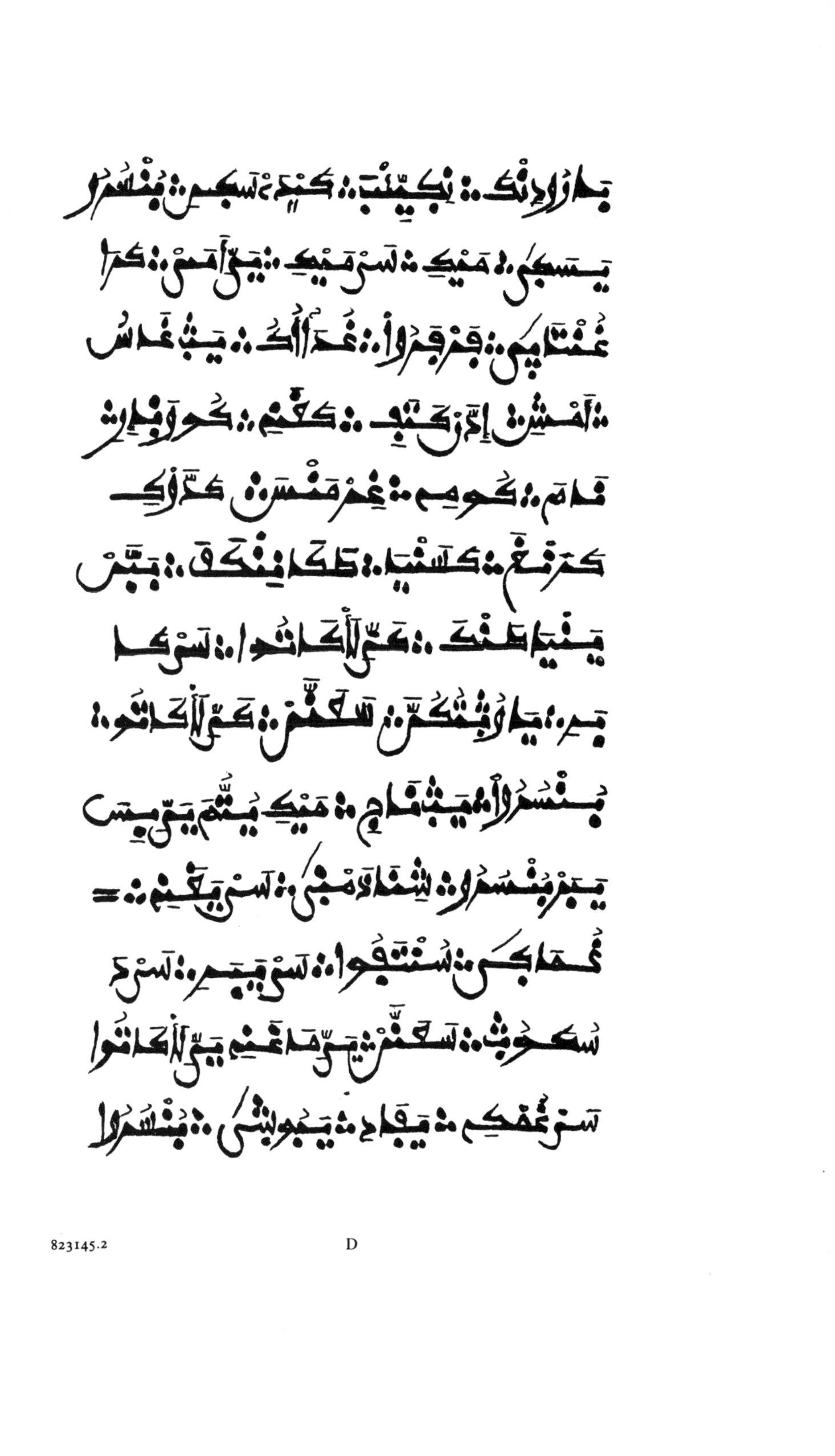

ya zō gida, ya che, 'Nā kashe nāma, ku tafi
ku daukō.' Su ka che, 'Mu je ka goda muna.' Sai
ya wuche gaba. Su-ka-tafi, ya nūna masu.
Su-ka-dauke nāma, su-ka-kāwō gida, su-na-
kākābi. Sai zāki ya che, 'Kūra kin gani,
ai da wuri kin che ba shi iyāwa.' Kūra ta che,
'Gaskīa ne ba shi iyāwa, kō yanzu
ba shi ya kashe wanan ba.' Sai zāki ya che, 'Ku bari
mu gani.' Da su-ka-gama wanan kilinbībi, sai
su-ka-kirāwō shi, su-ka-che, 'Yanzu mun giyāra
gida mun kāre, mu-na-sō abinchinmu
shi zama guda daia. Idan wanan yā je dāji

---

came home (and) said, 'I have killed some game, do you go and bring it in.' They said, 'Let us go; you show us (where it is).' So he passed on in front. They went on. He showed them (the place), they lifted up the meat, they brought it home. They were astonished. And the lion said, 'You have seen, hyena; formerly you said he was not capable (of killing game).' The hyena said, 'It is true, he is not able. Even in this case, it is not he who has killed it.' And the lion said, 'You wait and we shall see.' When they had finished this plotting, then they called him to them and said, 'Now we have finished making the home proper for living in (by killing the game) we are desirous that our food should be the same for all. If this one has gone to the bush

يدواغدا ∴ يبث قداكبشناقم ∴ كتقيم ∴

كدّ وكوا ∴ لسكيث ∴ مجي كغدا امز ∴ لسن

يبوث غمب ∴ لسكتقيم ∴ ييقوقدا مسن ∴ =

لسكدّ وكوا اقدام ∴ لسككدا ورو ∴ غمدا اد لسقد

كدكدام ∴ لسن داك ∴ يبث كوار ∴ كنغم

آ؛ دورو ∴ كنقب ∴ بدا شعيارا ∴ كوراتبث ∴ ع

قسعيا بن ∴ بدا شعيارا ∴ كوا ايقدم ∴

بدا شم يكشن ∴ وقنب ∴ لسن داك يبث ∴ كبم

نغنم ∴ د لسكغم ∴ وقم كلقبيب ∴ لسن

لسعكرا ورشن لسكيث ∴ يقنم ∴ منقيلو

غدا امنكدا بن ش مقدا لسوا ∴ امنشنم ∴

شغم ∴ غدا ام من ∴ امدن ∴ وقم يا بن دام ∴

yā kasō nāma mu tāru mu chi. Idan gari ya wāye wanan shi tafi, shi kasō, mu tāru, mu chi; mu dinga yin hakanan.' Bunsurū ya che, 'Ya yi mani dādi.' Yau gari ya wāye, zāki shi ya fāra zua, ya kasō bauna. Su-ka-tāru su-ka-chi. Gari ya wāye, dāmisa ya tafi ya kasō, su-ka-tāru su-ka-chi. Da gari ya wāye, kūra ya tafi dāji, ya kasō nāma, ya kāwō, su duka su-ka-tāru, su-ka-chi. Da gari ya wāye, su-ka-che, 'Bunsurū sau-ran kai.' Ya che, 'To.' Bunsurū ya tafi dāji, zāki ya bi sau sa. Ya boyē, ya gani wada shi ke yi, shi kashe nāma, sai ya gudānō maza shi-na-ba su lābāri, sai kūra ya che, bai yarda ba, sai yā gani. Aka-jima

---

and has killed game we shall meet together (and) eat. When it was dawn, this one goes (and) kills, we meet, (and) eat; (and) we continue to do so.' The he-goat said, 'That is just what I want.' So when dawn came, the lion first went. He killed a bush cow. They met (and) ate. Next dawn the leopard went (and) killed; they met together (and) ate. When it was dawn the hyena went to the bush; he killed meat (and) brought it back, (and) they all met (and) ate. When dawn came they said, 'He-goat, it is your turn.' He said, 'All right.' The he-goat went to the bush, (and) the lion followed his spoor. He hid, and saw what he did to kill game. Then he ran back quickly (and) was giving them the news, but the hyena said he would not believe (consent) unless he has seen. In a little while

بداكسوقدام ∴ متدارمث ∴ إمّ رغمر بداوايرن

وقمر شنّف ∴ شكسوا ∴ متدارمث ∴ مدمغ يمكن

∴ بنسروا ∴ يث بديم دادي ∴ بوغم بيوايس ∴

داك ∴ شم بقدوذر ∴ يكسوا بوقد ∴ لسكتار ∴

سكث ∴ غمر بيوابي ∴ دامسن بيتف ∴ يكسو

لسكتار سكث ∴ غمر بيوابي ∴ كورا ∴ يتّج

داج ∴ يكسوندام ∴ بكاور ∴ سوذك ∴ لسكتار ∴

سكث ∴ دغمر بيوبي ∴ سكب ∴ بنسروا سو

ونكن ∴ يث ثو ∴ بنسروا ∴ يتنج داج ∴ داك

يب سوسن ببوبيّن ∴ يغنم ∴ ودشجي ∴ شكشل

قدام ∴ سن يغدا قوا مغدا ∴ شند بدا سن لا بداو ∴ =

سن كورا ايث ∴ بن بمدب ∴ سن بدا غنم ∴ أكجم

sai bunsurū ya zō. Ya che, 'Nā kashe nāma, ama ba ni iya dauka.' Su-ka-che, 'Mu je, mu daukō.' Su-ka-tāshi. Ya wu--che gaba. Su-ka-tafi, ya nūna masu bauna, ta-na kwa--nche, sai shi ya kōmō gida. Su kūa su-ka-yā--yāge nāma, su-ka-kāwō gida. Wata rāna kuma, da zaa shi, sai dāmisa ya bi shi, ya gani, ya kōmō, shi-na--gaia masu. Kūra ya che, shi dai sai yā gani. Tukuna bunsurū ya zō ya che, 'Nā kashe nāma, ku je ku daukō.' Dada sun shiga tsōrō(n)sa. Sai su-ka tashi, maza maza ya kwatamta masu wurin da nāma shi ke. Sai su-ka-je, su-ka-daukō, su-ka-kāwō. Wata rāna kuma, da zaa shi, kūra ta bī shi;

---

then the he-goat came. He said, 'I have killed game, but I cannot carry it.' They replied, 'We will come to lift (it).' They rose up. He (the he-goat) passed on in front. They went (and) he pointed out to them a bush-cow, lying; then he went back home. And they tore apart the meat (and) brought it home. Another day also when he (the he-goat) was about to go (to hunt) the leopard followed him. He saw. (he returned (and) told them. The hyena said, as for him He would not credit it) till he has seen. Soon after the he-goat came, (and) said, 'I have killed game, you come and lift it.' By this time they have entered into fear of him, so they rose up very quickly, (and) he directed them to where the game was. Then they went (and) lifted (and) brought (it). Another day also, when he was going off (to hunt), the hyena followed him;

سن مفسر ويذوا ∴ يبث ما عشي ∴ ما م ∴ آما با معي
∴ بزرك ∴ سكبث مبجي ∴ مذ زكوا ∴ سكتاش بيو
ث غجب ∴ سكتبم ∴ بنو ما مسن بجو ما تكا كو
مث ∴ سن شي يكو مو اغدا ∴ سوكو ∴ سكيد
يا غمي ما م ∴ سككا ور غدا ∴ و تمر امي كم ∴ د دا اش
سن دا مسن ببيش يخنم ∴ يكو موا ∴ يشنا
غيا مسن كورا ∴ يبث شم دز ∴ سن ميا غم
∴ تكس ∴ مفسر اوا ∴ يذوا ∴ يبث ما كبشنا حم ∴
كجي ∴ كد زكوا ∴ دد ∴ سنشغ ∴ طوو رسث
سن سكتاش مغ مغ ∴ يكتمنا مسن ورند
نا ما شبكي ∴ سن سكجي ∴ سكد وكوا ∴ =
سكا او و ∴ آ تمرا امي كم ∴ د دا اش ∴ كورا ∴ تبيش

ta-na sanda, har ya je ya gani gumāke. Sai ya kyale, su-ka-shudē, saanan ya bi sau(n)su. Da ya kusa da su, sai ya dauki kara nan guda uku, ya sainya tsakānin baban dan yātsansa, sai ya tuma, ya yi lākātō, sai wani baban gumki da shi ke bāya, shi kuma ya tuma, ya fādi. Kūra kūa shi-na-gani, sai ya gudānō, partab! partab! ya zō gida, shi-na-fadi. Sai bunsurū ya zo, ya che, 'Ku tāshi, ku je, ku daukō nāma.' Sai su-ka-tā--shi, ya wuche gaba, ya kai su, su-na-fida nāma. Kūra kūa, tsōrō ya kāma shi, idan ya gani bunsurū, zaa shi wuchewa bāyansa, sai

---

she was following him stealthily till he (the he-goat) went and saw (some) hartebeest. Then he did nothing till they passed, then he followed their tracks. When he was near them, then he took his straws, three in number. He set them between his big toes, then he leaped up, turned head over heels, and one big hartebeest which was behind, he too leaped up and fell. The hyena too was looking on. Then he ran off in great haste. He came home and told (what he had seen). Then the he-goat arrived and said, 'You, get up, go (and) bring in the meat.' So they rose up, he went in front (and) took them to the place (and) they took off the meat. As for the hyena, fear seized on him; if he saw the he-goat was going to pass behind him, then

تُنْدَ سُنْكَ ا ∴ حَرْبِجِكِ يَقْنِمْ ∴ قَمَاكُمْ سَيْنْ ∴

يَكْبُوْ ∴ سُكَشُوْ دِسُ ∴ سَغَمْنْ ∴ يَبِسُوشِنْ ∴ ع

يَكُسَرْ دُسُوا ∴ سَنْ يَمَدُّوْرِكِ ∴ كَمْ قَمْنْ ∴ غُمْدَا اُكُ

بِلَسَنْبِيَا ∴ طَكَافِمْ ∴ يَمَبْنْ دَمْ قُيْمِ طَفُلْسُوشْ تَسْ

يَنْتُمْ ∴ يَيْمْ لاَعَدَا مْتُوا ∴ سَنْ وُقَبَبْمْ غُمْكِيمْ ∴ =

دَشِكَبِيَا سَ ∴ شِيكُمْ ∴ يَنْتُمْ يَقَلاَدِ ∴ كُوَاكُوْ

شِنَاغُنِمْ ∴ سَنْ يَغُدَا مْقُوا ∴ قَرْقَتَبْ قَرْقَبْ

∴ يَخُوْغُمَا ∴ شِنَا قَجِ ∴ سَنْ بُنْسُرُ وَايَذُوا ∴

يَبْ كُتَنَاشِنْ كُجِي كُدَّوْ كُوقَدَامْ ∴ سَنْ سُكَنَا

شِنْ يَبُوقْ غُمْجَ ∴ يَكَنْيُسُنْ سُنَدَ قِيْبِرْ مَدَامْ

كُوَاكُوْ ∴ طُورُ اَبْيَا كَدَمَا شِنْ اِدَّرْ يَغُنِمْ

بُنْسُرُ وَا ∴ دَ اَشِنْ وُبْنُوَا ∴ بَا يَقُسْنْ سَنْ

kūra shi tāshi, shi kōma wani wuri. Idan bunsurū ya bi nan, sai kūra shi bi wani wuri, har kūra ya gaji, ya che, 'Haba abōkīna me na yi maka, kō-ina na bi, ka-na-bi na?' Bunsurū ka kyale, har su-ka-zō gida. Su-ka-chi abinchi, su-ka-kāre. Kōwa ya shiga dāki. Sai kūra ya je wurin zā-ki, su-ka-tada dāmisa, su-ka-yi shāwara, su-ka-che, 'Wanan ya fi karfinmu, idan ba mu gudu ba, wata rāna mu ma shi kashe mu.' Sai su-ka-fita, su-ka-gudu, bunsurū na kwāna. Mafāri ke nan, zāki, da kūra, da dāmisa, su-ka-shiga dāji, da wuri makwobtan bunsurū ne. Shi ke nan. [10]Kungurus kan kūsu.

---

the hyena rose up and moved to another place. If the he-goat followed there, then the hyena went to some other place, till the hyena got tired (and) said, 'Haba! my friend, what am I doing to you, that wherever I go you keep following me?' The he-goat did not reply, till they came to the house. They finished eating the food. Every one entered the house. But the hyena went to the lion, (there) they woke the leopard, (and) they held a council, (and) said, 'This thing is too much for us. If we do not flee some day, as for us, he will kill us.' So they came out and ran away. The he-goat was asleep. That was the first time the lion and the hyena and the leopard went to live in the bush. Formerly they were neighbours of the he-goat. That is it. Off with the rat's head.

مُنْسُرَا ؞ أَدّٖن ؞ وَفُورِي ؞ شِكُومَ ؞ مِشِن شِنَدَ ؞ كُوَرَا

؞ كُورَا قَمْ ؞ وَفُوُرِي ؞ شِبَ كُورَا سَنْ بِمّٖن يَا

كُو ؞ مَنِيّمَكْ ؞ أَبُوكِينَا حَبَ مِيبْ ؞ يَحْجِ

قَمْ ؞ يِكِلُو ؞ بُنْسُرَا ؞ بِمْنَا كَنَدَ ؞ إِقَا قَمْ

سَكَذُ وَغَدَا ؞ سَكَثِ ؞ أَمْنَثِ سَكَكَا بُرَن ؞ ي

كُوَرَا ؞ مِيشَغْ دَاكِ ؞ سَنْ كُورَا ؞ يِحِرُ وُنْغ

اكِ ؞ سَكَنَادَ دَامِسَن ؞ سَكَمّ شَادَرَ ؞ سَكَثْ

وَقَمْ ؞ بِيَافِ كَرِفَنْمُ ؞ إِدّٖن بِمُغَدْبِ ؞ أَقَرَانَ

مُومَا ؞ بِشْكَشَمُ ؞ سَنْ سَكِحَتَ ؞ سَكَفْدُ

بُنْسُرَوَ اتَاكُوامَدَ ؞ مَقَاوِي بَكَنّٖن ؞ دَاكِ دَكُورَا

دَدَامِسَن ؞ سَكِشِغْ دَاج ؞ دَوُو ؞ مَكَبْنَن

بُنْسُرَوُنُن ؞ شِكَنّٖن

فُنْفُرْسِنْكِن

فُوسَنْ

No. 26.

Wanan tātsunīar [1]alkume che.

[2]Gātanan, gātanan. Ta je, ta kōmō. Būzūzu shi ne [3]ya yi [4]gayā, ayi masa shibchi. Ya je, ya gaya ma za- -kara. Zakara ya che, 'Yaushe?' Ya che, 'Jibi.' Ya che, 'In ji ba ka ga ma [5]muzūrū ba?' Ya che, 'Aa.' Ya che, 'Kar ka gaya masa.' Būzūz ya che, 'Tō.' Da fitansa, sai ya je gidan muzūrū, ya fada masa. Muzūrū ya che, 'In ji ba ka gaya ma kare ba?' Ya che, 'Aa.' Ya che, 'Kar ka gaya masa.' Da fitansa, sai ya je gidan kare, ya gaya masa. Kare ya che, 'In ji, ba ka gaya ma [6]kūra ba?' Ya che, 'Aa.' Kare ya che, 'Kar ka gaya mata.' Ya che, 'To.' (df) Da fitansa, sai ya je gidan kūra, ya gaya mata. Ta che, 'In ji ba ka gaia ma dāmisa ba?' Ya che, 'Aa.' Ta che, 'kar ka gay masa.' Sai ta che, 'Tafi gida.' Da fitansa, sai ya je

---

This is a story about a beetle. A story, a story. Let it go. Le come. The beetle made an arrangement for people to come and as him with his thatching. He went and told the cock. The cock sa 'When (is it)?' He said, 'The day after to-morrow.' He (the cock) sa 'You did not tell the cat, did you?' He said, 'Oh no.' He said, 'Do tell him.' The beetle said, 'All right.' On his coming away then he w to the house of the cat (and) told him. The cat said, 'I suppose you not tell the dog?' He said, 'Oh no.' He said, 'Do not tell him.' Wh he left (there) he next went to the dog's home (and) told him. The d said, 'You did not tell the hyena, did you?' He said, 'Oh no.' The d said, 'Do not tell her.' He said, 'All right.' On coming away from th then he went to the house of the hyena, and told her. She said, 'Let hear, you did not tell the leopard?' He said, 'Oh no.' She said, 'Do tell him.' Then she said, 'Go off home.' On leaving her, next he went

وقن قاطو فيز الفجب

غد قنن غد قنن قجو تكومواْ بودور شيبن

يتي غيا ايمسـ[illegible] م شبنث يجن يغيا مد

كر دم كر يث يو شبن يث جيم يث اِنج بكغيا

مدوروك يث عادم يث كر كغيا مسلن بودور

يث قوا دي قتنلس سن يجي غد مدورو يقد لمس

مدورو ايث انج بكغيام كرمب يث عادم يث

كر كغيا مسن دي قتنلس سن يجي غد قكرم يغيا

مسن كبر من يث اِقج بكغيام كوراب يث

عادم كبرن يث كر كغيا مسن يث قوا دي

دي قتنلس سن يجي غد نكورا يغيا مسن قث

اِقج بكغيام دا مسرن يث عادم قث كر كغيا

مسن سن قث تي غد ا دي قتنلس سن يجن

gidan dāmisa ya gaya masa. Dāmisa ya che, ‘ In ji ba ka gaya ma mainya dawa ba ? ’ Būzūzu ya che, ‘ Aa.’ Dāmisa ya che, ‘ Kar ka gaya masa.’ Ya che, ‘ Tō.’ Da fitansa, sai ya je gidan zāki, ya gaya masa. Mainyan dawa ya che, ‘ Tō.’ Ranan gaya ta zō. Zakara ya fāra zūa, ya ishe būzūzu, su-ka-tāshi, su-ka-gewaya bāyan gida, su-na-yankan yanta. Aka-jima, sai muzūrū ya zō, ya yi salama. Sai zakara ya che. ‘ Wa ke salama ? ’ Būzūzu ya che, ‘ Muzūrū ne.’ Sai zakara ya che, ‘ Ai na che kar ka gaya masa ? ’ Ya che, ‘ Ai, ban gaya shi dai [7]yā ji lābāri ne ya zō.’ Zakara kūa yā zō da māsū(n)sa, guda bīū, ya kafa, ya gudu, ya shiga dāki, ya bar su, ya bōyē. Muzūrū ya zō, ya che, ‘ Wa ke da māsū ? ’

---

to the house of the leopard and told him. The leopard said, ‘ You di tell the great one of the forest, did you ? ’ The beetle said, ‘ Oh no.’ leopard said, ‘ You must not tell him.’ He said, ‘ All right.’ On le him he next went to the home of the lion, he told him. The one of the bush said, ‘ All right.’ The day when all the people we assemble came. The cock was the first to come. He met the beetle, they rose up (and) went behind the house (and) were cutting grass. Sh after the cat came (and) hailed, and the cock said, ‘ Who is hailing ? ’ beetle said, ‘ It is the cat.’ Then the cock said, ‘ What ! Did not I say were not to tell him ? ’ He replied, ‘ No, I did not tell him ; it is he hi has heard the news (and) come.’ Now the cock has brought his spears in number. He stuck them in the ground, he fled, he entered the h (and) left them. He hid (himself). The cat came (and) and said, ‘ W do the spears belong to ? ’

غد فد امس ؞ مكفيا مس ؞ د امس ؞ ميث ابج ؞
بكفيا م ؞ مفيد ترب ؞ بود ود ؞ ميث عاع ؞ د امس
يث كر كفيا مس ؞ ميث قوا ؞ د فتفس ؞ سن بجن
غد فداك ؞ ميفيا مس ؞ مفيم دا ؞ ميث قو ؞ راقم
غيا اتد و ؞ د كر ؞ ميقد ارد ر ؞ ميد ابش ؞ بود ود ؞
سكتا اش سك فلو ميا ؞ ميد ميف غد [illegible] ؞ سنا ابكس
ميفيس ؞ اكجم ؞ اسر مد ور ور ؞ ميد و ا ؞ ميي سلم ؞ اسف
د كر ميث واكر سلم ؞ بود ود ؞ ميث مد ور و فش سو
د كر ميث ؞ اغا اث كر كفيا مس ؞ ميث اغ بنفيا مس
شيد ميا ج ؞ لابا و ميش ؞ ميد وا ؞ د كر اكو ؞ ميا دوا
د ما سو سر ؞ غد ابجوا ابك ؞ ميفد ؞ ميشغ داك
ميم سر ؞ مبو مبس ؞ مد ور ور ؞ ميد ور ؞ ميث واكد ما سو

Aka-che na zakara na. 'Ina zakara?' 'Shi-na dāki.' Sai muzūrū ya je, ya būdē kōfa, ya kāma shi,
ya kashe. Sai būzūzu ya zō, ya che, 'Kāwō in bō-
-ye maka har mu gama.' Ya ba shi, ya kai wani dāki, ya rufē. Su-ka-je, su-na-aiki. Aka-jima, sai kare ya yi salama. Muzūrū ya che, 'Wa ke salama?' Būzūzu ya che, 'Kare ne.' Sai muzūrū ya shiga dāki, ya bōyē. Kare ya zō, su-ka-yi gaisua da būzūzu, sai ya gani māsū, ya che, 'Wa ke da mā-
-sū?' Aka-che, na zakara ne. 'Ina zakara?' Muzūrū ya kashe. 'Ina muzūrū?' 'Shi-na dāki.' Sai kare ya shiga dāki, ya kāma muzūrū, ya kashe. Būzūzu ya che, 'Kāwō in bōye maka, har mu gama aiki.' Ya ba shi, ya kai dāki, ya rufē. Su-ka-je.

He was told they belonged to the cock. (He said), 'Where is the cock?' 'He is in the house.' Then the cat came (and) opened the door, (and) caught him (and) killed him. And the beetle came (and) said, 'Bring (him) (and) I will hide him for you till we have finished.' He gave the cock to him. He took it to another room (and) covered (it up). They went back (and) were at work. Soon after the dog hailed. The cat said, 'Who is that calling out his arrival?' The beetle said, 'It is the dog.' And the cat went into the house (and) hid. The dog came. He greeted the beetle; then he saw the spears (and) said, 'Whose are the spears?' He was told they were the cock's. 'Where is the cock?' 'The cat has killed (it).' 'Where is the cat?' 'He is in the house.' Then the dog entered the house. He seized the cat (and) killed it. The beetle said, 'Bring (it) here that I may hide it away for you till we have finished the work.' He gave him (and) he took it to a room, (and) covered (it up). They went off.

آكَبْ مَدَ كَمَرَ اُبُهُ ؞ اِقَّا دَ كَمَرَ ؞ يِشْنَا دَاكِ ؞ سَسِ

مُدُ وُرُ ؞ يِجُ ؞ مِيبُ وُدَ مِ كُوقَ ؞ يَكَ مَا لِشْ ؞

يَكَشْبُ ؞ سَسْ بُوُ دُ وُرُ ؞ يِيخُرَا ؞ مِيشْ كَدَ وُرُ ؞ اِنْبُو

يِمَحَكَ ؞ حَمْ مُحَمَ ؞ يِبَا لِشْ ؞ يَكَمْ وَنْدَ اكِ ؞ مِيرُ وُبِ

سَكَجُ ؞ سَنَا أَيْكِ ؞ اَكِجَمْ سَسْ كَمَرُ ؞ مِيمْ سَلَّمَ ؞ ـ

مُدُ وُرُ ؞ يِيشْ وَاكِ سَلَّمَ ؞ بُوُ دُ وُرُ ؞ مِيشْ كَمَ مُبُ ؞

سَسْ مُدُ وُرُ ؞ مِيشَغَ دَاكِ ؞ مِيجُ وُبِكِ ؞ كَمَ مُ يِيدُ وُرُ ؞ سَكَ

كَيِلْسُوا ؞ دَبُوُ دُ وُرُ ؞ سَسْ مِيغَنْغَ مَدَ سُوا ؞ يِيشْ وَاكِ كَمَ مَا

سُوا ؞ آكَبْ مَدَ كَمَرَ اُبُهُ ؞ اِقَّا دَ كَمَرَ ؞ مُدُ وُرُ اَبِدَا كَشْبُ

اِقَّا مُدُ وُرُ ؞ يِشْنَا دَاكِ ؞ سَسْ كَمَرُ ؞ يِيشَغَ دَاكِ ؞ يِكَدَمْ

مُدُ وُرُ ؞ يَكَشْبُ ؞ بُوُ دُ وُرُ ؞ يِيشْ كَدَ وُرُ ؞ اِمْبُو يِمَكَ

؞ حَمْ مُحَمَ اَيْكِ ؞ مِبَا لِشْ ؞ يَكَيِدَ اكِ ؞ مِيرُ وُبِ ؞ سَكَجُ

Su-na aiki. Aka-jima, sai kūra ta zō, ya yi salama. Kare ya che, 'Wa ke salama ?' Būzūzu ya che, 'Ban sani ba, kamar kūra che.' Ya che, 'Bari in je, in gani.' Sai ya che, 'Shiga nan.' Kare ya shiga dāki. Kūra ta zō. Su-ka-yi gaisua. To gani māsū, ta che. 'Wa ke da mā- -sū ?' Ya che na zakara ne. 'Ina zakara ?' 'Muzūrū ya chainye.' 'Ina muzūrū ?' 'Kare yā chainye.' 'Ina kare ?' 'Shi-na dāki.' Sai kūra ta shiga dāki, ta kāma kare, ta kashe. Būzūzu ya zō, ya che, 'Kāwō in bōye maka har mu gama aiki.' Kūra ta ba shi, ya ja, ya kai dāki, ya rufe. Su-ka-je su-na aiki. Aka-jima, sai dāmisa ya zō, ya yi salama. Sai kūra ta che, 'Wa ke salama ?' Būzūzu

---

They were working. In a little while the hyena came (and) hailed. The dog said, 'Who is hailing?' The beetle said, 'I am not sure ; it appears to be the hyena.' He said, 'Wait till I go and have a look.' And he said, 'Get in here.' The dog got into the house. The hyena came. They exchanged greetings. She (the hyena) saw the spears. She said, 'Who possesses the spears ?' He (the beetle) said, 'They are the cock's.' 'Where is the cock ?' 'The cat has eaten (it) up.' 'Where is the cat ?' 'The dog has eaten it up.' 'Where is the dog ?' 'He is in the house.' Then the hyena entered the house, caught the dog (and) killed it. The beetle came (and) said, 'Bring (it) here, that I may hide it for you till we have finished the work.' The hyena gave it to him ; he drew (it) along, put it in the room, (and) covered it up. They went back. They were working. A short time passed, and the leopard came. He hailed them. And the hyena said, 'Who is that wanting admittance ?' The beetle

سند أيك ∴ أبجم ∴ سن كورا ∴ قد وال ∴ ثم سلم ∴

كبر يث وابكو ∴ سلم ∴ بود وإ ∴ يث بنسنيب ∴

كمن كوراث ∴ يمث بلم إفجو ∴ إثغنم ∴ سن يث

شغفن كبر يشغ ∴ داك ∴ كور اقدوا ∴ ـ

سكر غيبسوا ∴ قغنم مدا سوا ∴ قث وابكو قا

سو ∴ يث مد كم ابكو ∴ إقاد كمر ∴ مدورو ∴

يا قنبي ∴ إقا مدورو ∴ كبر ∴ يا قنبو ∴ إقا

كبر ∴ شقداك ∴ سن كور اقشغ داك ∴ ـ

تكام كبر ∴ تكشبو ∴ بودود ∴ يدو ∴ يث

كداو ∴ إثبويمك ∴ حرمحم أيك ∴ كورا ∴

قبا شن يجمو يكمو داك ∴ ميرفو ∴ سكجو

∴ سند أيك ∴ أكجم ∴ سن دامسو يغ وا ∴ يمس

سلم ∴ سن كور اقث وابكو ∴ سلم ∴ بودود ∴

ya che, 'Dāmisa ne.' Kūra ta che, 'Ai na che kar ka gaya masa?' Ya che, 'Ban gaya masa ba, kō yā ji lābāri ne.' Sai kūra ta yi zai zai, zaa ta gudu. Sai būzūzu ya che, 'Kar ki gudu, tafō ki bōye nan, ko yā zō gaishe ni ne.' Sai kūra ta shiga dāki, ta bōye, dāmisa ya shigō. Su-ka-yi gaisua da būzūzu, su-ka-dinga yankan yanta, sai ya tada kai, ya gani māsū, kafe. Ya che, 'Būzūzu wa ke da māsū?' Ya che, 'Na zakara ne.' 'Ina zakara?' 'Muzūrū yā kashe.' 'Ina muzūrū?' '[8] Kare yā kashe.' 'Ina kare?' 'Kūra tā kashe.' 'Ina kūra?' 'Ta na dāki.' Dāmisa ya tāshi, [9] sannū, ya shiga dāki. Kūra ta zaabura, zaa ta gudu, sai ya sainya mata akaifa

---

said, 'It is the leopard.' The hyena said, 'Oh! Did not I say you must not tell him?' He replied, 'I did not tell him, perhaps he has heard about it.' And the hyena ran here and there (looking for a way to escape. And the beetle said, 'Do not run away come here, hide in this place, perhaps he has only come to greet me.' The hyena got inside. Then (the leopard) exchanged greetings with the beetle. They were working away at cutting the grass, when he (the leopard) raised his head (and) saw the spears stuck (in the ground). He said, 'Beetle, who possesses the spears?' He replied, 'They are the cock's.' 'Where is the cock?' 'The cat has killed (it).' 'Where is the cat?' 'The dog has killed it.' 'Where is the dog?' 'The hyena has killed it.' 'Where is the hyena?' 'She is in the house.' The leopard rose up softly and entered the house. The hyena leaped up, to run away, but he stuck his claws in her

يِبْ دَا اِمَسَ فَرِ ؞ كُوَ وَاتَبْ ؞ اَاَ فَاذِبْ ؞ كَرْكِيَا

مَسَ ؞ يِبْ بِنْكِيَا مَسَرِ ؞ كُوِيَا اَبَا وَيِبْنِ ؞ سَسْ

كُوَ وَا ؞ يِبْرِ ظَمْ ظَمْ ؞ دَا اَمْغُدُ ؞ سَسْ مُوَ دُوَرُ ؞ يِبْ

كَرْكِغُدُ ؞ اَمْ فُوَا ؞ كُمُوِيَتِّنْ ؞ كُوَيَا دُوَ غِبْشِتِّنِ

سَسْ كُوَ وَا ؞ تَيِشْغُ دَاكِ ؞ اَمْبُوِيَنْ ؞ دَا اِمَسَرْ يِشْفُوَا

سْكَتِّ غِبْسُوَا ؞ كُمُوَ دُوَرُ ؞ سْكَدِ مْغُ ؞ يِنْكَنْ ؞

يِنْتَنْ ؞ سَسْ يِتَنَا دَكِّنْ ؞ يِغُنِي ؞ مَاسُوَا اَكِيفِنْ ؞ يِبْ

بُوَ دُوَرُ ؞ وَاكَمْ مَاسُوَا ؞ يِبْ فَدَ كَمْ اَيِفُنْ ؞ اِمَّا

دُكَمْ ؞ مُدُوَوَرْ ؞ يَا كَشِبْنْ ؞ اِمَّا مُدُوَرُ ؞ كَمْ بَرِيَا كَشِبْنِ

؞ اِمَّا كَمْ بَرِنْ ؞ كُوَ وَا اَتَا كَشِبْنِ ؞ اِمَّا كُوَ وَا ؞ اَتَنَا دَاكِ

؞ دَا اِمَسَرْ يِتَنَا شِنْ ؞ سْغُفُوَا ؞ يِشْغُ دَاكِ ؞ كُوَ وَا

تَرَا بَمْ ؞ دَا اَمْغُدُ ؞ سَسْ يِتَسْنِيَا مَتَنَ ؞ اَكِيفِنْ ؞

يِلَاجْ

ga chiki. Ya falke, sai hanji ya fitō, sai kūra ta fadi; ta mutu. Sai alkume ya zō, ya che, ‘Bari mu bōye ta, har mu gama aiki.’ Su-ka-ja su-ka-kai dāki, su-ka-aje, su-ka-ja askunia, su-ka-rufe kōfa dāki. Su-ka-kōma bāyan gida, su-na-yankan shibchi. Gaya na-tārua, māsu-aiki su-ka-tāru dayawa, su-na-yankan yanta. Aka-dade, su gada, su barēwa duka, su zōmō, su bachīa, su mājē, su hargini, su gumki, su bauna, su gīwa, duka su-ka-tāru, da kurēge, da kū-sa, da nāmun dāji mainya mainya, da kankanāna. Hata tsuntsāye duka sun tāru wurin gayan būzūzu.

---

body. (She) fainted, and the intestines came out, and the hyena fell, (and) died. Then the beetle came (and) said, ‘Let us hide her away till we finish the work.’ They dragged (and) brought (it) into the room, (and) set it down. They drew the mat for covering the doorway (and) shut the door of the house. They went to the back of the house. They were cutting grass. The helpers were (by this time) assembling, and many workers had assembled (and) were cutting thatching grass. They went on increasing in numbers, duyker, all the bush-buck, hares, bush-goats, ‘mājē’ (?) hargini (?) hartebeest, bush-cow, elephants, all assembled, and jerboas, and rats, and the great beasts of the forest and the small. Even all the birds have assembled to assist the beetle (in his getting grass).

تمثك ⁝ يبعلكى ⁝ آسن قنجم ⁝ يبفتوا ⁝ آسن
كوراقبام ⁝ تقحف ⁝ آسن الفبى ⁝ يبذر ⁝
يب ⁝ بمر فبويت ⁝ قم محم أيك ⁝ سكجن
سككن كراك ⁝ سكآجى ⁝ سكجا ⁝ أسكنيا ⁝ =
سكرفى ⁝ كوفداك ⁝ سككوم ⁝ بايزنجدا
⁝ سنايكز ⁝ شبت ⁝ تميافقاروا ⁝ قداسدأيك
سكتار ⁝ كقيو ⁝ سنايكز مستو ⁝ آكم جمن
سغدا ⁝ سبرموا ⁝ دك ⁝ سذ ومو ⁝ سبثن ⁝
سدابكو ⁝ سحرغمن ⁝ سخمكى ⁝ سبوقمن =
سفيوا ⁝ دك ⁝ سكتار ⁝ دكم مجلن ⁝ دكو
سا ⁝ دقمرجاج ⁝ ممترمفمن ⁝ دقمقتان ⁝ =
قتم طغرطابمن ⁝ دك ⁝ سمتار ⁝ ووز ⁝ تميز بجدوكد ⁝

Sai zāki kadai ne bai zō ba. Ana-nan ana-
-aiki ankusa gajia, sai zāki ya zō.
Ya kwanta kusa da su. Ya yi nīshi. Sai gaya
ta wātse. Mainya mainya su-ka-dinga tāke
kankana. A-tāke kankana dayawa. Sai zāki
ya tāsō, ya zō, ya gani, ya che, 'Ina alkume?'
Ya che, 'Gā ni.' Sai zāki ya che, 'Gā tāwa
gaya nan, fitō ka kwāche, kō bai yi maka
dādi ba?' Ya che, 'Yā yi mani dādi.' Sai zāki ya juya,
ya yi tafia tasa. Būzūzu ya yi ta kwāsa nāma,
ya kwāshe, ya tāra. Shi-na-chin abinsa da maatarsa. Ashe
sun gama bāki ne, da zāki ya yi hakanan. Mafāri
ke nan, idan ka-na-sō ka sāmu abinchi
11 alhāli ka-na-jin yunwa, sai ka gama

And it was only the lion that had not come. And they were all working and getting weary when the lion came. He laid down near to them (and) roared. Then the assembled helpers scattered. The great ones kept trampling on the small ones. Many of the small ones were trampled. Then the lion rose up (and) came forward. He looked (and) said, 'Where is the beetle?' He said, 'Behold me.' And the lion said, 'Look at (what) my alliance (with you has done). Come out and collect them. Or is it not pleasing to you?' He said, 'It has pleased me.' Then the lion turned round (and) went his own way. The beetle collected the meat, and pulled it off, (and) heaped it together. He was eating his spoils with his wife. Of a truth they had arranged it all with the lion to do all this. That was the origin (of what you do now) if you want to get food when you feel hungry; for you join

سن واك ∴ تكد يفغن يبنغ ورڤ ∴ إنّا فرن أمر

أنبك ∴ أنكسن غمجن ولسن واك ∴ يغرا ∴ =

يكونت ∴ كسد سوا ∴ يبي نيبيش ولسن غيد

تواطي ∴ منومني ∴ سكدنغ ∴ فاتكي ∴

فنفرن أمّا تكي ∴ فنفرن دتيّجو ∴ سن واك ∴

يتنا سوا ∴ يغدو ∴ يغنم ∴ يب إنّا ألفجي

يبغان ∴ [illegible] سن واك ∴ يب غدّا نّاون ∴

غيّا منّ وبتوا ∴ تكوا نشي ∴ كو يبنيّقك

دادعب ∴ يبتيا يقمن ∴ دادي ∴ لسن واك ∴ يجون =

يبي تجيا فسن بودود ∴ يبي تكواسن ∴ فادم ∴ =

يكوا نسكن يتّاون ∴ شتّا فنن أمغسن ∴ د ماقرسن آشبن

سنغم ∴ بلكيبني ∴ د واك ∴ يبيّ تكمّن مغاري ∴

بجنّن إدّن تكنّا سو ∴ تكسلم ∴ أمنش ∴

ألحالم ∴ تكنّا جنّن يمغو ∴ سن تكغم ∴

da mai-[12]karfī tukuna, saanan ka sāmu.

Shi ke nan. [13] Kungurus kan kūsu. Kūsu ba yā chi kai na ba, sai in chi kai, dan banza.

---

with some powerful person first, then you get (it). That is it. Off with the rat's head. The rat has not eaten my head, rather will I eat its head, son of a worthless fellow.

فَ دَمِنكَمْ بَجِ تَكُمْ سَعَنَّمْ مُحَمَّدَ ⁘ سَمكَسْ

شِبِكَنَّ فَنْغَمْ سَنْ كَمْ كُو مُنْ كُو سَنْ جَجِيَاتِ

كَيْنَابْ . سَنْ إِمْشِ كَيْعِ فَيْنْدَا

No. 27.

Wanan tātsūnīar [1]gizo che de zāki.

Gizogizo ya tafi [2]sun kīfi. [3]Ya kāma kīfi dayawa. Shi-na-[4]banda, sai zāki ya zō, ya che, 'Gizō me ka ke yi nan?' Gizō ya che, 'Ina-banda kīfi ne.' Zāki ya che, 'Ba ni guda in chi.' Ya ba shi, ya chi. Ya ji dādi, ya che, 'Kāra mani.' Sai ya kāra masa, ya chi. Sai ya che, 'Kāra mani kuma.' Sai gizo shi-na-kūka. Sai zāki ya che, 'Gizo kū-ka ka ke yi?' Gizō ya che, 'Aa, ba kūka na ke yi ba, hayāki ke shiga mani idānu.' Sai zāki ya che, 'Dauki duka, ka ba ni, in chainye.' Sai ya dauki duka, ya ba shi, ya chainye. Shi-na-kūka. Aka-jima, sai [5]makwarwa ta zō ta-na-kūka, kuker! kuker! Sai gizō ya che,

---

This is a story about the spider and the lion. The spider went to fish. He caught many fish. He was frying them when the lion came (and) said, 'Spider, what are you doing there?' The spider replied, 'I am frying fish.' The lion said, 'Give me one to eat.' He gave him (and) he ate. He found it was sweet (and) he said, 'Add some more.' He added some more (and) he ate. Then he said, 'Add some more again.' But the spider was crying, and the lion said, 'Spider, you are crying.' And the spider said, 'Oh no, I am not crying; the smoke is getting in my eyes.' And the lion said, 'Lift them all (and) give me to devour.' And he lifted them all (and) gave him, (and) he ate them up. He (the spider) was weeping. Soon after the bush-fowl came along crying kuker! kuker! And the spider said,

وقن قا هو فتمير غدب د داك

غد غد :: يتف صر كيبه :: يكا مكيجه ديو ::

شنا بنكر :: لسر داك يدوا :: يب غدو مكجيتنر

غدو يب إنا بند كيجيبنر :: داك يب بار غدا

إقت :: يجاشر يث :: يجدا ، يب كاو امر :: اسر

يكدو امسر يث سر يب كاو امر كحم :: سر

غد شنا كو كر :: سر داك يب :: غد كو

كو كجر :: غدو يب عاع با كو كر نكب

تيا كي :: بكشغا مر اد انحو :: سر داك يب دوك

دك :: كبار افتقيو :: سر يدو كي دك يباش

يتنيو :: شنا كو كو :: آ كجحم سر مكرو اقدر

تنا كو كر :: كجر كجكر :: سر غد و ايب

'Yar nema, dūbe ta, ta-na-yi mani tākama, kō gaishe ni ba ta yi ba, sai ka che ba ni ya yi mata zāne nan ba.' Sai zāki ya che, 'Gizō kai ka yi mata?' Gizō ya che, 'Ni na yi mata.' Sai zāki ya che, 'Gizo ba ka yi mani?' Dōmin wauta. Sai gizō ya che, '[6]Naa yi maka.' Da wuri kua ya [7]kyale. Sai zāki ya dinga lālāshinsa, saanan ya yarda, Gizō ya che, 'Ama da wia.' Zāki ya che, 'Da wane abu ake yi?' Gizō ya che, 'Da gawurtache bauna, saanan a-bidi baba kazaura.' Sai zāki ya che, 'Ab! wanan bābu wia.' Sai zāki ya shiga dāji maza maza, ya sāmu bauna gawurtache, ya kashe, ya jāwō, ya kāwō. Su-ka-fēde. Gizo ya rēde fāta, ya che, 'Sauran kazaura.'

'Daughter of a profligate! Look at her, she is showing off her airs before me. Even a greeting she does not give me, even you might suppose (say) it was not I who gave her (her) spotted plumage.' And the lion said, 'Spider, was it you who made them for her?' The spider said, 'I made them for her.' And the lion said, 'Spider, will not you make them for me?' For he was a fool. And the spider said, 'I will make them for you.' (Now) at first he was going to refuse, but the lion implored him, and at last he consented. And the spider said, 'But it is difficult.' The lion said, 'What is it done with?' The spider said, 'By means of a huge bush-cow, next a big kazaura-tree.' And the lion said, 'Tut, that is not hard.' Then the lion went quickly off to the bush. He found a big bush-cow (and) killed it. He dragged it (and) brought it. They skinned it. The spider cut the skin in strips, (and) said, 'There remains the kazaura-tree.'

يرقمو ؞ دوبت ؞ تندا يقرقا عمو ؞ كو غنبش
بتيب ؞ لسر كب بدام تيمت ظا بنتنب ؞ لسش
داك يب ؞ بمغدو كنكيمت ؞ غدو يب فينيمت
لسر داك يب غدو بدا كيمن ؞ دو مرو قمل ؞ لسر غدو
يب ؞ تا يمك ؞ دو كوّ بدا فبو ؞ لسر داك يد مغ
لا لا الشفمس ؞ لسعنر ميير دا ؞ غدو يب آما دو يب
داك يب دو بندا با ابكن ؞ غدو يب دا غمور تب
بونمك ؞ اسعنر ابد ببك عورا ؞ لسر داك يب
عنبو نمر بدا مب ويا ؞ لسو داك يشغ داج ؞ مدمد
يسدا مو بحونمو غدا يتب يكبشن ؞ بجاو يكدا ور
فكعبجبر ؞ غدو يبر مجر مبقدا ؞ تب لسو نكدورا

Ya che, 'Sai kā je kā gani kazaura, ka [8]banke ta da kirjinka, da [9]karfī, idan ta mōtsa, ka sākewa ta, wanan ba ta yi, sai wada ka banka, ba ta mōtsa ba, ita ke yi.' Yau, zāki ya shiga dāji, shi-na-neman kazaura. Idan ya ga wanan, sai shi zābura, shi banke ta, ta yi mōtsi. Hakanan har ya sāmu wata kazaura mai-girma, ya banke ta, ba ta mōtsa ba har sau uku. Saanan ya zō, ye kirāwō gizō. Gizo ya che, 'Sauran, runfa, a-dōra nama.' Akai, zāki ya kariō itāche, su-ka-yi runfa, su-ka-dōra nāma. Su-ka-fūra wuta. Saanan gizō ya che zāki shi zō shi kwa--nta. Zāki ya zō, ya kwanta gūtsun kazaura. Gizō ya dinga daurinsa da kīri, ya tanke shi duka, ya rika

---

He said, 'Still you have to go (and) look for a kazaura-tree. Hit it hard with your chest (and) if it moves, leave it; such an one will not do. Only one that when you beat against it does not move, it will suffice.' So the lion entered the bush in search of a kazaura-tree. If he saw one, then he sprang at it, (and) beat against it. It moved. And so on, till he found a huge kazaura-tree (which) when he shook it, did not stir after (testing it) three times. Then he came and called the spider. He said, 'There remains a rack for putting the meat on.' It (the meat) was brought, the lion broke sticks, (and) they made a rack, (and) put the meat on it. They kindled a fire. Then the spider said the lion was to come and lie down. The lion came and lay down at the foot of the kazaura-tree. The spider began to tie him up with the (bush-cow) hide; he bound him up completely, (and) kept

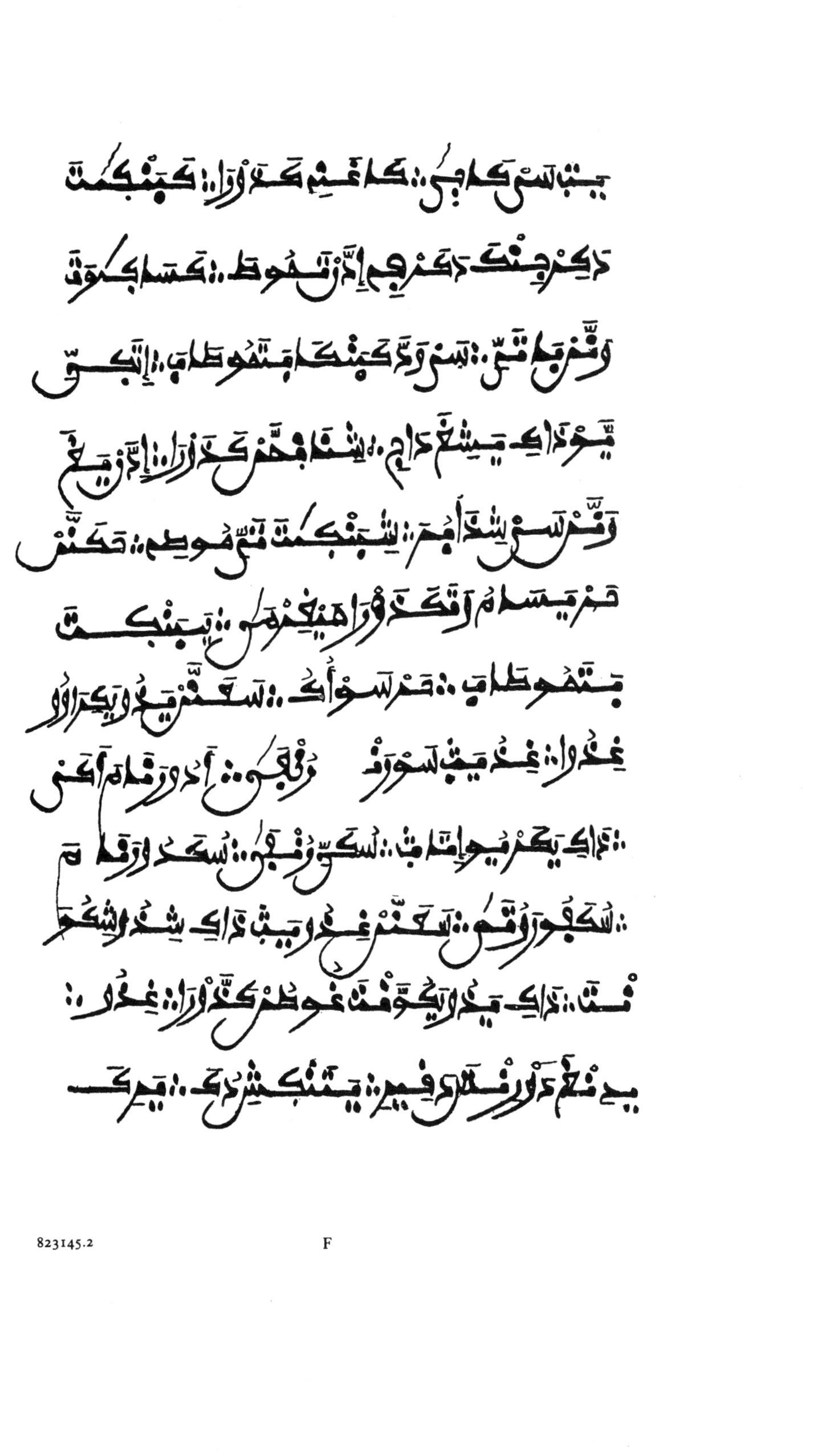

tanbaya sa, 'Ina ne, bai tanko ba?' Sai zāki shi mōtsa, shi ji wurinda shi ke iya mōtsi, shi che, 'Nan ne bai tanko ba.' Sai gizō shi tanke da keau, shi che, 'Mōtsa in gani.' Shi mōtsa, idan ya gani wurinda shi ke iya mōtsi, sai shi tanke da keau. Hakanan hakanan har ya tanke shi, ba shi iya mōtsi kuma. Saanan ya daukō [10]churakai ya sa wuta. Su-ka-yi ja zur. Sai shi daukō guda daia, shi nāna masa, shi che, [11]'Chuwai! kifina, chuwai! gargazata, chuwai! rājiata, chuwai! gwandōna, chuwai! kulumeta, chuwai! gīwaruata.' Har ya zāne jikin zāki duka da churakai. Ya kwāshe nāma, da shi, da [12]maatar tasa, da yāyansa. Su-ka-kai gida, su-ka-bar zāki kwanche gūtsun kazaura, har zāki ya lālāche

---

asking him, 'Where is it I have not bound?' And the lio squirmed about, that he might perceive where he could move, (and said, 'Here is a place you have not bound up.' Then the spide trussed him beautifully and said, '(Try) and move that I may see He moved. If he saw the place he could move, then he fastened i up well. And thus till he bound him that he could not stir agai Then he lifted up the skewers and put them in the fire. The became red hot. Then he lifted up one and pressed it (against th lion) and said, 'Chuwai! that 's for my fish. Chuwai! that 's for m gargaza (a kind of fish). Chuwai! that 's for my "kulume" fis Chuwai! that 's for my "elephant of the water" (a kind of fish) and so on till he had spotted all the lion's skin with the skewer He carried off the bush-cow meat, he and his wife and childre They reached home, and left the lion lying at the foot of th kazaura-tree, until the lion wasted away

تنبيس ؞ إمافج منتنكب ؞ تسن كراك شموط

شج ورفد شكم عتم موطم ؞ شب تنفنبم منتنكب

شر تسن غمخرا ؞ تننكم عم قتو ؞ يشب موط إنفغنم ؞ شمو

ط ؞ إدن يغنم ورفد شكم عتم موطم ؞ تسع شتنكي

قتو ؞ تكنق وكنق ؞ تخ ينبكشو ماشعن موطم

كم ؞ سعنق يدر كو نخو ركي يسوقط ؞ سكي قدادر

؞ تسر شد ركو غدع ادمو ؞ يشقا قا قمس ؞ يشب قتوى

كيفيسا ؞ قتوى غمر غذات ؞ قتوى واجيات ؞ قتوى

غموفد وقص ؞ قتوى كلبقا ؞ قتوى غميووات ؞ قم

يقداقبح وجكم كداك دك دقو ركم ؞ يكوا بشر فا

كم درشم دقا قاقمسن د يا يفس ؞ سككنى غدا ؞

سكبر كداك كوفب غموطمر كفورا ؞ قمر كداك يبدالاث

ya kusa mutūa. Sai gara ta zō. Ta che, ‘ Mutun, mutun dan Adam, idan kā yi masa rāna, sai shi yi maka dare.’ Sai zāki ya che. [13] ‘Asha haba gara, yanzu kaman da ni ke nan mutun shi yi m rāna, in yi masa dare ?’ Sai gara ta lāshe kīri. Zāki ya tāshi, da tāshinsa, sai ya lāshe gara. Ya wuche ya shiga dāji. Shi-na-neman gizō, shi-na-yāwō. Shi-na-tafi kamar zaa shi fādūa, sai ranan ya gamu da kwarangaman barēwa. Sai zāki ya che, ‘ Ke barē--wa ina zaa ki ?’ Ta che, ‘ Ina yāwō ne.’ Daga nīsa bai kusa da ita ba, bale shi san kōwānenē. Ya che ‘ Ba ki ga gizō ba ?’ Ta che, ‘ Aa, Ala shi tsarē ni da ganin gizō, mai-mugun kai, ai wanda ke neman gizō, ai shi ma,

---

(and) was near to death. Then a white ant came along. She said, ‘ M man, the son of Adam, if you have made it day for him, he makes it ni for you.’ And the lion said, ‘ Come now, do not say so, white ant. N placed as I am here, if a person made it day for me, would I make it ni for him ?’ Then the white ant licked the strips of hide through, (and) lion got up, and on getting up, licked up the white ant, and passed on (a entered the bush. He was searching for the spider, and walking ab He went along as if about to fall, and one day he met a very thin bu buck. And the lion said, ‘ You, bush-buck, where are you going ?’ S said, ‘ I am walking.’ From some distance off (he spoke). He (the li did not go near him, much less did he know who it was. He said, ‘ H you not seen the spider ?’ He said, ‘ No, may Allah protect me fr seeing the spider, the evil-headed one. Now surely he who is seeking spider, as for him,

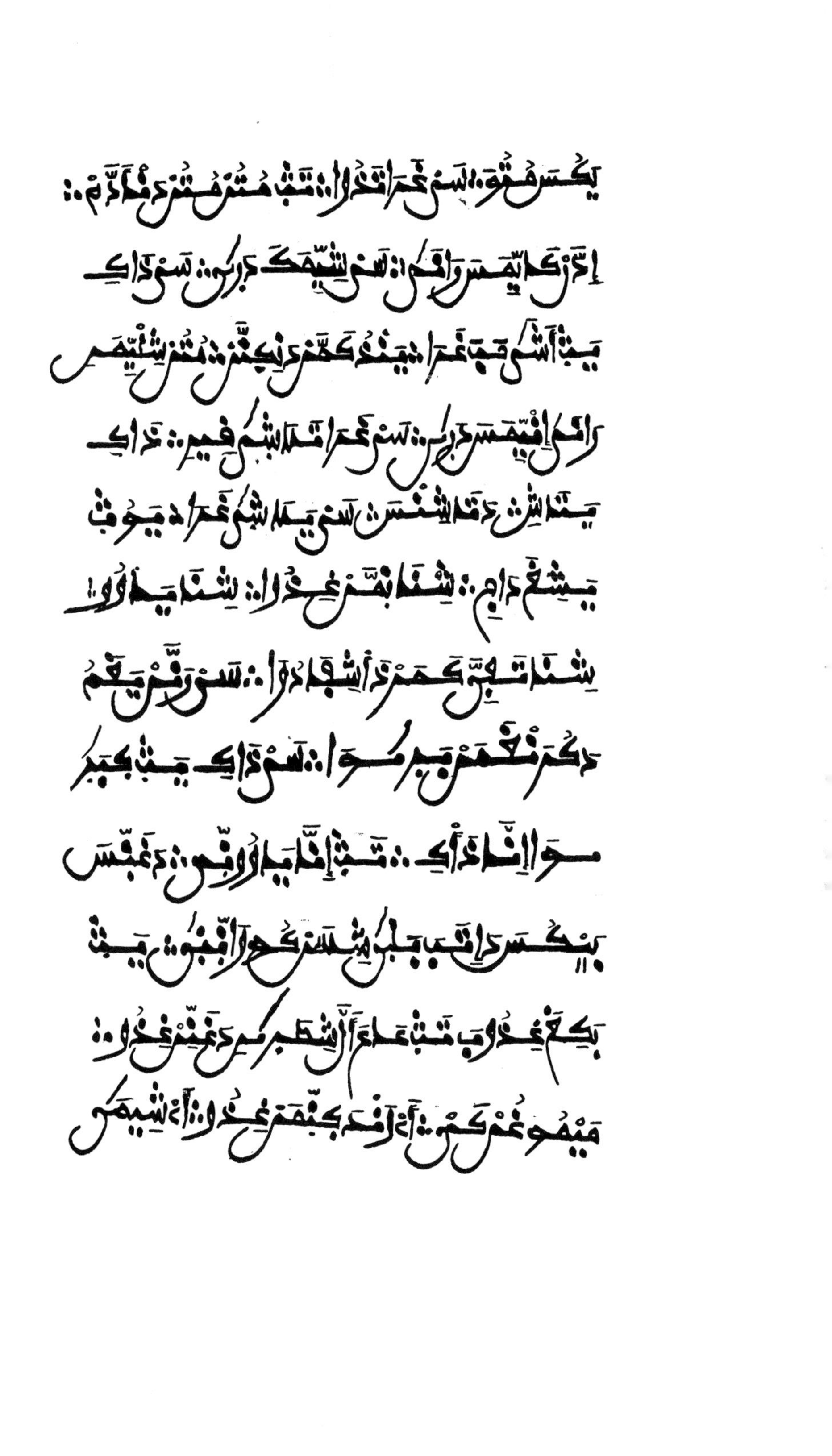

[illegible]
[illegible]
[illegible]
[illegible]
[illegible]
[illegible]
[illegible]
[illegible]
[illegible]
[illegible]
[illegible]
[illegible]

[14]yā fī shi mūgun kai.' Sai zāki ya che, 'Me ya fāru?' Sai ta che, 'Ai kwānanga barna shi ke yi chikin dāji, ba ka gani wada na zama ba, nā lālāche, mun yi fada da gizō, sai ya nūna mani hannū, nā lālāche, bai bugē ni ba, kōwa ya yi fada da shi idan ya nūna masa hannu, sai mai-shi shi lālāche.' Sai zāki ya che, 'Dōmin Ala barēwa idan kin gane shi, kar ki che ina bidansa.' Sai barēwa ta che, [15]'Nā ji.' Ashe gizō ne ke chiki. Zāki kūa tsōrō ya kāma shi. Sai gizō ya yi maza maza, ya yāda fātar barēwa, ya kōmō, shi-na-fadi, 'Ina [16]zākin shi ke?' Har ya chika da shi. Ya che, 'Gā ni, an-che ka-na-bida na.' Sai zā-ki ya fadi kasa, shi-na-afi, shi-na-fadi, 'Nā tuba, ba ni bidanka.' Gizō kūa, shi-na-zāgi, shi-na-fadi, 'Gōbe in kāra ji ka-na-bida na, [17]kaa gani, ai nā che idan ba ku kiyāye ni ba, chikin dājing

---

he has surpassed him in evil.' And the lion said, 'What is the matter And she said, 'Oh, in these times evil is he doing in the bush. Do n you see what I became? I have wasted away. We have quarrell with the spider, and he pointed his hand at me and I wasted awa He did not strike me; whoever fights with him if he points his hand him, then he who has this done to him wastes away.' Then the li said, 'For the sake of Allah, bush-buck, if you have seen him, do n say I was looking for him.' And the bush-buck said, 'I have hear Now really the spider was inside. As for the lion, fear seized hold c him. Then the spider made haste; he threw off the bush-buck sk (and) came back, (and) was saying, 'Where is that lion?' till he m him. (And) he said, 'See me, I am told you are looking for m But the lion fell down (and) prostrated himself and said, 'I ha repented; I will not follow you.' And the spider, too, was sweari and saying, 'To-morrow if I hear you are following me you will se Moreover, I have said if you do not obey me in this bush

يا فيشه موعمر كحو : لسحو داك يتب ميقارو : لسو

قتب آى كوا قنع بمر فالشكو نكمر داج : بكغنم ودا

نعمب : كدالالاث : فنبقد غدو : سر ينو فاهم

فنوا فدالالاث بنبغنب : كوا ايرقد دشه : إدرو

ينو فاملا فنوا لسر ميشم شدالاث : لسو داك ميث

دو تمراآ مرلو : إدركنغنبش : كم كتبا إفا بدفش

سر بمر موا فتبا فام : آبشر غدو قم بكنكم : داك كو

كوررما كا ماش : لسر محدو يرمعمد : يتبادو قاتم

بمر موا : يكومو ا : شناقد : إقادا كنشبكم :

تمر بثكد شم : يثعمار آفث كنا بد امكر : لسو دا

ك بقادكسر شنا آف : شناقد فا قوب : باوم دنك

غدو كو شندا غم شناقد غوبمرز : اوكادر : كحا

بعامر كا غنيم : آى فاث إدرو بكفيا بمنب نكمر ابغنغ

[18]kaa ga wia.' Sai ya che, 'Anbar ku ne, ku ke rēna mutāne, tāshi munāfiki.' Shi ke nan. [19]Kungurus kan kūsu.

Kūsu ba yā chi kaina ba, sai in chi
kai, dan banza.

---

you will see trouble.' And he said, 'You are pardoned, you (who) despise people. Get up, you hypocrite.' That is it. Off with the rat's head! The rat has not eaten my head, rather will I eat the head of the son of the worthless fellow.

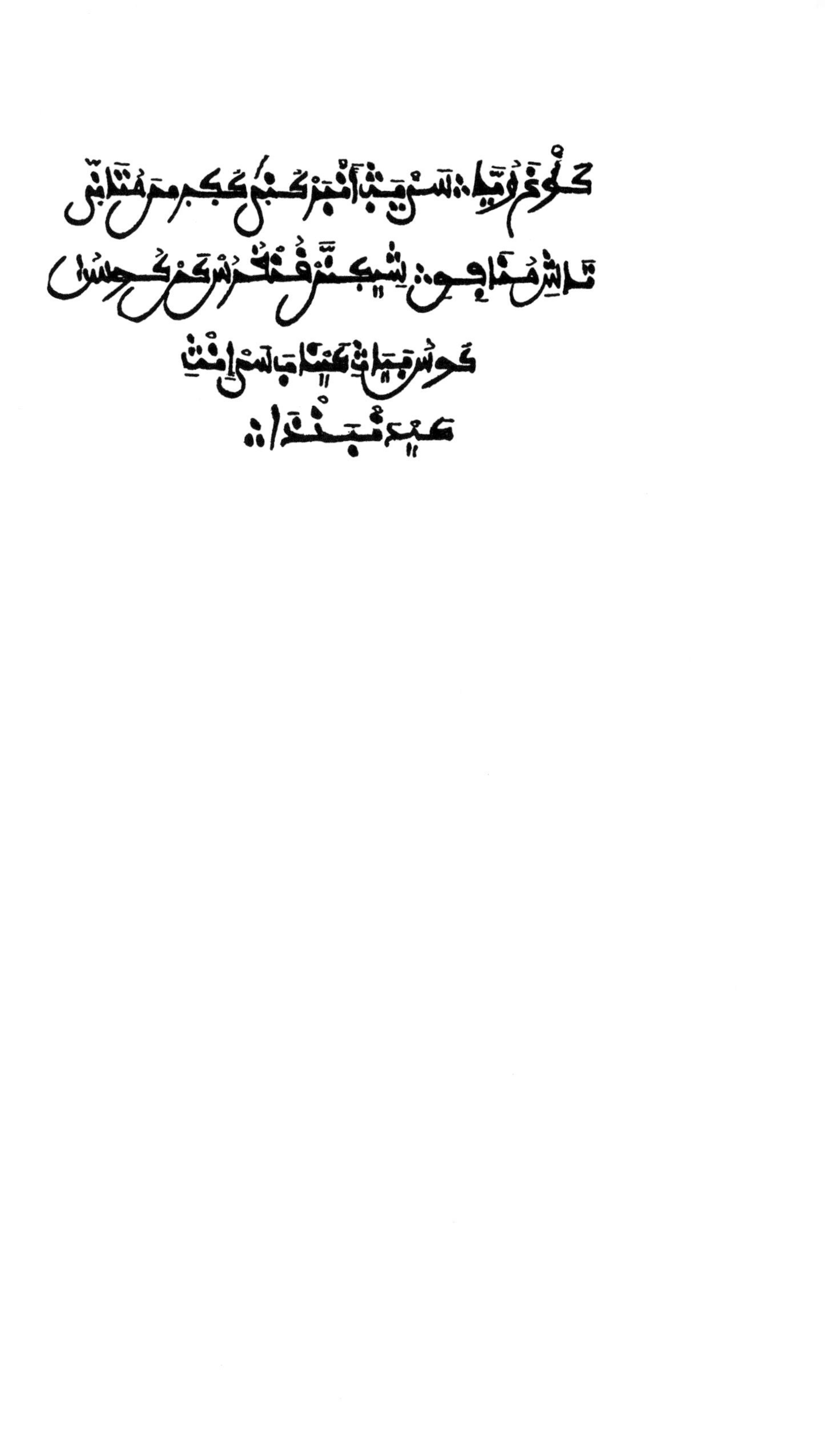

[illegible]

[illegible]

[illegible]

[illegible]

No. 28.

Wanan tātsūnīar [1] gizō da hankāka che.

Wata shēkara aka-yi yunwa, bisa, kasa, bābu abinchi. Hankā--ki su-na-zūa tsakar rua, su-na-dēbō baure, su-na-kāwō gida su-na-chi. Wata rāna gizō [2] ya ji lābāri, da su-ka-kōmō gida, sai ya daukō katanga, wai shi [3] zaa shi dīban wuta. Ya bidi dankō, ya līke duwāwunsa da shi, ya tafi gidan hankāka. Ya ishe, [4] su-na-chin baure, su-na-zuba wani kasa. Sai ya je bisan baure, ya zamna. Ya gaishe su. Ya tāshi. Baure ya mane ga gūtsunsa. Ya dēbe wuta, ya tafi gida, ba su sani ba. Ya kai gida, ya aje. Ya kashe wuta ya kōm ya zamna bisa baure, ya mane masa, ga gūtsu. Ya dēbi wuta, ya kai gida, ya aje baure. Ya kashe wuta, ya kōmō kuma

---

This is a story about the spider and the crows. A certain ye there was a famine, above, (and) below there was no food. Th crows used to go to the middle of a river and pluck figs (from a tre that stood in the water) and bring them home (and) eat them. On day the spider heard about this, (and) when they (the crows) cam back home, then he took up a piece of broken pot, saying he wa going to get some fire. He (then) sought for some wax and plastere his testicles with it (and) went off to the crows' home. He came o them eating figs, and they were throwing some down on the groun Then he went on top of the figs, (and) sat down. He greeted then He rose up. The figs stuck to his bottom. He drew some hot ashe from the fire (and) went home. They did not know what he ha done. He took (the figs) home (and) put them aside. He put ou the fire, (and) went back, (and) sat down on top of the figs; (they) stuck to his bottom. He drew out some fire. He took (them) hom (and) put the figs aside. He put out the fire (and) returned again

ونرتلطو فيير غدود قنككب

وتبشكر ؛ أكجي محو مسر كسدا ؛ مدا مبا أمنث ؛ قنكلا

كم لسند ذر طكر زوار ؛ لسنا بموبمورس ؛ لسنا كدا ورغدا

لسندق ؛ وقترا قم غدو مجي لابدار ؛ دلسكو مو غدا ؛

لسن بد روكو اكتنلغ ؛ ورشم دا أشر دمبغو قس

ييمجدر نفوا ؛ يليبغي درا رفسر دلشم ؛ ينق غم ن

حنكدك ؛ بيا أشي لسنا [illegible] شر مجو رسو ؛ لسندب

ونكسر ؛ لسن بجي مسر مجورس بغمر يغمشمس

يتدا شر مجو رس بحبش غفوطنس ؛ يدمب وقرينق

غدا بلسنيب ؛ يكي غدا ايا جي وتي يكو موا

يغمر مسر مجو رس ؛ يحمنمسر غفوط يدمب وقس

بكي غدا ايا جي مجو رس ؛ بكسبو وقر بطو مو كم

har sau uku. Hankāka ta che, 'Wani irin dība wuta ke nan, ka-na-zūa, ka-na-kashēwa, ka-na-kōmōwa?' Sai gizō ya che, 'Aa ba kashēwa na ke yi ba, mutua ta ke yi da kai(n)ta.' Hankāka ta che, 'Karīa ne, dōmin baurenga ka ke kōmōwa.' Hankāka ta dībi baure, ta ba shi, ta che, 'Ba dōmin mūgun hālinka ba, [5] daa sai mu di--nga zūa tāre.' Sai gizō ya fādi da kūka, 'I! i! i! Dōmin uwayenmu sun mutu kuma ba mu rīka zumunta. I! i! i! Ai da uwayenmu zaa su mutūa, su-ka-che mu rīka zumunta, kōwa ya [6] shāmu abinchi shi bai da--n uwansa.' Sai hankāka ta che, 'Bari kūka, tafi gida, idan gari ya wāye, da asuban fārin ka zō, mu tafi da kai.' Gizō ya che, 'Tō.' Ya shārē

(and did so) three times. A crow said, 'What kind of way is that to get fire? You are going, (and) quenching it (on purpose) (and) coming back again.' But the spider said, 'No, no, I am not quenching it, it died out itself.' The crow said, 'It is a lie; because of these figs you keep coming back.' The crow picked out a fig (and) gave him, (and) said, 'If it was not for your evil nature, then we might have gone together (to where the fig-tree is). And the spider fell down with sobs, 'Ē! ē! ē! Since my parents have died, we have not made any friends again. Ē! ē! ē! No, when my parents were about to die, they said I must make friends (with people); whoever jot (got) food was to give his fellow creature.' And the crow said, 'Stop crying, go home. When it is dawn at the very first streak come, we will take you.' The spider said, 'It is well.' He dried

كم لسوا كُ ،، قنكدا ك قتبٌ ،، وَبَا رفع ميب وتمو بكنّ

كنداء وكندا كبشوا كندا كومُوا ،، لسن غدو ويتٌ

تدا غ ،، بدا كبشوا نجييب ،، مُتو تجيّو ء كيتٌ

،، قنكدا ك قتبٌ ،، كم يدا بن ،، دو وقن بجوو نغ ،،

كجكو موا ،، قنكدا ك قتع ميب بجوون قتبا

شن ،، قتبٌ بادو وقن مو غمن قدا لنكب ،، داسن مح

نغ دو قدا ون سنو غدو وبقدا ء كو غكن ،، ايبه

دو وقن غموا ايغم ،، سنمنتكم بدا مرك ء منتا

،، ايبه ،، أء ء غموا يغم ءاسمشو ،، لسعب

مرك ء منتا ،، كوا ايشدا م أمنتٌ شجم ء

نغو مس ،، لسن قنكدا ك قتب بم كو كن

تعغدا ،، اكن غمر بدا وا ايكى ،، دا اكمن وقدا ون

كدو وقتبه دكن ،، غدو ويتٌ شو ،، يشدا بن

hawāye, ya tafi gida. Da aka yi kwānan fārin, sai gizō
ya tāra [7] yāyi, ya fūra wuta wajen gabas, gabas ta yi haske.
Sai ya zō, ya tada hankāka, ta-na-kwāna, sai ya che,
'Asubā [8] tā yi.' Sai hankāka ta che, 'Haba gizō, ai kai ne
ka sa wuta, tafi tukuna, sai kāji sun yi kūka,
saanan ka zō.' Da zūansa, ya kwanta kadan. Sai ya tā-
-sō, ya būde akurkin kāji. Shi-na-bugunsu. Su-na-
-kūka. Sai ya zō, ya tāda hankāka, ya che, 'Kun ji
kāji su-na-kūka.' Hankāka ta che, 'Haba gizō,
ai kai ne ka ke bugan kāji, tafi, sai lādan [9] yā yi kiran
sala, saanan ka zō.' Ya kōma gida. Da zūansa, sai
ya dinga kiran sala, '[10]Ayāhu akubai, ayāhu akubai.'

---

his tears (and) went home. When people were having their first sleep then the spider collected straws (and) kindled a fire towards the east, (and) the east became bright. Then he came and found the crow asleep, and he said, 'Early dawn has come.' But the crow said, 'Come now, spider, it is you (who) made a fire. Off with you, in the meantime till the fowls have crowed, then you can come.' On his going off he slept a little; then he got up (and) opened the fowl-house, (and) was beating them, (and) they were crowing. Then he came (and) met the crow, (and) said, 'You have heard the fowls are crowing.' The crow said, 'Come now, spider, was not it you who were beating the fowls? Off you go, and not until the muezzin has called to prayer must you come.' He, (the spider) went off home. On his coming, then he began to call to prayer, 'Yallah is yate, yallah is yate' (Allah is great).

توابي ؞ ميتف غدا ؞ داكيكوا امن قارن ؞ لسن غرو

يتاروبا ؞ يفجورنا رجن ؞ غجبس ؞ قمو فسكي

لسن يذو يتم فنكاه ؞ قتاكوا امن ؞ لسن ميث

اصبا قاب ؞ لسن فنكاك قبث ؞ حبن غذو اءكيبنق

كسارتن ؞ قد تكرن ؞ لسن كاجي لسنيكوكس

لسعمن كغوا ؞ دذ امس ؞ يكوفتا عمن ؞ لسن يتا

سوايبو دن اكرعن كاجي ؞ لشنا بغنس ؞ لسا

كوكن ؞ لسن يذ ويتا فنكاك ؞ ميث كنج

كاجي سفا كوكن ؞ فنكاك قبث حبن غذو ؞

اءكيبنق عجبغن كاجي ؞ قف لسن لادو يا يكرن

صلن ؞ لسعمن كغوا ؞ يكوم غدا دو امس لسن

يدي نغ كرن فصلن ؞ ايا اكبو ايا اكبن ؞ =

Sai ya kōmō, ya tāda hankāka, ta che, 'Ai kai ne,
ina-ji ka ke yi.' Sai ta che, 'Tafi gida, idan gari ya wā-
-ye, [11] naa zō in tāshe ka, kar ka zō kuma.' Saanan
gizō ya hankura. Da asubā ta yi, sai hankāka
ta je, ta tāshe shi. Su-ka-yi masa tarbachen fikāfikai,
su-ka-tāshi, su-ka-tafi tsakar gulbi, su-ka-hau
baure, su-na-dība. Sai idan ya gani zaa su dība
wani, sai shi che, 'Nāwa ne, ni na gane shi tunda fārin,
kar ku dība.' Sai su bari, shi je, shi dēbe,
shi sa māla. Hakanan har ya dēbe baure duka,
ya bar su. Hankāka da ta kāwō shi ta che, 'Tō gizō
ba (ka) ga abinda na ke fadi ba?' Sai su-ka-yi fushi (sk)

Then he went back, (and) met the crow. (And) she said, 'Oh no, it was you. I heard you doing it.' And she said, 'Go home. If it is dawn, I shall come (and) waken you. Do not come again.' Then the spider had patience. When dawn came then the crow came and roused him. They (the crows) gave him a feather each, (and) they rose and went to the middle of the river (and) climbed the fig-tree (and) were plucking the fruit. But (the spider) when he saw they were about to pick one (of the figs), then he said, 'That is my one, I saw (it) long ago; you must not pluck it.' And they desisted, and he came, (and) plucked it (and) put it in his bag. And thus (he did) till he had plucked all the figs and let them (get none). The crow who had brought him said, 'All right, spider, do not you see the thing I was saying (about your bad character)?' And they (the crows) got angry,

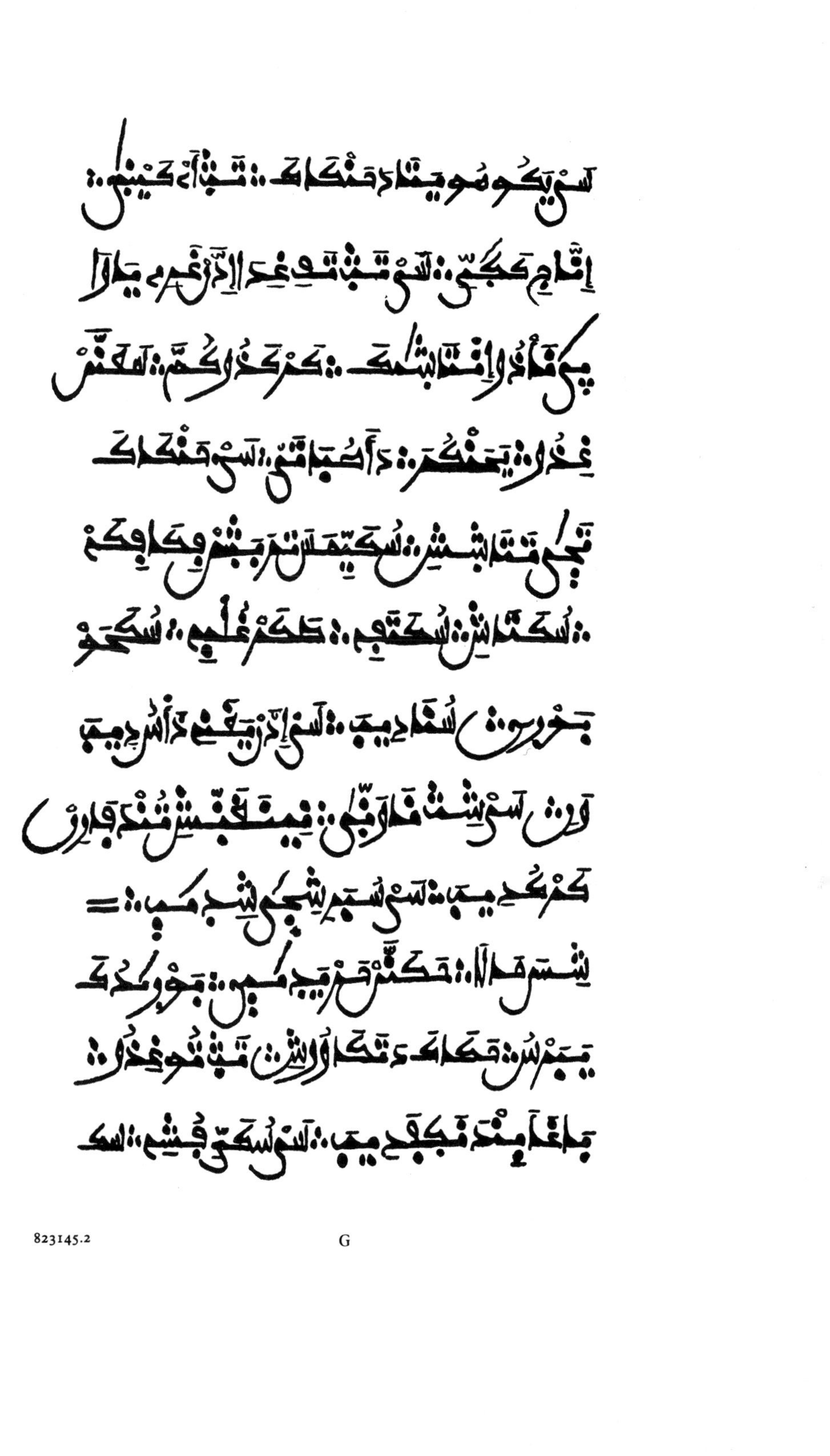

[illegible]

su-ka-kwāche fikāfikaisu, su-ka-tāshi, su-ka-zō gida, su-ka-bar shi [12] tsugunē, bisa baure. Ya rasa wurinda zaa shi bi, gaba rua, bāya rua. Shi-na nan har rāna ta kusa fāduwa, sai ya che, 'Bari ni ma in tuma, ai su ma tuma su-ka-yi.' Sai ya tuma, sai ya fādi chikin gulbi, punjum! Sai gidan kada. Sai ya che, '[13] La iya, ashe nan ku ke.' Sai ya dinga kūka. Su-ka-che, 'Ina ka fitō, ka zō, ka-na-kūka?' Sai ya che, 'Yā-ya ku bar tanbaya. Tun zāmanin kākaninku, dōmin kin ji ina yārō, na bache, a-ka-yi bida, aka gaji (ba g) ba aganē ni ba, sai yau Ala ya kāwō ni.' Shi-na-kūka da hawāye shabshab! har su-ka-che, 'Bari kūka hakanan kuma, ai kā zō gida ne.' Sai su-ka-ba shi dāki wurin da kada

---

(and) snatched out their feathers, (and) rose up (and) went home, (and) left him squatting there on top of the fig-tree. He could not think where to go, water in front, water behind. He was there till nearly sunset, and he said, 'Wait, I too must jump, for it was merely a jump they (the crows) gave.' So he jumped, but he fell into the river, plump! And it was the home of the crocodile. And he (the spider) said, 'There is no God but Allah, this is the place you are.' And he commenced to cry. And they (the crocodiles) said, 'Where have you come from, that you come (and) are weeping?' And he said, 'Children, leave off asking. Since the days of your grandfather, that you may understand I must tell you I was then a boy, I was lost. I was sought for till they were weary, and have not been seen except to-day (when) Allah brought me here.' He was weeping, with tears falling splashing, till they said, 'Stop crying like this now, for now you have come home. Then they gave him a room where the crocodiles

سُكَكُوَاشِ وَكَدَ وَكَيْسِ ۞ سُكَتَا اِشِ سُكَّ وَغَدَا

سُكَبَمْ شِ طِغُنُّ مَسَّ بَجُوكُوشِ يَمْ سَرُوفْدَ دَ أُلْشِبَ

غَمْبُ وَاهْمَا نُورُوَا ۞ شِنَا قَمْ حَمْرَ اِمْنِي تَكُسْ قَدِي وَا ۞ سَنْ

مَيْشِ بَمْ فِيَبِهِ اِفْشِمْ ۞ أَءْ سُوصُو فُصُو سُكَيُّ ۞ سَنْ

يَشِمْ ۞ سَنْ مَيْقَادِ فِكِسْ غُلِّبِهِ فُنْجُمْ ۞ سَنُوغُدْ وَكَمْ

سَنْ مَيْشِ لَايَا ۞ آشِنْشَكُبُكُ ۞ سَنْ مَيْدِ مُنْغَ كُوكُ

سُكَشِ اِنَا كَبِنُو ۞ كَدُ وَكَنَا كُوكُ ۞ سَنْ مَيْشِ يَا

يَا غُمْبُ تَنْبَمِيُ ۞ شُنْغُرَ امْتِّمْ كَدَا كِنُّكْ ۞ دُ وَقِّسْ

فِنْجِ اِمَّا مِيدُ وَاشْبِيشِ ۞ أَكِيُّ مِدَا ۞ أَكِغْجِ ۞ بَدَ غَمْ

بَا غَمْبُنْ فِبَ ۞ سَنُو مَيُّو أَلْ يَكَاوُرِنْ شِنَا كُوكَيْ

دَ قُوَامِهِ شِبْشِبْ ۞ حَمْ سُكَشِ بَمْ كُوكُو حَكَمْشْ

كُتَمْ أَءْ كَدَا دُ وَغَدَا امْبِي ۞ سَنْ سُكَبَا اِشْ دَاكِ وُوفْدَ كَدَ

kada ke kwai. Achikinsu, wani mai-hankali, ya che, 'Ku bari mu gani idan gaskīa ne shi danginmu ne.' Sai ya che, 'Ayi kunun lāka aba shi, idan ya sha, gaskīa ne, idan bai sha ba, karīa shi ke yi.' Yau sai aka-yi kunun lāka, aka-ba shi chike da kworīa, da aka-kai masa. Sai ya che, 'Yāya wa yā gwoda maku irin abinchin nan, na mutānen da wuri?' Sai ya fūde gūtsun kworīa, ya gina rāme, ya aza kworīan bisansa. Kunun ya yōye duka, ya shiga rāme. Sai ya che, 'Yāya ku tafō ku dauki sūdi.' Sai yāra su-ka-zō, su-ka-dauki kworia, su-ka-che, 'Ashe danginmu ne.' Dākin da aka-sa shi, akwai kwai kada chiki, guda dari da guda daia. Da zaa ashiga kwāna, sai ya che. 'Tō yāya, idan

---

crocodiles laid eggs. (Now) among them (the crocodiles) one who had all his wits about him said, 'Wait, let us see if it is true he is one of our family.' So he said, 'Let some mud gruel be made (and) given him. If he drinks it is true (what he says), if he does not drink he is telling lies.' So they made mud gruel (and) gave him a calabash full, which they brought him. And he (the spider) said, 'Children, who has shown you this kind of food of the people of long ago?' But he bored a hole in the bottom of the calabash He dug a hole, he set down the calabash over the hole; all the gruel drained through and went into the hole. And he said 'Children, come and take what is left.' And the children came (and) lifted up the cup, and said, 'Truly he is of our family. (Now) in the room where he had been put there were the crocodiles eggs, one hundred and one in number. When he was going in to sleep, then he said, 'All right, children, if

كد بجكون ∴ أشكفتس ونجمنكلي ∴ يتكتمر

مغنم ∴ إدن غنسكيا قبي ∴ شيم مغفصبن ∴ وسن يتف

أيكنزلاكي ∴ أجا اشن ∴ إدن يا شا غنسكيا بكي ∴ إدن ربش

شاب كمريا اشبكي ∴ تيجولسع أكيكنزلاكي ∴ أكبا اشن

ثبكم كمريا ∴ دأعكيمسن اسن ميتب يأيا ∴ ورياغدا

مكا إرنغ أمنيشنفشن ∴ مفتابن دوري ∴ سنيمجودس

غوطم كوربا ∴ يغمرا امون ∴ مدغ كوزيم بسنفسن

كنن قيبو بيودك ∴ بيشغو وامن ∴ لسن يتب يايمن

كتبو كدوركسودي ∴ اسن يدوا اسكغ وا ∴ سكدوري

كوريا ∴ سكتب اشي دمغفصبو ∴ دا اكنم أكسلا

لشن ∴ أكوزكوبجكد تكي ∴ غمدا ادري دغمدا دس

∴ د دا أعيشغن كجوافكي ∴ اسن يتب ثوجيأيا ∴ إدن

kun ji pus! ku che, Tūsan bākō, tūsan bākō.' Ashe ya yi haraman chinye kwai kada. Ana-nan dare ya yi, sai gizō ya dauki kwai kada, ya jēfa wuta, sai kwai ya pashe pus! da ya ji zāfin wuta. Yāra su-ka-che, 'Tūsan bākō, tūsan bākō.' Sai uwa--yensu su-ka-dinga yi ma yāra fada. Sai ya che, 'Ku bar su, ai jīkōkīna ne.' Yau idan aka-jima, sai ku ji pus! 'Tūsan bākō, tūsan bākō.' Hakanan har ya gashē kwai duka, sauran guda daia. Da gari ya wāye sai aka-che, 'Yāra ku daukō kwai nan a-kidaya.' Sai ya che, '[14] Ku bai, ku bai, ni nā daukō.' Sai ya je ya daukō, aka-zāna. Aka-che, 'Ajie nan.' Sai ya ch

---

you have heard pop! you must say, It is the stranger breakin wind, it is the stranger breaking wind.' Of a truth he had the evi design of eating up the crocodiles' eggs. Then when night cam the spider lifted a crocodile egg and cast it on the fire (and) th egg broke pop! when it encountered the heat of the fire. Th children said, '(It is) the stranger breaking wind, (it is) the strange breaking wind.' But their parents began to scold the children but he (the spider) said, 'Leave them alone, are they not m grandchildren.' Now, every now and then you heard pop! and 'It is the stranger breaking wind, it is the stranger breaking wind. And so (he went on) till he had put all the eggs on the fire excep one solitary one. When it was dawn they were told, 'Children lift up the eggs and let them be counted.' But he (the spider) said 'Stop, stop, I have lifted them.' Then he went and lifted one, anc marked (it). They said, 'Set it down here.' But he (the spider said,

كُنْجِ فُسْ ۰ كُثْبِ ثُوسْنِ بَاكُو ثُوسْنِ بَاكُوا
اُشِكُ يَا تِّ قَمْ مَرْ فُنْيِكِ كُوَيْكَدَ ۰ أَقْدَ اَقَّمْ دُرُسِ
يِتُّو سِنْ غَذْرَ ابِدّ وُكِ كُوَيْكَدَ ۰ يَبِجِدُ وُتَ ۰
سَنْ كُوَنْ يَقِشْ فُسْ ۰ دِ يَجِ ذَا فِنُوتَا ۰ يَادَرَا
فُكُثْبِ ثُوسْنِ بَاكُوا ثُوسْنِ بَاكُو ۰ آسُو غُوَا
مِنْسْ ۰ سِكِدِ مْغَ يَمِيدَ وَاقِدَ ۰ سَنْ يِبْ مُكُبَرْسُنْ
آتِ جِيكُو كِيِنَّا بُنْ ۰ يَخَاعَرْ آكِجَمْ اَسِنْ كُجِ فُسْ
ثُوسْنِ بَاكُو ثُوسْنِ بَاكُوا ۰ حَكُكَّرْ قَمْ
يَقْبِشْ كُوَيْدِكَ ۰ اَسُووَنْفُدَ ادَتُّ ۰ دَ غَمْرِ
يَحَوَابِمْ ۰ اَشُوأَكِثْ يَادَوَاكِدَ وُكُو ۰ كُوَيْثَمْ
آكِدَ ابِيَا ۰ اَسَنْ مِيثْ كُجِبُ كُجِبُ ۰ نُفِيِتَا دُوكُوا ۰
سِنْ يِجِي يَتِمْ وُكُو ۰ أَكَذَاوَ ۰ أَكِثْ اِبِشَمْ ۰ اَسَنْ يِبْ

'Aa bari in dinga kai ina kōmōwa.' Aka-che, 'Tō.' Ya rika daukōwa, ana-zānāwa, shi-na-zūa, shi-na-lāshe zānen da aka-yi, shi-na-kōmōwa da shi. Hakanan har ya chika guda dari da guda daia. Saanan aka-che ya chika. Shi ke nan dada ya che, '[15] Nā gani gida kuma, naa tafi in daukō kaninku, da māta, in kāwō zama daia, kōmi mutun shi ke bida bābu kamar mahaifa.' Sai su-ka-che, 'Tō, bābu laifi, ka zō maza ga jīkōkinka, ka zō ku di- -nga wāsa da su.' Ya che, 'Tō.' Sai su-ka-che, 'Akai shi gulbi, a-fishē shi.' Aka-kai shi, aka-sa jirgi.

'No, no, let me keep taking (them) back and returning (with another).' They said, 'All right,' (and) he kept bringing them backward and forward; it was marked; (and) he was going back and licking off the mark they had made and returning with it (the same egg). And so on till he had reached one hundred and one; then they said he had accounted for all. Things were thus when he said, 'I have seen home again. I shall set out and get your younger brothers and (my) wives that I may bring them, (and we may all) become one (family). Whatever a man may seek for there is nothing to compare with those who bore him.' And they said, 'It is well, there is no harm in that. Come back quickly to your grandchildren, come and play with them.' He said, 'All right.' And they said, 'Let him be escorted to the river and taken over.' He was escorted and put in a canoe.

عَدَاعَ بِمِ اِنْدِ نَمْغَ هَوِ : اِمَدَا كُومُووَا : اَعَثِ

ثُو : بِيمِ كَدِ وُكُووَا : اَمَّدَا اَمَدَا وَا : شِنَدَ دُوَ :

شِنَدَ الاشِمُ ذَابِتَّنْدَ اَكِي : شِنَدَ كُومُووَا :

دَاشِمِ : مَكَتِمُ تَمْ بِيِنْكَ نُكَدَا دُوِي دَغُدَا دَسَّ

نَاسَكَتِمُ اَعَثِ بِيَا اِنْكَ شِبِكَتِمُ : دَ دِ بِيثِ مَدَا غَنِمِ

غِدَا كُتَمَّ : شَمَدَا اُتِفِ اِمُدَ وُكُوَا : فِتِنْكُ

دَمَدَا تِمُ اِنْكَدَا وُرِ : دَمَدَا دِنْ : كُومِيمِ مُتُمُ فُتِبِدَا

بَدَا بُ تَكَتِمُ مَمَبِكُو : اسَ سُكَثِ ثُو بَدَا بُ لِيبِعِ

: تَكَذُو مَدَ غَدَا جِيكُو كِنْكُ : تَكَذُو كُدِ

نْغَ وَاسَو : دَسُو : بِيثِ ثُو : اسَ سُكَثِ

اَكِيشِ غُلِيمِ : اَبِشَمُشِ : اَمَكِيشِ : اَكَسِبِ رِغِمِ

Ana-tūka shi har su-ka-kai tsakan rua. Saanan
wani mai-hankali ya che, ‘A-je, a-dūba kwai, a-gani.’ Aka-je,
aka-dūba, aka-gani, kwai guda daia ya saura.
Aka-che, ‘A-yi maza a-kōmō da bākō nan. Sai aka-je ba-
-kin rāfi, ana-che, ‘A-kōmō da bākō nan.’ Wanda
ke tūka shi kuruma ne, ba shi ji kwarai. Idan aka-che,
‘A-kōmō da bākō nan.’ Sai gizō shi che, ‘Tō, kā ji,
wai a-yi maza da bākō nan, sābon rua yā zō, yi maza.’
Hakanan har aka-fishē shi, ya yi tafia tasa. Shi ke nan.
[16] Kungurus kan kūsu.

He was paddled until he reached mid-stream. Then one of the crocodiles who was smart said, ‘Let us go and look at the eggs.’ (So) they went and looked, and saw one single egg was left. And they said, ‘Let this stranger be brought back at once.’ And they went to the edge of the river and were saying, ‘Let the stranger be brought back.’ The one who was paddling was deaf, he did not hear very well. And when they said, ‘Let the stranger be brought back,’ then the spider he said, ‘There you are, have you heard, They say, Hurry up with the stranger, as a freshet has come down. Make haste.’ And so (he said) till he was across; (and) he went his way. That is it. Off with the rat’s head.

أَنَا قُوكَدَاشِ ⁘ قَمْ سُكَكِي طَكَمْ رُوَا ⁘ سَغَنَّ ⁘

وَنِمْعَنْكَلِمْ يِبْ أَجِي أُدُوبْ كُوسْ ⁘ أَغْنِمْ ⁘ أَكَجِي

أَكُدُوبْ ⁘ أَكَفْنِمْ ⁘ كُوسْ مُعَادَتِ يَسُوَوْ ⁘ =

أَكَبْ أَيِمَدْ أَكُومُودْ بَاكُوقَنَّ ⁘ تَسِ أَكَجِي بَا

كِرْ رَاجِ أَنَا قِنُو أَكُومُودْ بَاكُوقَنَّ ⁘ وَفَمْ

بِكُتُوكَدَاشِ كُرْ مَا فُجِ بَاشِجِ كُرْ ⁘ إِدَرْ أَكَبْ

أَكُومُودْ بَاكُنَّ ⁘ تَسِ غِدَرْ وَشَبْ تُوكَادِ ⁘

وَبَا يِمَدْ دِبَاكُوقَنَّ سَامُورْ وَابَادْرُ ⁘ يِمَدْ

مَكَنَّ قَمْ أَكَجِبْ شَكَمِشِ بِي تَجِبَا تَسِ ⁘ نِشِيكَنِّ

فُغْنُرْ سِكَمْ فُوسِ ⁘

No. 29.

Wanan tātsūnīar [1]gizō che.

Gizō ke da [2]maata tasa, sūnanta [3]wāke, ta-na da sānīarta. [4]Ta haifi da, namiji, ta mutu, ta bar [5]dan. Shi-na nan. Maatar gizō ta-na-kīwonsa har ya girma. Ranan gizō ya kwanta chīwō na karīa, sai ya che, ta tafi ta yi bōka, ta gani, me ya fāru, chīwō nan ya ki kārēwa. Sai ya gwoda mata wurin wani [6]tanbō. Ya che, 'Akwai wani bōka nan, mai-idō guda, tafi wurinsa, ki yi dūba.' Shi-na kwanche, shi-na nīshi, 'i! i!' Da fitanta, sai shi kuma ya fita, ya bi wani wuri, ya yi maza maza, ya je, ya shiga chikin tanbō. Da zūanta, sai ya che, 'Marhabi da maatar abō-

---

This story is about the spider. The spider had a wife. Her name was Bean (and) she had a cow of her own. It bore a son, (and) died (and) left the son. It was there, (and) the spider's wife was looking after it, until it got big. One day the spider was laid up with a pretended illness, and he said she (his wife) must go and consult a wizard (and) see what was the matter with this sickness, that it refused to get better. And he showed her where there was a certain ruin, (and) he said, 'There is a certain wizard here, with one eye; go to him (and) consult the lots.' He was lying down, and groaning 'ē! ē!' On her going out then he too went out, (and) took another way, (and) proceeded very quickly, (and) went (and) entered the ruin. When she (the wife) came then he said, 'Welcome to my friend's wife.'

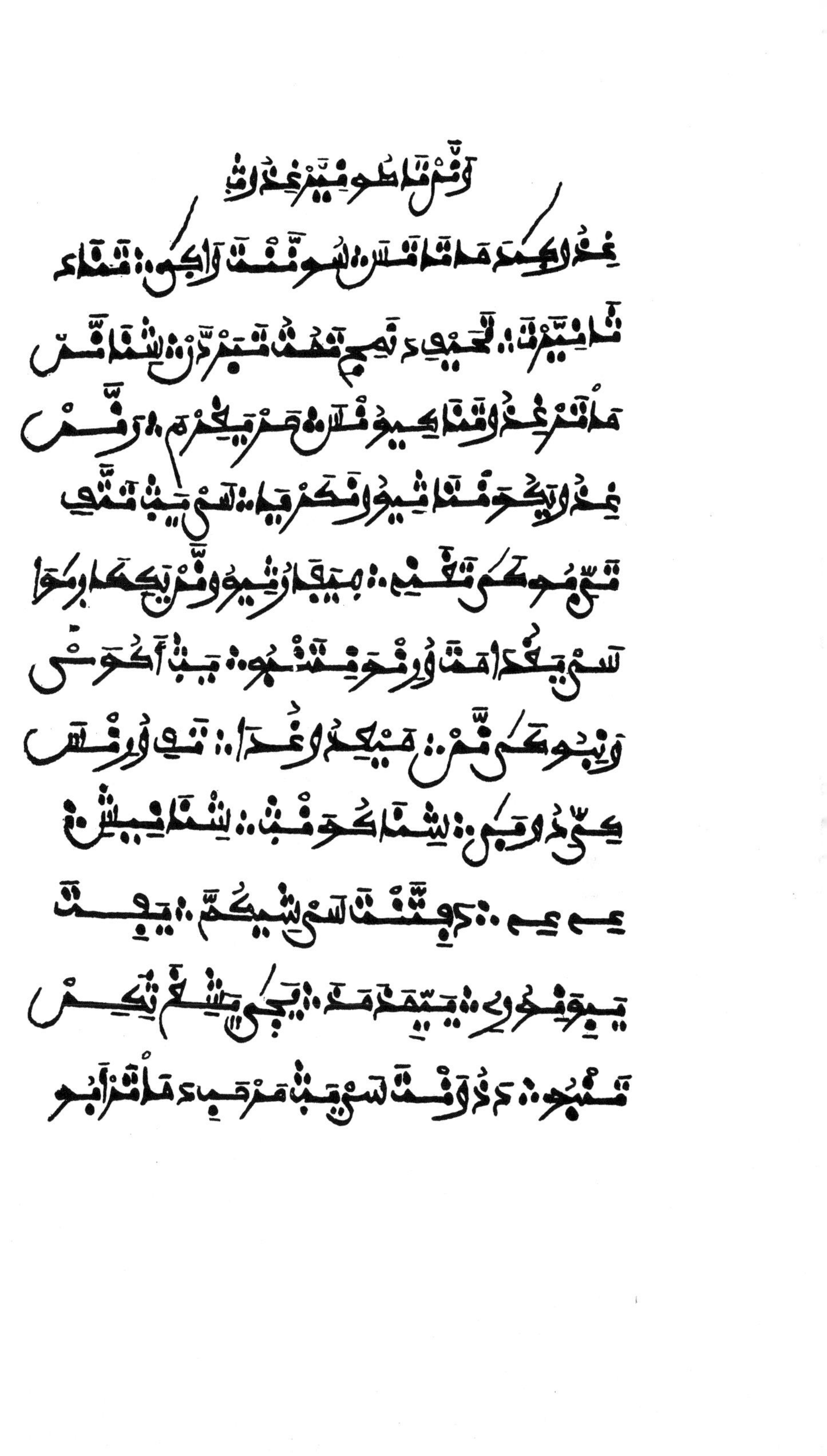

[illegible]

[illegible]
[illegible]
[illegible]
[illegible]
[illegible]
[illegible]
[illegible]
[illegible]
[illegible]
[illegible]
[illegible]
[illegible]

-kīna.' Su-ka-yi gaisua. Ta zube kurdi, ta che, 'Mijina ne, ba shi da lāfia, dōmin hakanan na zō, a-dūba mani.' Sai ya che, 'Hakanan mi-jinki shi-na nan kwanche, chīwonsa ya yi tsanani, idan ba [7] sāniar nan nāki ki ba shi ba, shi tafi da ita dāji, wurinda bābu kōwa, bābu kuda, shi kai nan, shi yanka, idan ba hakanan ki-ka-yi ba, sai shi mutu.' Maatar gizō ta che, 'Tō bābu laifi.' Sai ta tāshi ta tafō gida. Kāmin ta isa gida, sai gizō ya rigāwō ta gida, ya zō, ya kwanta, shi-na-nīshi, 'ī! ī!' Maatarsa ta zō, ta ishe shi, ta che, '[8] Nā kōmō, bōka ya che in gaishe ka.' Sai ya che, 'Kāka shi ke, me ya gaya maki, chīwō nāwa na mutūa ne, kō [9] naa yi rai?' Ta che, 'Ya che wai ka tafi dāji

---

They exchanged greetings. She poured out cowries (and) said, 'It is about my husband. He is not well, (and) for that reason I came that you may search out the cause for me.' And he said, 'This is how matters stand. Here is your husband lying down; his illness is very severe. If you do not give him this cow of yours, that he may go to the bush with it, to some place where there is no one, not (even) a fly, and he take it there, and kill it; if you do not act so then he must die.' The spider's wife said, 'It is well; there is no harm in that.' And she rose up, (and) went home. When she got home the spider had already got there first; he went, (and) lay down, (and) was groaning, 'ē! ē!' His wife came (and) found him (and) said, 'I have returned. The wizard says I must greet you.' And he said, 'How is it? What did he tell you? Is my illness to be fatal, or shall I get better?' She said, 'He says you must go to the bush

يَكِينَا ∴ لُسَحِي غَمْيِسُوَا ∴ تَغُمْبِي كُرْدِي ∴ تَثْبِتْ مُجِينَا

بُكِي مَا لِشِدَ لَلَّفِجِي ∴ دُوفِمَّرْ قَكَنْ مُدُوَا ∴ آدُرْ قَبَا قَمِنْ لَسِي

يَبْ قَكَنْ بِمُنْكِ شِنَا مَرْ كُومُنْبْ ∴ قِيُو فُسَرْ

يَا يِطَلْفِي ∴ إِدَّرْ قَبَا فَا فِيرْ قَمْرْ قَالِكِ ∴ كِبَا لِشَبْ ∴

شِتَفِ دَاِتَ دَاجِ وُرْفَدَ يَابُ كُووَا ∴ يَابُ كُدَا ∴

شِكِنْ مَرْ شِيَبْنِكِ ∴ إِدَّرْ قَبَا قَكَنْ فِكِيبَ لَسَرْ شِمُتْ

مَا اَنْتَرْ غِدُورْ تَثْبْ تُووبَابْ اَبِجِي ∴ لَسَرْ تَحَا لِشَ قَتَفِجُو

غِدَا ∴ كَلَا لِيَّرْ قَا لِسَرْ غِدَا ∴ لَسَرْ غِدُو بِيمِ بِمَا وُرَفْ غِدَا

يِدُرْ ∴ يِكُو فُنْتَ شِنَا فِيشْ يِمِ يِمِ ∴ مَا اَنْتَرْ سَرْ تَدُرْ

قَالِشِشْ ∴ قَثْبْ مَا كُومُوَا ∴ بُوكِي يَابْ إِنْفِيفِنْكِ

لَسَرْ مَثْبْ كَالِكِ شِكِي ∴ جِبِفِيَا مَكِ ∴ قِيُو وَنَارَ ∴

تُخُتْوَا فِي كُوفُنْ أَيْمَرُ ∴ تَثْبْ يَابْ وَيِكَنْفِ دَاجِ

da sānīar nan, wurinda bābu kuda, ka yanka.' Sai gizō ya tāshi ya che, 'Hi him! har nā ji [10]shauki, shauki?' Yanzu sai ya tāshi, ya zamna, maatarsa ta che, 'Ka-na-iya zūa?' Ya che, 'Naa [11]yayafa hakanan.' Sai su-ka-tāshi, su-ka-kāma sānīa, su-ka-shiga dāji da shi. Su-ka-je wani wuri da bābu kōwa, su-ka-che yārō shi tsuguna, shi yi bāyan gida, su gani, kō akwai kuda. Yārō ya tsuguna, ya yi bāyan gida, sai kuda su-ka-zō dayawa. Sai su-ka-che, 'Tāshi.' Sai yārō ya tāshi. Su-ka-kāra gaba, su-ka-che shi tsuguna. Ya tsuguna ya yi tōrōtsō. Sai kuda guda uku su-ka-zō. Sai su-ka-che, 'Tāshi.' Ya tāshi. Su-ka-kāra gaba, su-ka-tāshi su-ka-tafi da nīsa, su-ka-che

---

with this cow, to some place where there are no flies (and) slaughter it.' At that the spider got up and said, 'Until I have got well, eh?' And now he rose up (from his bed) and sat down. His wife said, 'Are you able to come?' He said, 'I shall cyawl (crawl) thus.' So he rose up (and) caught the cow (and) entered the bush with it. They came to a certain place where there was no one, and they told (their) boy to sit down, and ease himself, that they might see if there were any flies. The boy squatted down and eased himself, but the flies came in great numbers. And they said, 'Get up,' and the boy rose up. They went on. They told him to squat down. He did so, (and) eased himself, but three flies came. And they said, 'Get up.' He got up (and) they went on. They rose up and went far away (and then) they told

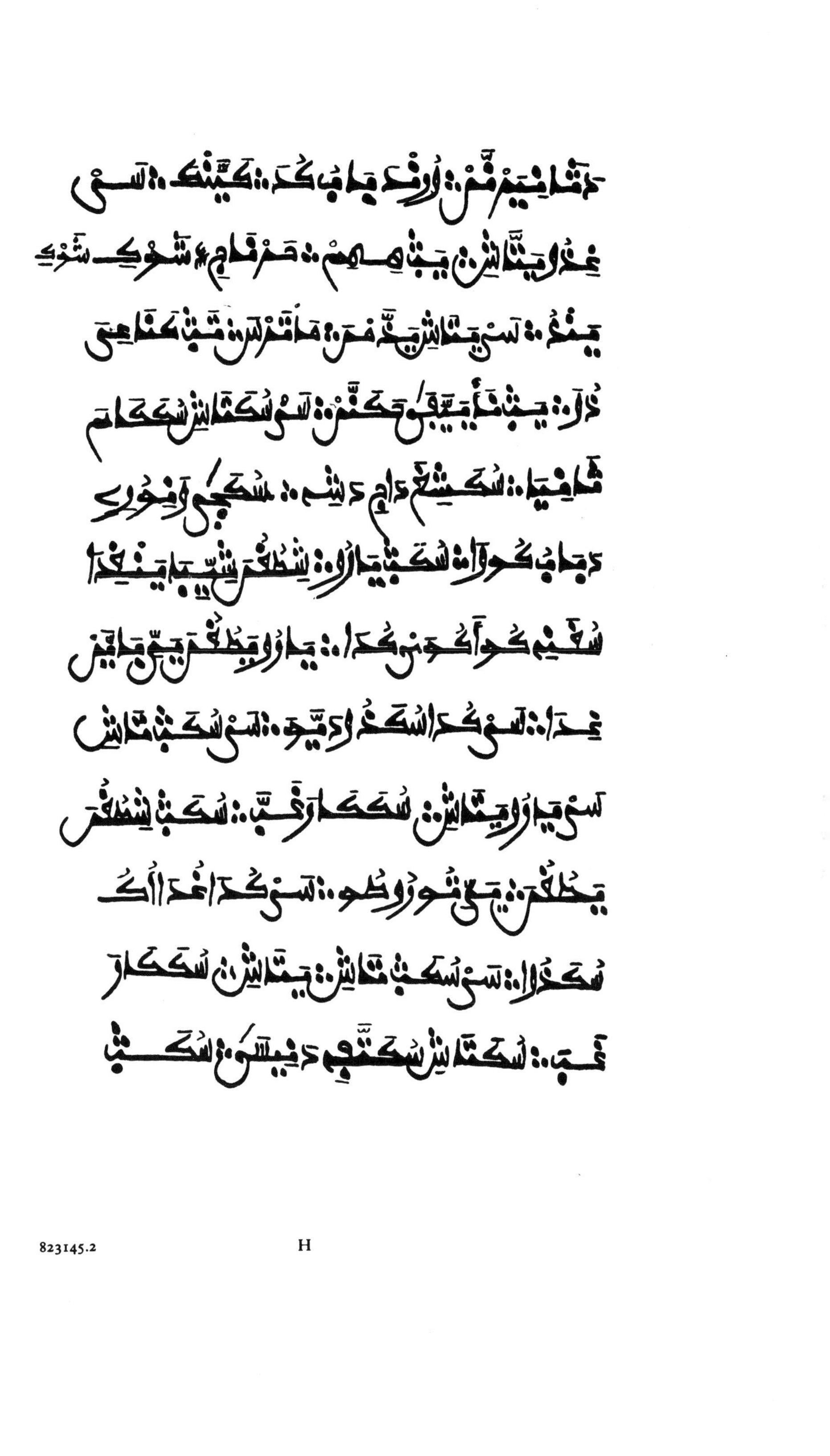

yārō shi tsuguna. Yārō ya tsuguna, ba su gani kōmi ba, sai kuda guda daia, rana kua ta kusa fādua, tā aza ganmō, tā yi jā zur! kamar garwāshi. Sai su-ka-che, 'Dōmin kuda guda daia, me zāa shi yi, mu yanka shi nan.' Sai su-ka-che, 'Mu yanka shi nan.' Sai su-ka-yanka sa. Su-ka-fēdē, da gizō ya gani jan rāna, kamar jan wuta, sai ya che, 'Yārō shi tafi. Ga wuta chan, yi maza ka dēbō.' Sai yārō ya yi gudu. Kāmin shi kai, rāna ta fādi, sai jan tsuliar Dōdō. Sai yārō ya kai wurin tsuliar Dōdō, sai ya dauki kara ya tsōkana, shi-na-che wuta che. Sai Dōdō ya che, 'Kai wānene?' Sai yārō ya ji tsōrō, ya che, 'Bābana wai ka zō.' Sai Dōdō ya tāshi, ya biyō

---

the boy to squat down. The boy did so, and not a thing did they see, but one single fly. (Now) the sun was near to setting, it has got big, it was fiery red like burning charcoal. And they said, 'Because of one single fly, what will he do? Let us slaughter it here.' Then they said, 'Let us kill it here.' So they slaughtered the bull. They flayed (it). When the spider saw the red sun, like red fire, then he said, 'Let the boy go. See the fire there; make haste and bring some here.' Then the boy ran off. By the time he got there the sun had set, and (nothing remained) but the red anus (of the bush spirit called) the Dodo. And the boy got to where the anus of the Dodo was. Then he took up a straw and poked it; for he was supposing it was a fire. And the Dodo said, 'Who are you?' But the boy was terrified (and) said, 'My father says you are to come.' And the Dodo rose up and followed

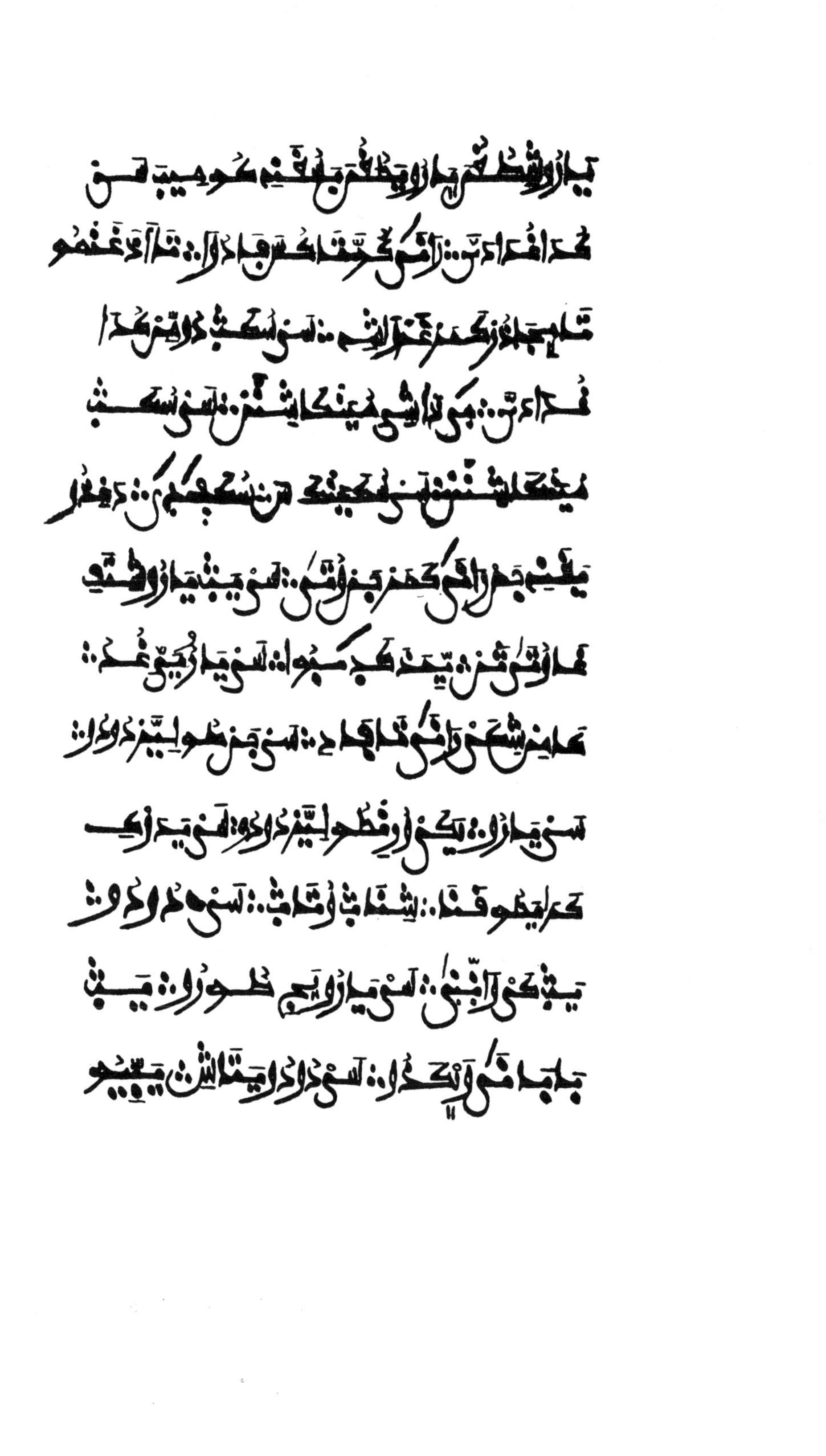

[illegible]

[illegible]

[illegible]

[illegible]

[illegible]

[illegible]

[illegible]

[illegible]

[illegible]

[illegible]

[illegible]

[illegible]

yārō, ya zō, ya ishe gizō. Sai ya kwanta, ya che, ‘ Gā ni.’ Sai gizō ya che, ‘ Wa ya kira ka ?’ Dōdō ya che, ‘ Danka ya kirāwō Sai gizō zaa shi bugun yārō. Sai Dōdō ya che, ‘ Kar ka buge shi.’ Sai ya bar shi, ya yanka nāma tsōka guda, ya bai wa Dōdō. Sai Dōdō ya che, ‘ Dan kankane abinan abōki kiran abōki ? Kārō dai, [12]dadi ne.’ Sai gizō ya kāra masa. Sai Dōdō ya che, ‘ Dan kankane abinan abōki kiran abōki ? Kāro dai, dadi ni.’ Hakanan hakanan, har Dōdō ya karbe nāman gizō duka. Sauran gizō, da maatarsa, da dansa. Sai Dōdō ya che, ‘ Dan kankane abinan abōki kiran abōki ? Kārō dai, dadi ne.’

---

the boy, (and) he came, (and) met the spider. Then he sat down a said, ‘ Here I am.’ And the spider said, ‘ Who called you ? ’ The Do said, ‘ Your son called me.’ And the spider was about to strike the b but the Dodo said, ‘ You must not beat him.’ So he refrained, (and) off one lump of meat (and) gave to the Dodo. And the Dodo sa ‘ For a little thing like this does a friend call a friend ? Add to increase it.’ So the spider added some more to it. But the Dodo sa ‘ For the sake of a little thing like this does a friend summon a frien Add to it, increase it.’ And so on, and so on, until the Dodo had tak all the spider’s meat from him. There remained only the spider, wife, and his son. And the Dodo said, ‘ For a little thing like this d a friend call a friend ? Add to it, increase it.’

يدارو. ميغو ويابشر غغو. سن يكو فتا ييب غغر

سن غغو ويب ايكر اك. دودو ميب دنك يكر اورر

سن غغو داش مغنيا ورو. سن دودو ييب عمر كبغش

سن ييمر شن يينك فام. فطو مك غعم ايبغو

دودو. سن دودو ييب دنفنفني امنر ابو كي

كر فا ابو كم. كا ورو ييم دي ميفن سن غغو.

يكا وامسن. سن دودو ييب دنفنفني امنن

ابو كم كر فا ابو كي كا ورد ييم دي ميفن.

مكنن مكنن قنر [illegible] دودو ييكمر بين

فامن غغو ودّك. سو وفغو اد ماقر سن

دد فسن. سن دودو ييب دنفنفني امنر ابو

كي كر فا ابو كي كا ورد ييم دي ميفن.

Sai gizō ya che, 'Nāma yā kāre, wane abu zaa ni ba ka?' Dōdō ya che, 'Kō kai dakai(n)ka ka ba ni, ban kia ba.' Sai gizō ya dauki dansa, tīlas, ya ba shi. Dōdō ya che, 'Dan kankane abinan, abōki kiran abōki? Kārō dai, dadi ne.' Sai ya dauki maatarsa, ya ba shi. Dōdō ya che, 'Dan kankane abinan abōki kiran abōki? Kārō dai dadi ne.' Gizō ya che, 'Kō ni dakaina kuma, zaa ka kāma.' Dōdō ya che, 'Tafō, shiga burgāme.' Dōdō kūa, bur-gāmen gīwa ke garēshi. Da gizō ya gani hakanan, akwai yāyan duma wurin, sai ya dinga kwāsan yāyan duman. Shi-na-zubāwa chikin burgāmen Dōdō, wai dōmin shi chika, har dīan duma su-ka-kāre. Dōdō

And the spider said, 'The meat is finished. What kind of thing must I give you?' The Dodo said, 'Even if you give me yourself, I shall not refuse.' But the spider lifted up his son by force (and) gave to him. The Dodo said, 'For the sake of this little thing does a friend summons a friend? Add to it, increase it.' So he took up his wife and gave him. The Dodo said, 'For a little thing such like this does a friend call a friend? Add to it, increase it.' The spider said, 'Even me too you are going to catch.' The Dodo said, 'Come, enter the sack.' Now the Dodo had a sack made out of an elephant's skin. When the spider saw this—(now) there were young pumpkins at the place—then he began to gather up the young pumpkins (and) was pouring them in the Dodo's bag, as he said, to fill it; (and he kept on doing this) till the young pumpkins were finished. The Dodo

لس غد ويب مدام ياكد ومن ؞ وف اب د افباك ؞

د ود ويب كوكن دكيك ؞ كبان وينفياب ؞

لس غد ويد وك دملس تيحس ؞ يمباش د ود ويب

دنقنقبن ابستن ابوك كم ند ابوك ؞ كد ود

د يبن ؞ لس يد وك مدتراس ؞ يباش ؞ د ود ويب

دنقنقبن ابستن ابوك كم ند ابوك كد ود يبد

يبن ؞ غد وبب كوفيد كينا كم د اككد ت

؞ د ود ويب تبفو شغ بم غد ابن ؞ د ود وكوبم

غمبنغيو ابغم مشن ؞ د غد وبغنم تحكمن

اكون يايبن دموورن ؞ لس يد مغ كو السن

ياين دمن ؞ شند مبا والتكم مرغد ابمغد ود ؞

ويد وتمن شنك ؞ حم د يير دمى سككد ولو ؞ د ود

ya che, 'Dan kankane abin nan abōki kiran abōki? Kārō dai, dadi ne.' Sai gizō ya che, 'Tō bābu wani abu sai ni kadai, idan ni zaa ka kāmāwa tō, ka kāma.' Sai Dōdō ya būde bākin burgāme, ya che, 'Tafō shiga.' Sai gizō ya shiga tīlas, ba da sōsa ba. Sai Dōdō ya damre bākin jika, ya tāshi. Shi-na-bidan itāche, dōmin shi gasa, sai rākumi ya zō, barwansa na bisa, da [13]banbadāwa su-na--yi masa kirāri. Ya wuche, bai che masa kōmi ba. Aka-jima, bunsurū ya zō, da barwansa, ya wuche. Aka-jima, sai kūsu ya zō, ana-yi masa kirāri, shi-na-tsale. Ana-fadi, 'Furub! bāta kāyan Dōdō. Furub!' [14]tuntoja.

---

said, 'For this little thing a friend calls a friend? Add to it, increase it.' But the spider said, 'Well, there is not another thing but myself. If you want to catch me, well and good, you can catch me.' So the Dodo opened the mouth of his bag (and) said, 'Come here. Get in.' And the spider entered by compulsion, not of his own wish. Then the Dodo tied up the mouth of the bag (and) rose up. He was searching for a tree in order to roast (them). And the camel came along; his servant was on top, and his followers were singing his praises. He passed on (and) did not say anything to him (the Dodo). Soon after the he-goat came with his followers, (and) passed. Soon after then the rat came; they (his followers) were singing his praises; he was leaping about. They were saying, 'Furub! Spoil the Dodo's bundle. Furub!' plucking (at the hair on the rat's back).

يث ؞ نقنقبن أبشر آن بوكم كم نا بوكم ؞
كاورد ئيم د يبشن اسغ غذ ورييث ثوبابا ورنا أم
اسغ نيكم ؞ ياآر زنيغ أعكاما دوا أثو ؞ ككام
اسغ دوردو ييبوذ بن يا كنبر غا بمو ؞ ييث ثقبو
يشغ ؞ اسغ غذ ورميشغ ؞ تيليشن با د اسو اسخ
؞ اسغ دوردو ريبع مبر يمر با كعر جك ؞ ييتاش ؞
يشنا بع نيل قاث ؞ دروقمن يشغ خصن ؞ اسغ وافيم
يغ ور ؞ بمر وقسر قا بنشن ؞ دمبجبداوا ؞ اشنا
يحسر كمراو ؞ ييوف بنشفسركو ميبا ؞ أكيم
بنشسر ريذ ور ؞ دبمر وقسن ييمحوث ؞ أكجسم
اسغ فوسن ميذ وأنا يمسر كراو ؞ يشنا عاليو
أنا قبع فبر مبا اث كا ايند ورد فبر بث ثنغم

Zaa shi wuchēwa, sai aka-che, 'Ai gā Dōdō chan, da wani abu gabansa.' Sai ya che, 'Mu je mu gani.' Su-ka-tafi, su-ka-i--she burgāme gabansa. Sai kūsu ya che, 'Kai, me ka ke yi nan.' Dōdō ya che, 'Kai sani wurin da dare ya yi maka.' Kūsu ya che, 'Ku kwanche burgāme nan mu gani.' Sai Dōdō ya yi fushi, ya tāshi, ya kāma kūsu, ya hade. Sai kūsu ya fitō masa ga shākira ya kuma hade shi ya fitō masa ga idānu, ya kuma hade shi sai ya fitō masa ga chibīa. Sai Dōdō ya fādi, ya mutu. Kūsu ya che, 'Ku kwanche kāya nan in gani.' Aka-kwanche. Sai ga gizō, da maatarsa, da dansa, su-ka-fitō. Sai kūsu ya che, 'Me ya kāwō ku nan?' Gizō ya che, 'Kā ji kā ji wada mu-ka-yi.' Sai kūsu ya che, 'Lālātache,

---

He (the rat) was about to pass, but they said, 'Oh! look at the Dodo there with something in front of him.' And he said, 'Let us go and see.' They went and found (the Dodo) with the bag in front of him. And the rat said, 'You, what are you doing here?' The Dodo replied, 'You, know when night overtakes you, and be wise (and sleep there). The rat said, 'Unfasten your bag that we may look.' But the Dodo got angry. He rose up, he seized the rat (and) swallowed (him). But the rat came out from his anus. He swallowed him again, but he came out at his eyes. He swallowed him again, but he came out at his navel. Then the Dodo fell down and died. The rat said, 'Unloose this bundle (and) let me see.' It was loosened. Then, behold the spider, and his wife, and his son, came out. And the rat said, 'What brought you here?' The spider said, 'So-and-so and so-and-so is what we did.' And the rat replied, 'Worthless one,

دأس ورْ يشوا ؞ آسن أكتبْ أ ؞ غدا دورد ورْ فثن دم ورف آب
كمبنلسن آسن مينْ فجى مغنم ؞ سكتفم ؞ سكم
شبى مبرْ غدا بوغ مهفلسن ؞ آسن فوس مينْ كغ مكجق
فمرشْ درا مينْ كغ آسر ور فد دمو مىتمحك ؞ فوس
مينْ محكو فنبْ مبرْ فلاقمن مغنم ؞ آسن دادور مينْ
فشم يتنا اشرْ ككام فوس ؞ تعجم ؞ آسن فوس مينْ جتو
مس غشا اكرا ؞ تيكم قد مشن مينْ جتو مس
غم د افو ؞ تيكم قد مشن ؞ آسن مينْ جتو مس
غشم مينا ؞ آسن دورد ويقا دمينْ ؞ فوس مينْ
ككو فنبْ كد امتن امغنم ؞ أككو فنبْ ؞
آسن غدا غدرد ما امرسن ؞ دم فسن ؞ سكجتو
؞ آسن فوس مينْ جيكا ورك فمرْ غدرد مينْ
كدم كدم ورد مكتى ؞ آسن فوس مينْ لالا امتبْ

kwāshi nāmanka ka tafi gida. Ala ya sō ka yau.' Sai kūsu ya yi [15]tafia tasa. Gizō ya kwāshi nā-mansa, ya kai gida, ya yi gaya. Aka-zō aka-yanyanka nāman Dōdō, aka-kai gida. Dōmin hakanan, mūgun kwadai, da mūgun rōwa, ba su da chau. [16]Kungurus kan kūsu!

---

take your meat, (and) get off home. Allah has been good to you this day.' And the rat went his way. The spider gathered up his meat (and) took it home, (and) summoned all the people. And they came (and) cut the flesh of the Dodo in pieces (and) took it home. And from this (you perceive) that evil longing and evil greed are not beautiful. Off with the rat's head.

كواش ما منك كتف غدا ⁘ آليداسوك يو ⁘

سن قوس يي قجيا مقس ⁘ غدو ⁘ بكواش قا

منس يكن غدا ⁘ يير غبيا اكدو ⁘ اكيقيك

قامر دودو ⁘ اكتكيغدا ⁘ دوير قكتن موغمس

كدد ⁘ دموغمر زرار با اسع قو ⁘ قنغرس

كرقوس ⁘

No. 30.

Wanan tātsūnīar

[1] gizō che.

Wani zāmani aka-yi yunwa, tudu da chikin rua bābu abinchi. Sai gizō da dīansa su-ka-rāme, ba su sāmun abinchi. Ana-nan ranan gizō [2] ya tafi wurin gīwa, ya che, 'Sar- -ki, Ala shi dade da raika, [3] shaki yuwa, dōyina, ta aikō ni garēki, wai in gaia maki, ba ta kwandō hatsi dari, in kāwō mata, idan kāka [4] tā yi, [5] taa ba ki dōki algarma, ama wai zanche, kunē na mainya, kar ki bari wani shi ji.' Gīwa ta che, 'Tō bābu laifi.' Gīwa ta bari aka-kāwō kwandō hatsi dari

---

This story is about the spider. Once upon a time there was a famine, on land and in the water there was no food. And the spider and his children had become thin for want of food. And things were in this state, when one day the spider went to the elephant (and) said, 'Chief, may Allah prolong your life. The shief (chief) of the shater (water), the hipopojmus (hippopotamus), sends me to you. She says I am to tell you to give her one hundred baskets of grain, and I am to take (them) to her. When the harvest season has come she will give you a great horse. Moreover, she says these words are only for the ears of the great ones, and you must not allow any one else to hear.' The elephant said, 'All right, there is no harm in that.' The elephant allowed them to bring one hundred baskets of grain

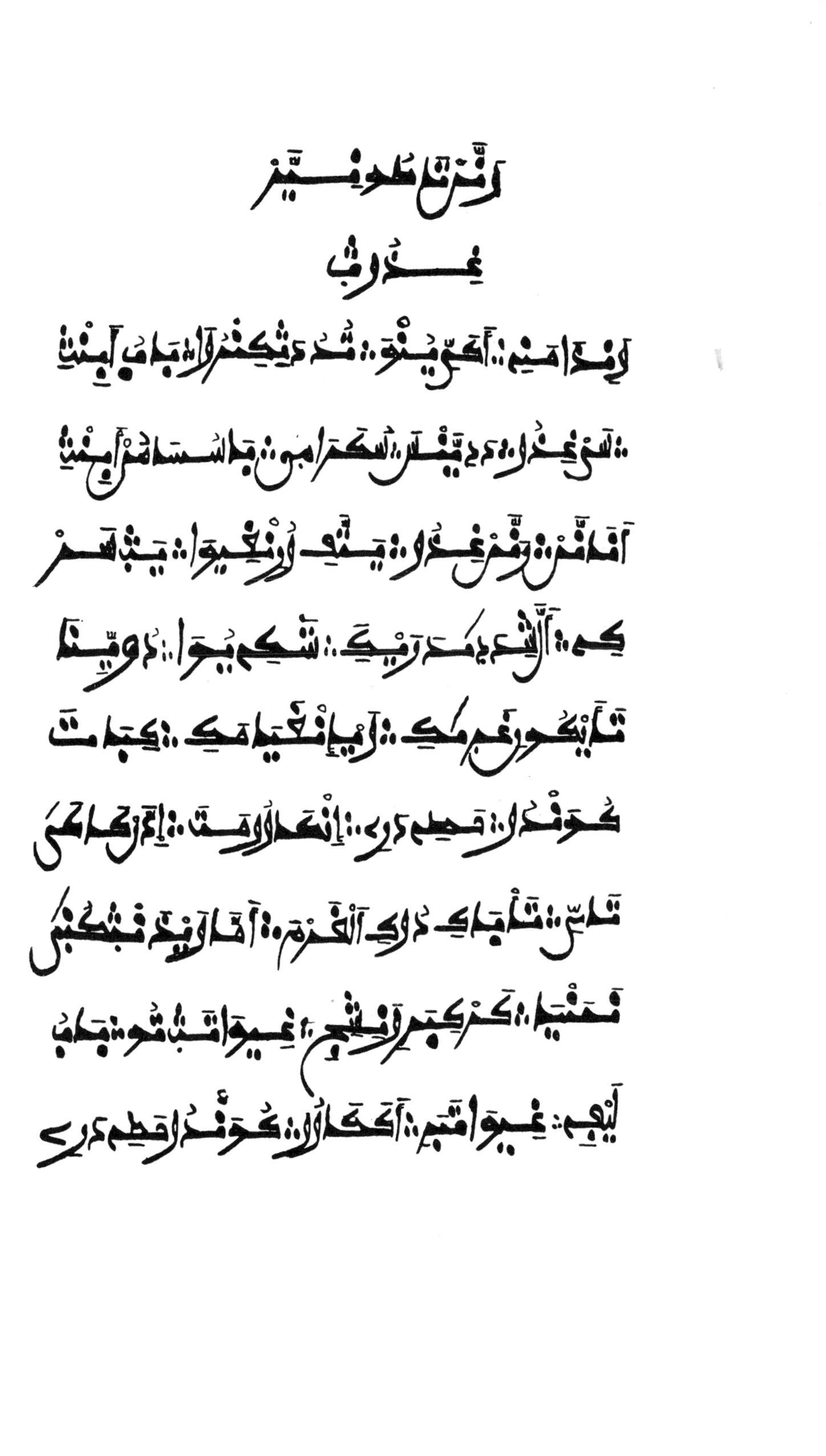

[illegible]

[illegible]

[illegible]

[illegible]

[illegible]

[illegible]

[illegible]

[illegible]

[illegible]

[illegible]

[illegible]

maza maza aka-bari samārin gīwa, su-ka-dauki su-ka-kai bākin rāfi. Da su-ka-kai, sai gizō ya che, 'Ku aje nan, ku kōma gida, in shiga in gaya mata. Ta bari samā-rinta su zō, su dauki, ai ku kun gama mai-wia.' Yau, samārin gīwa su-ka-kōma gida. Shi kūa, da su-ka-tafi, sai ya kōma gidansa, ya kirāwō [6] maatarsa da yāyansa, su-ka-kwāshe hatsi duka, su-ka-kai gida. Da gari ya wāye, sai ya je bākin rāfi, ya shiga chikin rua. Ya je fādar dōrina, ya taras fādanchi, ya chika. Sai ya wuche, ya tafi, har wurin zaman dōrina, ya zamna, ya che,

---

at once, (and) some youths of the elephants were allowed to lift them (and) take them to the edge of the river. When they had brought them then the spider said, 'Lay them down here, (and) go back home. I must go into the water and tell her, (the hippopotamus), that she may allow her young men to come and lift (them). For your part, you have finished the hardest of the work.' So the elephant's young men went back home. He indeed (the spider) when they had gone off, went to his home and called his wife and children, and they carried off all the grain, and took it home. When it was dawn, then he went to the river bank, (and) entered into the water. He went to the court of the hippopotamus' house (and) met the councillors. He went among them, (and) passed on, (and) went till he came to where the hippo was sitting, (and then) he sat down, (and) said,

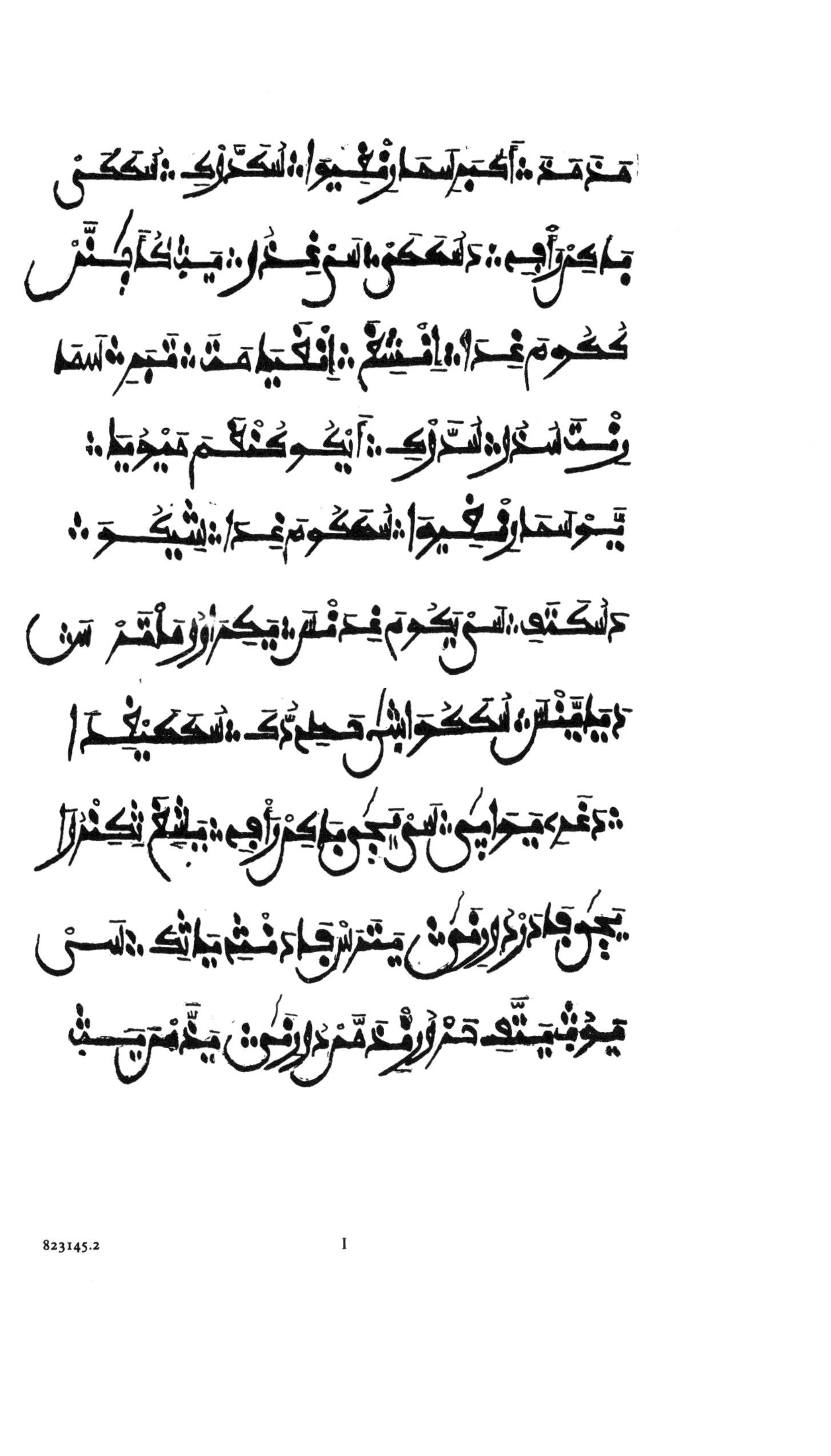

'Ala shi dada da rai sarki.' Dōrina ta che, 'Āmin [7] gizāma na kōki, ina aka-fitō?' Sai gizō ya che, 'Gā mu dai, [8] yanju ina-zamne, shaki tudu gīwa ta aikō, aka-yi kira na, na je, ta aikō ni wurinki. Wai in gaia maki, ta-na da tūō, ba ta da abin mia, ki ba ta kwandō kīfi dari, idan kāka tā yi, taa ba ki dōki algarma.' Dōrina ta che, 'Bābu laifi.' Sai gizō ya yi maza maza, ya che, 'Wai zan--nchenku na mainya, kar ki gaia ma kōwa, ke kūa kar ki tanbaye ta, sai ta waiwaie ki.' Dōrina ta che, 'Bābu laifi.' Dōrina ta bari aka-kāwō kwandō

'May Allah lengthen your days, O chief.' The hippo said, 'Amen, spider (husband) of the koki (fem. spider), whence came you?' And the spider replied, 'Behold me, I was living until just jow (now) as ujal (usual) when the shief (chief) of the land, the elephant, sent and had me called (to her). I went, (and) she sent me here to you. She bade me tell you that she has grain foods, but has nothing for making soup with, (and) you must give her one hundred baskets of fish. When the harvest season has come round she will give you a great horse.' The hippo said, 'That is all right.' And the spider made haste to say, 'He says, your words are only for (the ears) of the great, you must not mention (it) to anybody, and you, too, you must not ask her (any more about all this) till she comes and mentions it first to you.' The hippo said, 'There is no harm in that.' (Then) the hippo let them bring baskets of

kīfi dari aka-sa samāri su-ka-dauka, su-ka-kāwō bākin rāfi, su-ka-aje. Sai gizō ya che, ' Tō, ku kōma, in tafi, in kirāwō samārin gīwa, su zō, su dauki.' Sai samā-rin dōrina su-ka-che, ' Idan mu-ka-tafi, wani abu ya zō ya chi fa.' Gizō ya che, ' Ku dai ku tafi, bābu abinda ke tabāwa, idan ku-ka-tsaya, samārin gīwa su-ka-zō, samārin wani sar-ki, da samārin wani sarki, baa su gamuwa, idan ku-ka-tsaya, su-ka-zō ba asan abinda zaa shi abkua tsakāninku ba. Saanan kun sa manyanku yawan magana ke nan. Chin wāke na yāra, kunburin chiki na mainya.' Sai baban samārin nan ya che, ' Gaskīa ne, mu je gida.'

---

fish, one hundred, (and) boys were made to lift them (and) bring them to the bank of the river; and they set them down there. Then the spider said, ' It is all right, you go back (now). I must go and call the elephant's young men to come and lift them.' But the hippo's young men said, ' If we went off something else might come and eat it up.' The spider replied, ' As for you, off you all go, there is nothing going to touch them. If you were to stand here, the youths from the elephants would be here, and (you know) the young men of one chief and the young men of another cannot meet. If you stood and they came, who knows what might happen among you all? And by that time you have put your elders at variance. Boys may eat beans, but it is (their) elders who get swollen bellies' (i.e. boys may quarrel, but their elders settle the case). Then the eldest of the lads there said, ' It is true, let us go home.'

كِيبِمْ دُرِي ؞ أَكَسْتَسَحَدُرِي ؞ سُكَدُرْكِ ؞ سُكَكَدُرُو

بَايِكُمْ رَأْفِ ؞ سُكَاجِي ؞ سَنِي غُرُوا ؞ مَيِبْ تُوكُكُوم

اِمْنَتِ اِنْكِمْ اَوُرْ ؞ سَمَدَرْ فُخْيُوا سَغُرُ سُحُّرْكِ ؞ سَنُو سَمَدْ

رُفِدُرُو فُرَى ؞ سُكَبْ ؞ اِدَّرْ مُكَتَنْجِ اَرُفْ اَبْ ؞ مِيغُرُ وِيشِقْ

غُدُرَا اِيبْ كُودَمْ غُتَقِ ؞ بَدَبْ اَمِبْنُدُ بِكَتَبَدَارَا ؞

اِدَّرْ ؞ كُكَمَلَتِّ سَمَدَرْ فُخِيُوا ؞ سُكَغُرْ ؞ سَمَدَرْ فُمُوَفِلْسَمْ

كِمْ ؞ دُ سَمَدَرْ فُمُوَفِلْسَمْ كِمْ ؞ بَاسِرْ غُمُوا ؞ اِدَّرْ ؞

كُكَمَلَّمْ ؞ سُكَغُرَا ؞ بَعَسَرْ اَمِنْدُ دَأْشَنَا اَبْكُوا

طَكَدَا مِنْكُبْ ؞ سَعَقَّنْ كُفُسَا مُنِيَّكِ مِيُو فُمُقَسْ

بَكَلَّنْ ؞ شِنُوا اِجُمْ فُسَمِيَا كُنُبْرَ نِشْكِ نَمْفُنِيَا ؞ سَنِي

زا

بَبَّرْ اَسَمَدَرْ فُقَّنْ ؞ مِيبْ غَسْكِيَا اِبِي ؞ مُجِكِّي غُدَا ؞

Su-ka-tafi gida. Gizō ya je, ya kirāwō [9] maatansa, da yāyansa, su-ka-kwāche kīfi duka, su-ka-tafi da shi gida, su-na-chi, su-na-tumkar igia. Su-ka-tumka igia dayawa. Da kāka ta yi, su-ka-tumka gindi mai-tsawō, kamar nan da [10] Bajimsō. Ana-nan, ranan aka-kōne dāji, sai gīwa ta che, 'Ku nemō gizō.' Aka-je, aka-nemō gizō. Ya zō. Aka-che, 'Ina alkawālin da mu-ka-yi da kai zūa ga dōrina ? Gizō ya che, 'Bābu laifi, naa tafi in gaia mata, jībi naa kōmō.' Gizo ya tafi, kwānansa uku, saanan ya kōmō. Ashe ya je bākin rāfi, ya bidi wani baban itāche, ya damra masa gindi. Ya kāwō bākin igiar

---

They went home. The spider went and called his wife and children, and they removed all the fish and went off home with them, and were eating them, and twisting string. They twisted an immense quantity of string. By the time the harvest season came they had twisted a long horse-rope, as (long as) from here to Bajimso. Now one day when the bush was burned (by the annual bush fires) the elephant said, 'You must look for and bring the spider.' (So) they went and sought for the spider. He came. They said, 'What about the promise we made with you with regard to the hippo ?' The spider said, 'There is no harm done. I shall go and tell her. The day after to-morrow I shall return.' The spider went off; for three days (he was gone) then he returned. Now what he had done was this (*ashe*). He had gone to the river bank, (and) searched out a huge tree, (and) tied the horse-rope to it. He took the end of the rope

سُكَتّوبِ غِدَا ؛ غُدُ رِيجِي يكُرَ اُورُمَا تَنْفُسَ ؛ كِ بِيَامِيُّسَ

سُكَكُو اَشْبِي كِيِيمِ دُكَ ؛ سُكَتِّيمِ كَاشِّيمِ غِدَا ؛ سَنَافَ

سَنَا تَمْكَرْ اِغِي ؛ سُكَتَمْكَ اِغِي كَمْ تِيو ؛ كَكَاكَ كَسِي

قَ تِّي ؛ سُكَتَمْكَ غِنْدِي ؛ مَيْطُوُرُ ؛ كَحَمْرَقَسْ

دَبِغِمْسُوا ؛ آقَّا قَمْرُ فَّرْ ؛ أَكَكُو نَبُودَاجِ ؛ تَسَسْ

غِيُوا تَبْ ؛ كُنْبُمُو غِنْدُرْ ؛ أَكِجِي أَكَنْبُمُوا غِنْدُرْ

يَنْدُرْ ؛ أَكَبْ اِقَّا أَلْكُوانْدَ مُكَي دَمَكْ ؛ دُرْ غَدُورْقَلِ

غِنْدُرْ يِبْ بَدَابْ آنِيجِ قَمَا أَقِيدِ اِفْغَيْلَمَتَّ ؛ جِيِيمِ

قَأْكُو مُوا ؛ غِنْدُرْ يِتِّفِ كُوا أَقَّنْسَرْ أَكِي ؛ تَسْعَنَّمْ

يَكُو مُوا ؛ آشْبِي تِيَا جِي مَاكَمْ رَأْفِي ؛ مِيجِي رِنْبَبْ

اِقَلَفْ ؛ مِيكَمْ مَرَ امَسَرْ غِنْدِي ؛ يَكَا اُوُمَا اِكَمْ اِغَيَّمْ

wurin gīwa, ya che, 'Gā igiar [11] dōkin da dōrina ta ba ki. Gōbe ake-fida dōki nan chikin rua, wai ki bidi baban itāche adamra masa igia. Idan gari ya wāye, idan ku-ka-gani itāche nan shi-na-mōtsi, ki bari samāri su kāma igia nan, su ja, dōki nan, ke nan.' Gīwa ta che, 'Ashe hakanan gizō?' Gizō ya che, 'I.' Gīwa ta che, 'Ala shi kai mu gōbe.' Da wāyewa gari, gīwa ta tāra samāri. Ashe gizō ya je, yā gaia ma dō-rina, ya che, 'Gīwa [12] tā ba ni dōki, in kāwō maki, ama ba ni iya jansa, ama igiarsa da tsawō, [13] nā jāwō, nā kāwō bākin rāfi, nā damra ma itāche.

---

to where the elephant was (and) said, 'Behold the rope of the horse which the hippo gives you. To-morrow they are going to take out this horse from the water, and she says you must look for a huge tree to tie the rope to. When it is dawn (and) if you saw (see) this tree shaking, let the boy seize this rope and pull it, for that is this horse (pulling the tree).' And the elephant said, 'Is it really so, spider?' The spider said, 'Yes.' (And) the elephant said, 'May Allah give us a to-morrow.' When the dawn came the elephant assembled the young men. Now of a truth the spider has gone and told the hippo saying, 'The elephant has given me a horse to bring to you, but I am not able to pull it; but its rope is long; I have dragged it along and have brought it to the bank of the river and have fastened it to a tree.

ورف غيوا ∴ ييث غدا إغييرُ دوركم دم ورفو تجارك

غوبي أكبع دوركتن ثكنر وا ∴ وربكيج مبس

إتاث أكد مرامسر إغيو ∴ إدرغم ييجوايو ∴ ادرو

ككغني ∴ إتدابثنر شنامو وطيم ∴ كبر لسمارى

سكام إغيتم ∴ لبجي دوركتن بكتن ∴ غيواتب

آشي مكتني غدو ∴ غدويث إي غيواتث

أرشكيم غوبي ∴ دراپو غمري ∴ غيوا

تتاولسحاوي ∴ آشي غدوايا جي يا غيا مدو

ورفو ييث غيواتابا ودرك إنكادور مك

∴ أقا بانيحو ونتس ∴ أقدا إغييز سرى طودو ∴ تا

جدو ∴ قاكدا ورباكرو أقي ∴ قادفرا ما إتابا

Idan gari ya wāye, ki bari sāmari su tafi, su jā, mahaukachin dōki ne.' Dōrina ta che, 'Tō.' Da gari ya wāye, samārin dōrina su-ka-fitō, su-ka-taras itāchen, da aka-damra ma igia. Shi-na-mōtsi, kamar shi chirē. Sai su-ka-kāma, su-na-ja. Mutānen gīwa, su kuma, su-na-ja. Idan mutānen gīwa su-ka-ja mutānen dōrina, sai akāra masu wadansu mutāne. Idan mutānen dorina su-ka-jaye mutā-nen gīwa sai akāra masu wadansu mutāne. Hakanan hakanan har marēche ya yi, su-ka-bari, su-ka-kwanta. Gari ya wāye, da asubā su-ka-tāshi

---

When it is dawn let your boys go and pull, for the horse is a rogue.' The hippo agreed. When it was dawn the hippo's boys came up (from the water) and found the tree to which the rope had been tied. It was swaying about as if it was about to be uprooted. Then they seized hold and pulled. The elephant's people also were pulling. When the elephant's people were pulling the hippo's people, then some more people were added. When the hippo's people were pulling the elephant's people, then more persons were added to them. And so it went on till evening came, and they desisted, (and) lay down. When it was dawn, very early they rose up

إِدَنْ غَمِرِ مِيدَاوَابِيِ : كِبَمِ لَسَمَدَارِ : سُتَيِي سُجِيَ :
مَمُكِيثُرِ وَرِكِيبِنِي : دُرُوفُنِي تَبُثُمُو : كِغَمِرِ
بِتُوَابِي لَسَمَدُو فُدُورُوفُنِي : سُكَبِنُوا : سُكَتَعَرِشْ
إِمَدَا بُثُرِ دَأَكَمَ مُرَامَاغِنِي : لِشَقَا مُوَطَمِ : كَتَمَ
فُتَبُرِ كُو : لَسِي سُكَكَامِ : سُكَامِ : مُتَابُنِشْ
غِيُوا : لَسُو كُتَمَ سُكَامِ : إِدَرُ مُتَابُنِي غِيُوا
سُكَجِي مُتَابُنِ دُورُوفُنِي : لَسِي أَكَادَارِ مَسِرَا وَمُفَشْ
مُتَابُنِي : إِدَرُ مُتَابُنِ دُورُوفُنِي : سُكَجَابِي مُتَا
بُنِ غِيُوا : لَسِي أَكَادَارِ مَسِرَا وَمُفُشْ مُتَابُنِي :
كَكَمَ كَكَمَ : مَمَ مَبِ مَبُثِيِنِي : سُكَبِرِ :
سُكَكُو مُتَا : غَمِرِ مِيوَابِيي أَصَبَا : سُكَتَابِشْ

su-na-ja, har rāna ta yi bisa. Sai dōrina ta che, 'Abari, atafi, atanbayi gīwa, agani wane irin dōki ta ba ni, aka-ja aka gaji.' Gīwa kuma ta che, 'Ku bari aje agani wane irin dōki ke nan dōrina ta ba ni, aka-ja aka gaji.' Yau yāra su-ka-tafi, sai su-ka-gamu tsakan dāji. Sai samāri gīwa su-ka-tanbayi samārin dōrina, su-ka-che, 'Ina zaa ku?' Su-ka-che, 'An-aike mu wurin gīwa, mu je, mu gani wane irin dōki ta bai wa dōrina, tun jia ana-ja, har dare ya yi, har gari ya wāye.' Samāri--n gīwa su-ka-che, 'Mu ma aikinmu aka-yi gun dōrina mu tanbaye ta hakanan. Ama da ya zama hakanan mu kōma gida. Ku kuma ku kōma, ku je

---

and were pulling till the sun was above (them). Then the hippo said, 'Let them cease, and go and ask the elephant and let them see what kind of a horse she give me, that had been pulled and pulled and tired (every one) out.' Now the elephant also said, 'You leave off. Let some one go and see what kind of a horse this is that the hippo give me, that they had pulled and got weary (pulling).' So the boys went off, and they met in the middle of the bush. Then the youths from the elephant's asked the youths from the hippo's and said, 'Where are you going?' They replied, 'We have been sent to the elephant to go (and) see what sort of a horse she had given to the hippo. Since yesterday they have been pulling at it, till night came, till dawn came.' The elephant's youths said, 'We too, our errand was with the hippo, that we ask her this same thing. But since things are so let us turn back. You too turn back (and) go

سُنَاجَ ؛ قَمْ وَافَلِي تَنِي بَسَنْ ؛ تَسِنْ دُورُفَ قَتَبْشْ أَبِرْ

أَقَفِ أَمُنْفَبُو غِيوَا ؛ أَغَنِمْ رَفَارِزْ دُورِكِ قَتَبَارْ

أَنْجِي أَكَغَجِ ؛ غِيوَا أَكُمَّ قَتَبْشْ كُبَرِ ؛ أَبِي أَغَنِمْ

رَفَارِزْ دُورِكِ بَكَّمْ دُورُفَ قَتَارِ ؛ أَنْجِي أَكَغَجِ ؛

يِيوْيِيَارَ ؛ سَكَتَقِي ؛ تَسِنْ سَكَغَمْ تَكَمْ دَاجَ ؛

تَسِنْ سَدَارِ ؛ غِيوَا ؛ سُكَتَبُنْجِي لَسَدَارُفُ دُورُفَشْ

سُكَتَبْشْ إِمَّادَ أَكِ ؛ سُكَتَبْشْ أَنْ أَيْكَمْ وُرُفَ غِيوَا

مُجِي مُغَنِمْ رَفَارِزْ دُورِكِ قَتَبُو دُورُفَشْ تُنْجِي

أَفَاجَ هَمْدُ دُو مُيِّي حَمْ غَمْ يِيوَا بِي ؛ سَدَارْ

نْغِيوَا سُكَتَبْشْ مُحُومِ ؛ أَيْكَمْ أَكُمَّ ؛ غِمْ

دُورُفَ مُتَبِّيَّ حَكَمَّ ؛ أَمَّادَ مِيَمَّ قَكَمَّ

مُحُكُومِ غِدَا ؛ كُوكَمَّ ؛ كُكُومِ ؛ كُجِي

ku fadi abinda ku-ka-gani, ku che karīa ne gizō ya yi, ba mu gani dōki ba.' Yau su-ka-kōma daga wurin nan, samārin dōrina su-ka-je, su-ka-gaia mata wada su-ka-yi. Samārin gīwa su-ka-je, su-ka-lābarta mata. Gīwa ta che, 'Ai dōrina ba ta bii na bāshi, ni ke biinta bāshi.' Dōrina kuma ta che, 'Ai gīwa ba ta bii na bāshi, ni ke biinta bāshi.' Alamari ya zō, ya bayana gizō ya yi karīa ne, ya karbi abinchinsu, ya chi. Sai dōrina ta aika wurin gīwa, ta che, kar ta yi fushi. 'Dōmin ita mai-girma che, ni kuma mai-girma che, idan mu duka mu ka yi fushi, abin ba shi giyāru ba.

(and) say what you had (have) seen; say it is a lie that the spider told, (and) that we have not seen any horse.' So they went away from this place. The hippo's young men went and told her what they had done. The elephant's youths went and told her (the elephant) the news, (and) the elephant said, 'What 's all this, I do not owe the hippo, the hippo owes me.' And the hippo said, 'What 's all this? I do not owe the elephant, the elephant owes me.' When the affair came to be discussed it became clear it was the spider that had lied, (and) received their food, (and) eaten it. Then the hippo sent to the elephant, and said she must not be angry, (saying), 'Because she is strong, and I also am strong; if we both get angry, the thing cannot be settled.

كُجِدِ أَبِنْدَ كُكَ قَنِمْ ∴ نَكَثْ عَرْيَا ابْنِ غُمَرُ

يَسّ بَطَغَنِمْ دُرْكِيبْ ∴ يَوْ سَكَكُوتَمْ ∴ دَغُوْرَنْشْ

سَدَارِفَدُرِنْ قُو ثَلَجِ سَكَقِيَا مَتَّا آرِ سُكَجّ ∴

سَدَارِفْغِيوَا سُكَجِ سَكَدَا بَرْ قَدَا مَتّ ∴ غَيْوَا

تَبْ آيِ دُرِقُ بَلْقَبِنْدَا بَاشِ ∴ نِكَبِنْتَ

بَاشِ دُرِقُ كُحَمْ تَبَ آ غَيْوَا ابَدَ تَبِنْدَا بَاشِ

نِكَبِنْتَ بَاشِ ∴ آلَّا امر ∴ يَغْدُرَا يَتِبَنْ غَمْرُ

يَا يَكْرِ يَالِفُ نَكَرْ بِ اَبِنْقَشْقَشْرِيَثْ ∴ سِس

دُرِنْحُومْتَا آيكَ دُرِنْخَيْوَا تَبْ كَرْتِي فُشِمْ

دَارِقَرَاتَ تَنِغَرْ قَلْبَ دَبِكَحَمْ تَنِغَمْ مَلْبَا آدَمْ نَ

فُودْكَ فُحَسّ فُشِمْ ∴ آبِنْبَقِمْ غَيَادَ رُبَ ∴ =

Mu bari mu yi fakō gizō.' Gīwa ta che, 'Gaskīa ne.' Dada su-ka-dinga bidan gizō. Ba su gane shi ba. Gizō yā bō--yē, ba shi fita har ya lālāche. Ranan yunwa ta chi kar--finsa, ya fitō, shi-na-bidan abinchi. Sai ya gani fātar barēwa, ta mutu, wani abu ya chinye ta, ya bar fāta, da kai, da kafāfu. Sai ya dauki, ya shiga chiki. Shi-na--yāwō. Sai ya gamu da gīwa. Gīwa ta gane shi, ta-na-zatō kwarangamar barēwa che. Sai gīwa ta che, 'Ke barēwa ba ki gani mani gizō ba?' Sai barēwa ta che, 'Gizō ki ke bida? Rufa ma kaiki asīri, tunda mu-ka-yi fada da shi, ya nūna mani

---

Let us desist, and lie in wait for the spider.' (And) the elephant said, 'That is true.' Then they continually sought for the spider. They did not see him. The spider was in hiding, and he did not come out until he had got weak and thin. One day when hunger had overcome his strength, he came out (and) was looking for food, when he saw the skin of an antelope, (which) had died—something had eaten it up, and left the skin, and head, and hoofs. Then he lifted it up and went inside. He was walking about when he met the elephant. The elephant saw him and thought he was a decrepit old antelope. Then the elephant said, 'You, antelope, will you not look for the spider for me?' And the antelope said, 'Is it the spider you are seeking? Keep that your secret. Since we fell out with him he pointed at me

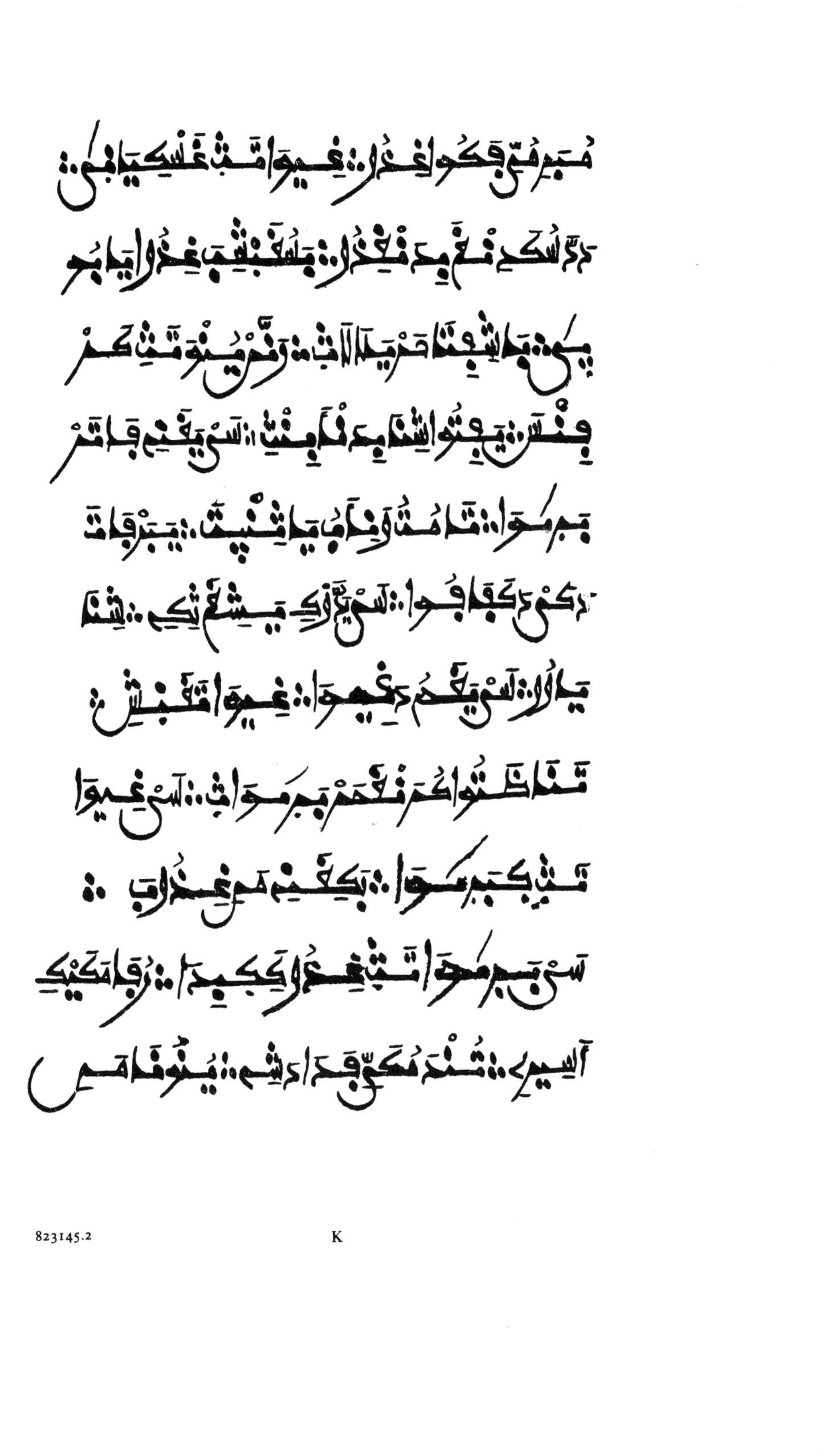

hannu na lālāche. Ba ni kamnar in gane shi. Yanzu, kōwa ya yi fada da shi, sai shi nūna masa hannu, shi lālāche.' Sai gīwa ta che, 'Shi ne ya yi maki haka?' Ta che, 'I.' Gīwa ta che, 'Idan kin gane shi kar ki che ina-bidansa.' Barēwa ta che, 'Tō.' Gīwa ta wuche, ta tafi. Sai gizō ya yāda fātar barēwa, ya gudu, ya chika da gīwa, ya che. 'Gā ni, anche ki-na-bida na.' Sai gīwa ta dinga makerketa, ta na che, 'Nā tūba, ba ni bidanka.' Ta na fitsāri daga tsayē. Sai ya che, 'In kāra ji wani shi-na-bida na, mu gamu da shi.' Ya kōmō, ya dauki fātarsa, ya shiga, shi-na-yāwō.

---

his hand (and) I wasted away. I do not want to see him. Nowadays whoever quarrels with him then he points his hand at him (and) he pines away.' And the elephant asked, 'Was it he who made you become like this?' She (the antelope) said, 'Yes.' The elephant said, 'If you have seen him you must not say I was seeking him.' The antelope said, 'All right.' The elephant passed and went on. Then the spider cast aside the antelope skin, (and) ran, (and) met the elephant (and) said, 'Behold me, they say you are seeking me.' Then the elephant kept shaking and saying, 'I repent. I am not seeking you.' He was making water through fear, from a standing position. Then he (the spider) said, 'If I hear again that some one is seeking me, we (I) will join with him.' He went back, lifted his skin, entered, (and) was walking along.

حسنو قتلا الاف ∴ تبدا نكمغر انغبشر ∴ يتغر ∴
كور ايبّو قدا دشيم لسن يشنو فدا مسر قشنو ∴
يشدا الاف ∴ لسن غيو امتب يشين يمو مّكي تحكي
قتب اي ∴ غيو امتب ادّ يكنغ نغبشر كمر يكب امقا
يعد فسر ∴ يبر موا امتب شو ∴ غيو اشوب ∴
تمتفي ∴ لسن غدر يتيّاد قدا امتمر يبر موا ∴ يعد
يتيكد غيو ايتب غدر اومتب يكنا يدا امني
لسن غيو اتحي فغ مبكمر بكنّا ∴ قتلا قما
شوقب ملفيجم نك ∴ قتنا فحلار دغطيس
لسن يتب انكدورم وينشنا يدا انّي مغم رشيم
يكو موتيدّم رك قدا امتمر لس يتشغ ∴ يشنا يدورو ∴

Aka-jima kadan, sai su-ka-gamu da dōrina. Sai ta che, 'Ke barēw kō kin gani gizō?' Sai ta che, 'Wanda ki ke bida nan, ni ba ni sō in ji sūnansa, dōmin shi ya bari na lālāche nan.' Sai dōrina ta che, 'Hakanan?' Barēwa ta che, 'I.' Dōrina ta che, 'Ida kin gane shi, kar ka che ina-nemansa.' Yau ta wuche. Sai gizō ya yāda fāta, ya kōmō, shi-na-fadi, 'Ina dōrina? Gā ni anche ki-na-bida na.' Da ta waiwaya, ta gane shi, sai ta fāda rua, punjum! Gizō ya sāmu kai(n)sa. Shi ke nan. [14] Kungurus kan kūsu.

Soon they (he) fell in with the hippo. And she said, 'You, antelop perhaps you have seen the spider?' But she said, 'This one who you are searching for, for my part I do not want to hear his name, fo he is the cause of my wasting away like this.' And the hippo sai 'Is that so?' The antelope said, 'Yes.' The hippo said, 'If yo have seen him, do not say I was seeking him.' So she passed o Then the spider threw off the skin and returned. He said, 'Wher is the hippo? Behold me, I am told you are looking for me.' O her (the hippo) looking behind she saw him and fell splash into th water. The spider (thus) saved himself. That is it. Off with th rat's head.

أَجِمَ كَدَّ وَسُ سُكَخُمْ دُ دُورِنْيَ وَسِنْ تَنْبَ بَكِبَرْ مُوَا

كُحُكَنْغَنَ نِغُدُ وَسِنْ مَنْبَ وَفْدَ يَكِبِدَ مُقَّرْ فَيِ بَا

فِسُو إِنْجِ سُوَ تَنْفُسَ دُوَ مِمَّرْ شَيْ يَبَرِ مَنَا امَا بِشَقَّرْ وَسِيِ

دُورِنْيَ تَنْبَ تَحَكَنْ بَرَّ بِمَ مُوَا اِشْبَ اِ ، دُورِنْيَ مَنْبَ إِدَّرْ

كِنْغَنْبِشِرْ كَخْرْ كِنْبَ إِمَا بَمَنْفُسَ يَتَّوَ مَنْوُبَّ وَسِنْ نِغُدُ

يَمِيدَ دَرَقَبَات يَكُوُ مُوَا اِشْنَا قِبَدِي إِمَّا دُورِنْيَ نِغَارْ

آمْنَ يِكِنَابِ عِرَامَيْ دَ مَتُوَيْ وَيَبَا مَنْغَبِشِرْ وَسِنْ تَبَقَادِ

وُرَّوْ فُنْجَمْ نِغُمْ وَبِسَلَامْ كَبِجَسْ شِيْ يَكِنْتَنْ فُنْقُمْسْ

كَمْ فُوسْ

PART IV

CUSTOMS AND ARTS

No. 31.

Wanan [1] bābi ne na [2] alaada aure
da [3] sūna.

Wada mu ke aure [4] nana, tafarkin Muhamadia.
Idan [5] kā gani yārinya, ka-na-sō, kō
budrua, sai ka bidi tsōfūa a gidanku.
Idan bābu tsōfūa mahankalchīa a gida-
-nku, ka je wani [6] gu, ka nema. Ka sai gōrō gōma
sha bīū, ka aike ta da su, wurin iyāyen
yārinya nan. Ta kai musu, ta che in ji ka, ta gaishe su.
Idan ta kai, idan su-na-sō su ba ka, baa su
tanbaya tsōfūa nan me shi ke sō, sai su [7] kyale har
ta kōmō sau uku. Saanan su che, 'Keauta nan

This is the opening of (a description) of a marriage and a naming ceremony. The way we marry here (is after) the Mohammedan fashion (lit. way). If you have seen a little girl you want, or a maiden, then you look out some old woman belonging to your household. If there is no sensible old woman at your own home, you look somewhere else for one. (Then) you buy twelve kola nuts, and send her (the old woman) with them, to the parents of this maiden (whom you fancy). She takes them to them, and says you have sent them. She greets them. When she has brought the gift, if they want to give you (the girl eventually), they will not inquire of the old woman what she wants, but they do and say nothing till she comes back three times. Then they say, 'These gifts

وقّن نجاميين نذ ألقاظ عويرن

د سوقني ۞

ولا ئجعويرن قّن ئقبقر فن ءمعقّدي تنّ ؛
إدّن ئكلغنم ئيارقّن ؛ كنّا سوا ؛ كو
ئدزرا ؛ تسركيج ؛ طوفوا ؛ أفد نك ؛
إدّن ئباب ؛ طوفوا ؛ ءمنكلتيا ؛ أغم
نك ؛ ئكجر ونّغ ؛ كجمن عسغ عورن ؛ غوم
؛ أشيوا ؛ ئكأبكت ؛ د سوا ؛ ورقعيا پين ؛
يارقّبنّن تكيمسن ؛ تقتّ إنجيك ؛ تغيشس
إدّن تكمن إدّن سنا سوا ؛ سبايك ؛ بلسن
تقبيطو فوقّن ؛ بّشجك سوا ؛ سنّ سكجي ؛ تقر
تكوموا ؛ سوأك ؛ سعقّن ؛ سبكو قّنّر ء

tā yi yawa, me shi ke sō?' Sai tsōfūa ta che, 'Lābuda wanche ya gani shi ke sō dōmin zumuntarku ta [8]sā--du da shi.' Idan ta-na da miji, idan mutāne gaskīa ne, tunda wuri, sai su che, 'Aa ta-na da miji.' Su che, 'Ama zuria dayawa, sai shi tarbi gaba.' Idan ba ta da miji sai su che, 'Tō, Ala shi sa mu ga nagari.' Sai su juye keautar da ka kāwō, su bāda tukwichi, dada ka shiga surukūta ke nan, ka-na-yi. Wata rāna ka kai nāma, wata rāna ka kai kurdi, wata rāna gōrō. Duka nan da mu-ka-kidāya ba da sai ka kai kaza ba, aa gworgwodō īkonka. Haka ka ke kai, har [9]uban, idan ya chika masa idō,

---

have become many, what is he wanting?' Then the old woman says, 'No doubt he saw what's-her-name and wants (her), in order that your house may be joined with him.' (Now) if she (the girl) had a husband since some time ago (betrothed), then, if they are truthful people, they say, 'No, she (already) possesses a husband.' (And) they say, 'But the family are many, so let him wait till some future time.' If she has no husband then they say, 'It is well, may Allah cause us to see good (come of this union).' Then they turn out the presents which you have brought, (and) give a return present. Then you enter this courtship stage. You are courting. One day you bring meat, another day money, another day kola nuts, all these things which we have enumerated, not only such you bring, oh no, but (anything else) according to your means. And thus you keep giving, till the father, if it is sufficient in his eye,

تلتن ؞ ميجو ؞ بشجسوا ؞ لسن طوبقوا ؞ تبث لابجم ؞

وفبنيفني ؞ ينجسوا ؞ دوومن ؞ ءمنتمك ؞ تحصا

د ؞ كرقشم ؞ إدّن ؞ تمتادمج ؞ إدّون ؞ متاقبن ؞ غمسكيا

بم ؞ شمتدورن ؞ لمن سشبهغام ؞ فمتادمج ؞ لسبا آما

تدوتن ؞ دميجو ؞ لسن لشترب غب ؞ إدّن ؞ ماتدمهم

لمن سنت ؞ مثوا ؞ أل شسام ؞ غمتكم ؞ لسن سبجومين

؞ بجومتن ؞ دككاوو ؞ لسباد تكيش ؞ دد ؞ كا

بشحم ؞ لسكوتا ؞ كسن ؞ كمتان ؞ وتمرامن ؞

ككن ؞ قام ؞ روقدان ؞ ككن ؞ كمنرحي ؞ وتمرامن

فوون ؞ دكنتمن دمككدايا ؞ بماد لسن كامكن

كداب ؞ عام ؞ غمغدون ؞ ايكوك ؞ قك

ككجكمكن ؞ اقم أبمن ؞ إدّن يشكا امسن ؞ إدون ؞

saanan su che, azō ayi rōkō. Saanan ka bidi gōrō gōma, da [10]kurdi alif, agama, asāmu dạtījai. Su je, su kai, su che, ' Gā shi. Wāne ya che mu kāwō, shi-na-rōkō aba shi wanche.' Saanan su karba, su aje, ku tafō gida. Saanan su juye, su bāda tāsa, akāwō gida tāre da tukwichi. Saanan kuma ka bidi kurdi, araba, da gōrō, aje, ayi ma uwāyenta adua. Mālāmai unguwarku, da su-ka-je, da mālāmai unguwar surukunaika, sai su ra--ba kurdin tsaka, da gōrō. Su, su dauki rabi, ku kuma, ku dauki rabi, ku zō gida, ku raba a junanku. Saanan kai, miji, ka bidi kurdi,

---

then says, they must come and ask (for the girl). Then you seek for ten kola nuts, and a thousand cowries, and when that is done, some persons of importance are sought, and they go (and) reach the place (and) say, ' Behold it. So-and-so said we were to bring (these), he is begging that he be given what's-her-name.' Then they accept it (and) set it aside, and you (all) come back home. Then they turn (the cowries) out and give back the cup, (and) it is taken home together with the return presents. Then you again seek cowries, (and) divide, (and) some kola nuts, and they are taken, and given with a prayer to her parents. Then the learned men from your town who have come, and the learned men from your father-in-law's, divide up the cowries in two portions—also the kola nuts. They for their part take half, (and) you (all), you take half, and you return home (and) divide it up among you. Then you, the man, seek cowries,

لَسَحَقَّنْ : لَسَبْ :: أَغْرِشْ آسِّ رُورُكْوا : لَسَحَقَّنْ : كَيجِ :.

غُورُو : فُلُوحَمْ :: شَمْ كُمْرِدِ :: أَلِفْ :: أَغْمَ :: أَسَامُ ::

دَقِيجَقْ :: لُسَجِي لَسَكَمْ : لُسَبْ غَدَاشِ رَامِلِي : مِيبْ

مَكَاوُرُ : فِسْنَا وُرُكْو :: أَبَدَاشِ رَفْتْ :: لَسَحَقَّنْ

فَسَكَمْ قِبَا :: سَأَجِلِي : كُنْتِبُوا اِغْدَا :: لَسَقَقَّنْ : لُسُجُوبِي

لَسَبَاءِ قَدَاسِ آكَدَاوُرِغْدَا :: قَدَاوَرُشْ دَمْتُكِينِشِ

لَسَقَّنْ : كُحَمَّ :: كَبِجِ : كُمْرِدِ :: أَرَبِ :: دَغُورُورُ

آجِكْ زَأَبِمَغُوا اِبَمْنَتَ :: أَدَعَمْ :: مَدَالَمْ :: أَمْلْغُورُكْ :

دَلُسَجِي :: دَمَدَالَمْ :: أَمْلْغُورُ : لُسُمْ كُتَنِيكْ :: لَسْ لَسَ

بَ غُمْرِدِ مَطَك :: دَغُورُر : لُسُو لُسَرْكِ :: زِمِّ ::

كُوكُحَمَّ :: كُدْرِكِ :: وَقِّ :: كُدُرِغْدَا :: كُحَرِبَا

أَبِوقَّمْكُ :: لَسَحَقَّنْ : كَيجِ : كُمْرِدِ ::

zanbar gōma, da gōrō, [11]kworia guda, da zanua bīū. [12]Mātan unguwarku su dauki, su kai. Idan aka-yi hakanan, aka-wanye, sauran aure. Idan yārinya ta chika, ba wani abu ake che ma chika ba, idan yārinya ta isa [13]marmarin namiji shi ne chika, to, idan tā isa aure, sai miji shi nemi zanen dauri, fudu, da [14]shāta, da mayāfi, da fatala, da dafuan akōkō. Shi akan-che [15]lālāta, da takalma, tāki bīū, da kurdi zanbar ishirin, da wuri zanbar gōma ne. Su ne akan-che kurdi-n tūō. Saanan abidi kurdi alif wa metin azuba karkashin lēfē. Zanua kua ajēra su

---

ten thousand, and kola nuts, one calabash full, and two cloths. The women belonging to your part of the town lift them and bring along. When all this has been done and finished, there remains the marriage. If the maiden is 'complete'—now by 'complete' I mean, if the maid has reached an age when she desires a man, that is 'complete'—well, if she has reached the marriage age, then the husband seeks four robes, and white cloths, and coverings (for the bed), and head kerchiefs, and dyed calico—this is called *lalata*, i. e. worthless—and slippers, two soles (pairs), and twenty thousand cowries, formerly it was ten thousand. And this last is called 'the food' cowries. Then twelve hundred cowries are sought and poured under (the cloths, &c., in the) basket. The cloths, too, they lay them out

دَقَبَرْ ؞ غُوم ؞ دَغُوزُرُ ؞ كُمْ يَا ؞ نُمْدَا ؞ دَطُنُو

؞ بِيُو ؞ مَاقَنْقُوزُكَ ؞ لَسَعُوكِ ؞ لَسَكَنْ ؞

إِدَّزُنْ أَكَتَّ قَكَقَّنْ أَكُوقَيِّنْ لَسُورَقْعُوزُسْ

؞ إِدَّزُنْ مَيَارِقَمْ ثَقَنْكَ ؞ مَاوَقِنْدَأَنْ ؞ أَكِنْثَمَّ ؞

ثَكَارِبْ ؞ إِدَّزُنْ إِيَدَرْقَمْ ثَقَاإِسَ مَمْ مَمْرَقَنْثِمْ ؞

ثِنْبِنْ ثَكَنْ ثَوَإِدَّزُنْ ثَقَاإِسَ عُوزُوثْ لَسْقَمْ

ثِنْبِهِ ؞ طَبَّنْ ؞ دَوُرُ ؞ قُدُ ؞ دَشَاقَّنْ ؞ هَمْ مَيَابِمْ

دَقَتَّلْ ؞ دَدَّ بُوقْقَكُوكُو ؞ يِشِيَأَكَنْثْ ؞ لَالَّامَ ؞

دَقَاهَلَمْ ؞ ثَدَاكِ مِيُّوا ؞ دَكُمْدِ ؞ لَاقَبَرْ عِشِرْ

دَوُرُ ؞ دَقَبَرْ غُومَنِّنْ ؞ سُوبَلِ ؞ أَكَنْثْ ؞ كَمْدِ

قَتُورْ ؞ لَسَعَقَّنْ ؞ آبِدِ كُمْدِ ؞ أَلِفْ ؞ وَمَتِّرْثْ

آدُمَا ؞ كَمْكِشِرْ ؞ لَبِّبُو ؞ خَلَمُو كُوتَّ ؞ آجِمَّا اُسْ ؞

achikin lēfe, aajie. Saanan abidi gōrō
ishirin, akai wurin uban maata, ache ana-so akāwō
lēfē. Idan ya gama shiri shi che, 'Tō.' Idan bai gama
ba shi che, 'Tukuna.' Gōrō nan shi ne akan-che 'gōrō
neman bāki'. Idan aka amsa, sai ku kai lēfē,
ama alif wa metin ni nan. Su ne akan che, 'rubudīnāli.'
Idan kun yi hakanan kun kāre, sai asa rāna
ache, ka kāwō kurdin [16] lalē. Su kuma alfen ne.
Idan aka-kai sai asa amarīa lalē.

Wanan fasalī ne
da zaa shi gwoda muna wada ake sainya
amarīa lalē.

---

in a basket, and they are set on one side. Then twenty kola nuts are sought and taken to the father of the wife (to be), and they say they want him to bring the basket. If he has everything prepared (for the final ceremony) he says, 'All right.' If he is not ready he says, 'Not just yet.' The name by which these kola nuts are known is 'the kola nuts which seek of the mouth' (i.e. seek an answer). If a reply is given, then you bring the basket, the one of the twelve hundred cowries. They are called *rubudinali.* If you have completed all this, then a day is fixed on which you are told to bring the 'henna' cowries. They amount to two thousand. When this is brought then the bride has henna put on (her feet). This now is a description of how they put henna on a bride.

أَشْكِنْ لَبَّجُنْ ∴ أَمِجِيبِي ∴ أَسَلَقَّتْنْ أَبِي غُورُنْ ∴

يشِيرُنْ ∴ أَكَرْوُرْ فَعَجَبَنْ مَا أَقَمُنْ ∴ آبْ أَمَدْ سُونْ ∴ أَكَارَرْ

∴ لَبُفُنْ ∴ إِدَّرْنْ ∴ مَيلَغَمْ شِيرْ ∴ شَبْثُونْ ∴ إِدَّرْنْ ∴ جَبَيْقَمْ

ج ∴ يَشَبْ تُكَّمْنْ ∴ غُورُو قَمَّنْ شِيبِنْ أَكَشَبْ ∴ غُورُرْ

بَغَمْنْ جَاكِمْ ∴ إِدَّرْنْ ∴ أَكَدَ أَمْسَنْ ∴ أَسَنْ كُكَنْ ∴ لَبِّيفُنْ

أَمَدْ آلِفْ ∴ رَبَتِيبِنْفَمَّنْ ∴ سُوبَفُمْ ∴ أَكَشَبْ ∴ رُبَعْ دِيتَلُو

إِدَّرْنْ ∴ كُفْمِ ∴ تَكَّقَّنْ ∴ كُنَكَاوُسْ ∴ لَسَنْ أَسَدَرَاقَمْ

∴ أَبْكَكَارُنْ ∴ كُمْرِدْ فَلَبَّلُنْ ∴ سُوكُمَّ ∴ أَلْفَجُمْ ∴

إِدَّرْنْ أَكَكَنْ ∴ لَسَنْ أَسَدْ أَمْرَ يَا الَّبْنْ ∴

رَفَّنْ قَصِيبَنْ ∴

دَدْ أَشْغُدْ أَمْرْ ∴ وَدْ أَجِيشَنْ

أَمْرَ يَا الَّلُنْ ∴

Idan matanbayi ya tanbaye ka ina hukumchin sa amar-
-īa lalē, ka amsa masa [17]jawābi ka che. Hakumchi
wada ake sa amarīa lalē. Idan aka-yi nufi za asa
amarīa lalē, sai abidō gainye lalē, asainya
achikin [18]dārō, azuba rua achiki, aajie chikin rāna.
Shi-na nan. Yārinya nan kūa, aaike ta dāji, kō
gōna, kō kauye, dōmin idānunta kar
shi gani. Idan ta kōmō da dare, aba ta tūō,
ta chi. Idan ta chi ta kāre, ta-na-sūdē hannu,
sai wata tsōfūa, kō kaka tata, kō bābā-
-nīa tata, ta dībi lalē, [19]ta zuba mata. Sai ta di-
-nga kūka, ta-na-kūka. Idan aka jima, sai ta yi kurum

If a questioner asks you the manner in which henna is put on a bride answer him in these words (and) say. The manner in which a bride has henna put on is this. If they wish to put henna on a bride then they seek fresh henna (and) put it in a large cup (and) pour water in (and) set it in the sun. It remains there. This maid also is sent off to the bush, or to an (outlying) farm or outlying village that her eyes may not look on (the henna). When she returns at night she is given food (and) she eats. When she has finished eating (and) is licking her (fingers) hand, then a certain old woman, perhaps her grandmother or her father's sister, takes up the henna (and) pours it over her. Then she cries and cries. She is crying. If they wait a little while then she is silent

إِدَّوْنْ مَتَنْفِيِّ ∴ يَتَنْبِيكْ ∴ إِفَّا مُكُخِشْنْ ∴ لَسَا أَقْز

يَالَلْبُوِّ ∴ كَا أَمْسَامَسَنْ ∴ بَجَوَابِ ∴ كَيْشْ ∴ تُكُمْشِ

وَدَا أَبَسَا أَمَرْ يَالَلْبُو ∴ إِدَّوْنْ أَكَيِّ ∴ فُبِجِ ∴ دَاعَسَا

أَمَرْ يَالَلْبُوِّ ∴ سَنْ أَمُدُوَا ∴ غَنْبِيُو ∴ لَلْبُوِّ ∴ آسَنْيِطْ

أَقِكِمْ دَاوُوِنْ أَدُبَمْ وَا ∴ أَنِكِمْ ∴ أَعَجِيكِ ∴ شِكِمْ وَافُسْ

∴ شَنَّا قَّمْ ∴ يَا وُفِيَتَّنْكُو ∴ أَعَيْجَكُتَ دَا إِجِ ∴ كُو

غُوفَمْ ∴ كُو كُوبِيَنْ ∴ دَوِقِّمْ ∴ إِدَا أُمُنْتَ ∴ كَرْ

شِخَيِ ∴ إِدَّوْنْ تَكُو مُوَا ∴ دَدُبَرْشْ أَبَاقَ ∴ قُوُوْنْ

قَنِشْ ∴ إِدَّوْنْ قَنِشْ تَكَا دُوَكَسْ ∴ قَنَا سُوبُرْ ∴ قَنْفُو

∴ سَنْ وَنْطُو بُجَوَا ∴ كُو كَاكَا قَتَ ∴ كُو بَابَا

فِيَا قَتَّ ∴ قَدِيبِ لَّعَلَبُو ∴ تَخُبَا مَتَ ∴ سَنْ تَجِ

فَعْكُو كَنْ ∴ قَنَا كُو كَكَنْ ∴ إِدَّوْ أَجِمْ ∴ سَنْ تَرْ كُرْ مَنْ ∴

Yan uwanta buduri sai su zō, su tayā ta kūka. Alaada su che hakanan, ba dōmin ba su sō ba ne. Idan aka-jima kadan, sai su fita, su tafi wurin wāsa. Idan dare ya yi kwarai, sai su tafi wurin samārinsu, su kwāna. Da asubāhin, su gudu, su kōmō dākin da aka sainya su. Idan gari ya wāye, idan ta na da abuya, sai abidi gōrō, atafi wurin iyāyenta, akai masu gōrō, ache ana-sō wanche ta zō, ta chi [20]abuyar amarīa. Sai su karbi gōrō su raraba ma dangi, dōmin, idan [21]zaa wurin aiki, su tāru, su tafi.

Now her sisters come and help her to weep. It is the custom for them to do so; they do not do so because they want to. In a little while then they come out, (and) go to where the dancing and rejoicing is. When it is quite dark, then they all go off to their young men, (and) sleep. At early dawn they run off (and) come back to the room where they had been put. When it is dawn (and) if she has any girl friend, then kola nuts are sought and they go to her (friend's) parents, (and) take the kola nuts, (and) say they want What's-her-name to come (and) act 'the bride's friend'. Then they receive the kola nuts and divide them up among the relations, in order that, if they are about to go to assist at the ceremony, they should assemble and set off.

ينغوقتنت ⁖ يجبور ⁖ تسن لسغرا ⁖ نستياق ⁖
كوكي ⁖ ألقاد سنب ححكنش بادرقس
ش بلسسو ببنو ⁖ إدرنش أكجم ⁖ نكمرن ⁖
تسن سبعت ⁖ لستبقم ⁖ أورفواسن ⁖ إدرن ⁖ عربس
يمان ⁖ كمرن ⁖ تسن لستبقم ⁖ أورفسعلا رفسن
سكوارن ⁖ د أصباحن ⁖ سغد سكومو ⁖
د اكرش د أكسنباسن ⁖ إدرن غم ميدا وايمن
إدرن قتنا د أبكم ⁖ تسع أمدي غوورن ⁖ أمبقم ⁖
ورفحيا مينت ⁖ أكيبمسن غوورن ⁖ أقب
أقلسوا ⁖ ورقب تقدوتين ⁖ أمبين أمم بيا
تسن سكم بغوورن ⁖ لستر وبا امد قنغ ⁖ دريمن
إدرن ذا عوو فحبك ⁖ سنتلرن لستبقم ⁖ =

Ita kūa, amarīa, ta-na-kwāna uku gidansu,
ana yi mata kumshi. Saanan ayi mata wanka da marēche,
saanan idan dare ya yi, atāru, da māta, da
buduri, da makada, ana-wāka da [22]gūda, da kade
kade. Arufa ma abuyar amarīa alkeba,
aaza ta bisa gōdīa. Idan ba asāmu gō-
-dīa ba, asāmu dōki, mai-lāfia, ta hau.
Ama batun nan da mu ke yi, amarīa [23]tā je
gidan mijinta tun dadewa. Wanan da za akai
bisa dōki, sūnanta, ‘amarīan bōkō.’
Idan su-ka-kai gidan angō sai su tsaya
waje, su-na-wāka, su-na-che, ‘Ba mu shiga ba,

She indeed, the bride to be, sleeps for three (days) at their (her parents') home (where) she is bound up (in cloths to keep the henna off her clothes). Then she is bathed in the evening, and then when night comes they (all) assemble, women and maidens, and the ones who play on drums, they sing and sound the *guda* with much beating of drums. And ‘the bride's friend’ is covered with a burnous, (and) she is set on a mare. If they cannot get a mare, a fine healthy horse is got for her to mount. But during all this time we have been talking about, the bride has already come to her husband's house, (since sunset). This one whom they were about to bring on horseback is called ‘the pretended bride’. When they (the dancers, &c.) get to the bridegroom's house then they stand outside and are singing, saying, ‘We do not enter,

إنّكو ؞ أمرقيا ؞ تنّا كوانّي ؞ أكّ ؞ غيم فسن
أمد يمّت كمّش سكنّ ؞ إيمّت وكّي ؞ [illegible] مبّ
سكنّ ؞ إدّن [illegible] ؞ أمّا و ؞ [illegible]
[illegible] ؞ أمّا واك ؞ [illegible]
[illegible] ؞ أمرقيا ؞ ألكب ؞ =
أدّ أنّ [illegible] ؞ إدّن [illegible] أسام ؞ [illegible]
[illegible] ؞ أسام ؞ دوك ؞ [illegible]
؞ أمّ [illegible] ؞ أمرقيا ؞ [illegible]
[illegible] ؞ [illegible] ؞ [illegible] أكّن
[illegible] ؞ سو [illegible] ؞ أمر [illegible] كو ؞
إدّن [illegible] أنّفوا ؞ [illegible]
[illegible] ؞ [illegible] ؞ [illegible] ؞

ba mu shiga ba, tsaitsaye, sai da bauya tsaitsaye.'
Dōmin akāwō masu tukwichi. Idan aka-kāwō masu
tukwichi sai su sabke amarīa su kai ta
dāki. Sai ta kwaranye alkeba, ta yes, ta fita
wurin wāsa, ama amarīa ta gaskīa, ita
ta-na dāki, kwanche. Idan mutāne sun wātse,
sai akai ta [24]dākin mijinta, su kwāna. Idan
ya iske ta budrua, sai shi bāda [25]kari, ko zō-
-be, kō mundūa ta azurfa, kō kurdi,
kō zanē, kō wani abu da shi ke da īkō.
Saanan su kwāna fudu dāki, da buduri
da samāri su-na-wargi. Ranan fudu, su fita,
su yi buki. Amarīa ta yi kwalīa, angō shi ma, shi yi;

---

we do not enter, (we) stand outside, unless (we are given a gift of) a slave, (we) stand without.' (They sing so) because they want a present. When a gift has been given they take the bride (the mock one) down from the horse (and) escort her into the room. Then she takes off the burnous (and) casts it down, (and) comes forth again among the revellers, but the real bride is lying down in the room. If the people disperse she is conducted to her husband's room, (and) they sleep together. If he finds she is a virgin then he gives her gifts, perhaps a finger ring or armlets of silver, or cowries, or a cloth, or something which is within his means to give. Then they sleep four days in the house, and the maidens and youths are playing and rejoicing. On the fourth day they come out (and) hold the marriage feast. The bride decks herself up, and the bridegroom, as for him, he does so too;

بموشغب ؞ طبنطيمي ؞ مسن دمبجوميا طبنطيمن
دوقمز آكاوو مسن ؞ تكيش ؞ إدن ؞ آكاوو مس
تكيش ؞ اسن لسسبكي ؞ آمزميا ؞ لسكيت
دابك ؞ اسن تكم فبي ؞ أنكب ؞ تبلس ؞ قوبت
ورفوا اسس ؞ آمدا آمزميا ؞ قفسكيا ؞ إم ؞
قندا دايك ؞ كفب ؞ إدن ؞ هتدا قبن ؞ سفوا ابن
مسن آكبت ؞ داكن هجنت ؞ لسكوا آملي ؞ إدن
بدا إسبكست ؞ بجدورا ؞ اسن شبادا كم ؞ كودو
بن ؞ كو منددا را ؞ تادوقلي ؞ كوكترد ؞
كوطبن ؞ كورنابا ؞ دشبكي دابيكو
؞ لسغمن ؞ سكوا آمن ؞ قجم ؞ دايك ؞ دمبدري
دلسمدا ري ؞ سندا وزغم ؞ وآمز فجم ؞ سبقت
ستنبكم ؞ آمزميا ؞ تم كلبا ؞ أفغوشيقا بشي

shi rufa alkeba. Shi fita, shi yi yāwō, shi gaida mutāne.
Shi ke nan. Hukumchi
amarīa yā kāre.

---

he covers himself with a burnous. He comes forth (and) walks about, (and) greets people. That is it. The bridal ceremony is completed.

[illegible]

[illegible]

[illegible]

No. 32.

Faslu.

Wanan fasalī ne na angwonchi. Idan matanbayi ya tanbaye ka,
iṅa wada ake angwonchi, ka amsa masa jawābi,
ka che, ‘ Idan yārō ka aure, randa aka-kāma amaṙīa,
sai tsōfin gidansu su je dākinsa, bai sani ba,
ashāfa masa [1] lalē. Shi kuma shi zamna dāki
shi yi lulubi. Samāri su dinga zūa wurinsa, su-na-
-zanche har akāwō amarīa.’ Shi ke nan.

Faslun.

Wanan fasalī ne zaa shi gaia mani wada shēkaran
yārinya ke kai, ta yi [2] haila, ayi mata aure.
Mafi karamchin shēkara da yārinya ke ganin haila,
shēkara tara, mafi yawansa gōma sha bīar.

Descriptions (of Customs).

This is a description with regard to the condition of being a bridegroom. If a questioner asked you what ceremony they have with regard to a bridegroom's condition, answer him words such as these, saying, ‘ If a boy is going to marry, on the day on which the bride is to be brought, then the old women of his house come to his room without his knowing it was going to happen, (and) rub henna on him. For his part he sits veiled in the house. The other young men (then) come and chat with him until the bride is brought.’ That is it.

The Descriptions.

This description which is about to be given will tell what year a girl reaches when she first had her menses, and is married. The earliest age which a girl has (lit. sees) her menses is nine years, and the latest fifteen years of age.

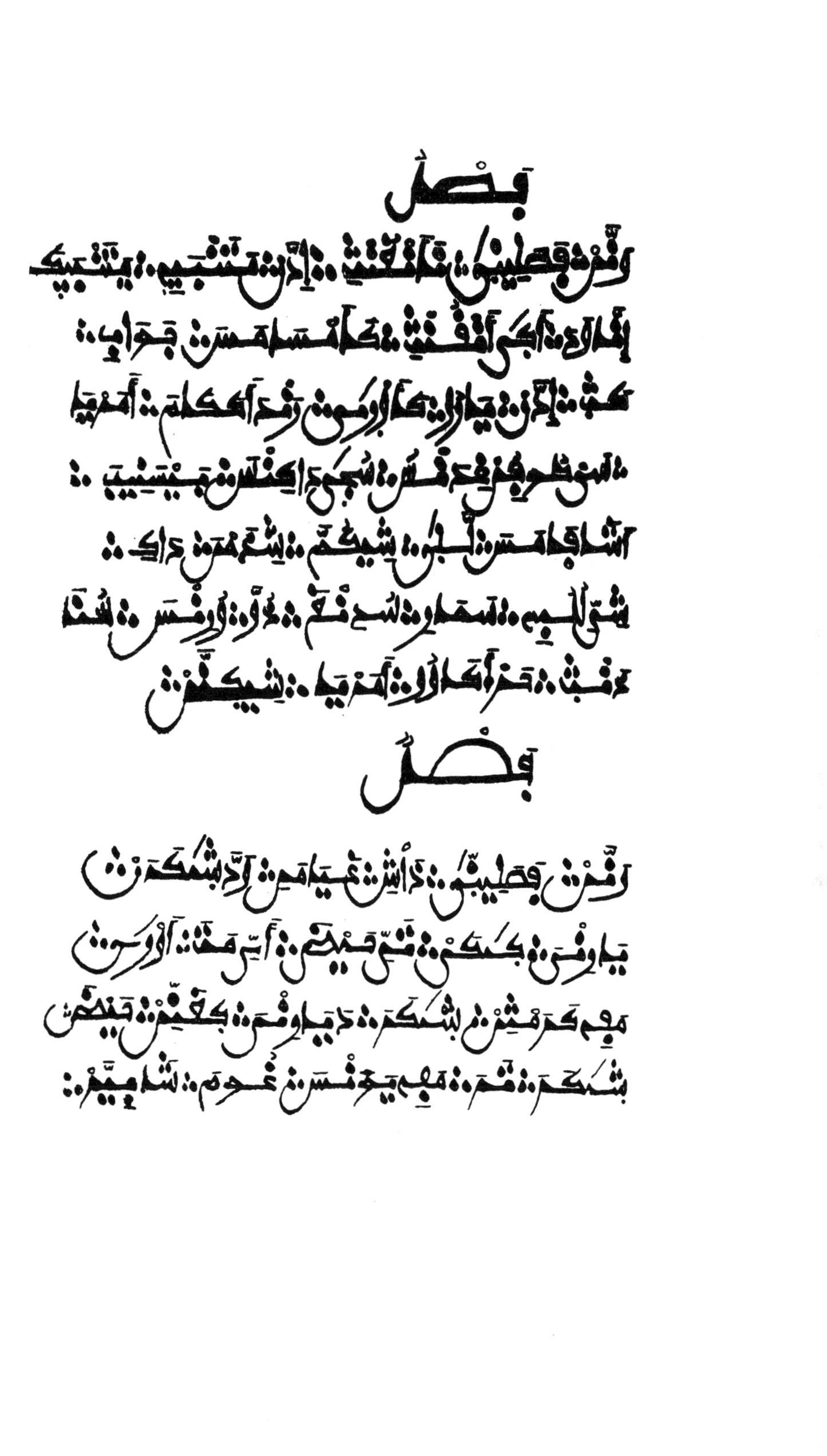

فصل

[illegible]

فصل

[illegible]

Mafi rinjaya shēkara gōma sha bīū wa [3] kīla,
in ji mālamai na [4] suna. Idan yārinya ta kai shēkara
gōma sha bīū, akai-ta gidan miji kō ba ta yi
haila ba. Idan aka-kai ta miji, shi bar ta, ama
ta-na tūō, ama ba ta kwāna wurinsa. Idan
ya gani ta yi haila, shi kirāye ta, ta kwāna
dākinsa banda sauran [5] mātansa.

Shi ke nan.

Most commonly it is said to be about twelve years of age; so say those learned men of holy repute. If a maiden reaches the age of twelve, she is taken to her husband's house, even if she has not had her menses. If she is taken (thus) the man leaves her alone, and she cooks (for him) but she does not sleep with him. If he sees she has had her menses he calls her, (and) she sleeps in his room without any of the rest of his wives (being there). That is it.

ميم ونجيا ∴ لشكر ∴ غوتم ∴ اشغبيوا ∴ ووفيل

إنج مالقة ∴ قشن ∴ إدرن ميلوفن ∴ تكن ∴ بشكم

غوتم ∴ تشغبيوا ∴ اكينتغع نيم ∴ نحوبتي

تيضن ق ∴ إدرن ∴ اككيت ∴ ميم شبرق ∴ امل

قند متوورد امابد تكوامي ∴ ورفسن ∴ إدرن

يغنيم ∴ قانتي تيضن لشكم ايت ∴ تحوارن

داكنسن ∴ بنع سوورن مافنسن

لشبكمن

No. 33.

[1] Faslun.

Wanan fasalī ne na hukumchin aure bajāwara. Idan mutun ya gani bajāwara kō [2] yā ji lābārinta, sai shi nemi wata tsōfūa, mai-hankali, shi aike ta kirāwō ta. Idan ta zō, su-ka-yi gaisua. Shi che, 'Lāfia? Na che akirāwō ki, nā gane ki ne, hankalina ya kwanta da ke, ina-son ki aure, kō Ala ya sa akwa--i kafa, mu sa hannu.' Idan ita kua ta-na-sō, sai ta che, 'Nā ji. Sai ku je wurin [3] waliyīna.' Idan kai kua ka-na da wani abu kusa, kamar silē, kō yar takofa, sai ka ba ta. Idan ta je gida, sai ka bidi gōrō, kō nāma, ka aika, akai ma uwāyenta, ache, in ji ka, idan sun [4] lāmun ta.

The Descriptions.

This is a description of the marriage of a woman of some age whose husband is dead or has left her. If a man saw a woman (widow or divorced), or has heard about her (whom he wishes to marry), then he looks out for some old woman of sense and sends her to call her to him. When she comes they greet one another, and he says, 'Is it well with you? I said you were to be called to me, I have looked on you, and my mind is at rest owing to your presence. I want to marry you, if perhaps Allah causes that an opportunity arrives that we may place our hands on.' If she too is agreeable then she says, 'I have heard, but you must go to my guardian.' Now if you have seen some little thing handy, as a shilling or a trifle like a sixpence, then you give it her. When she goes home then you seek kola nuts or meat, and send (them) to be given to her parents from you, if they have consented (to give) her.

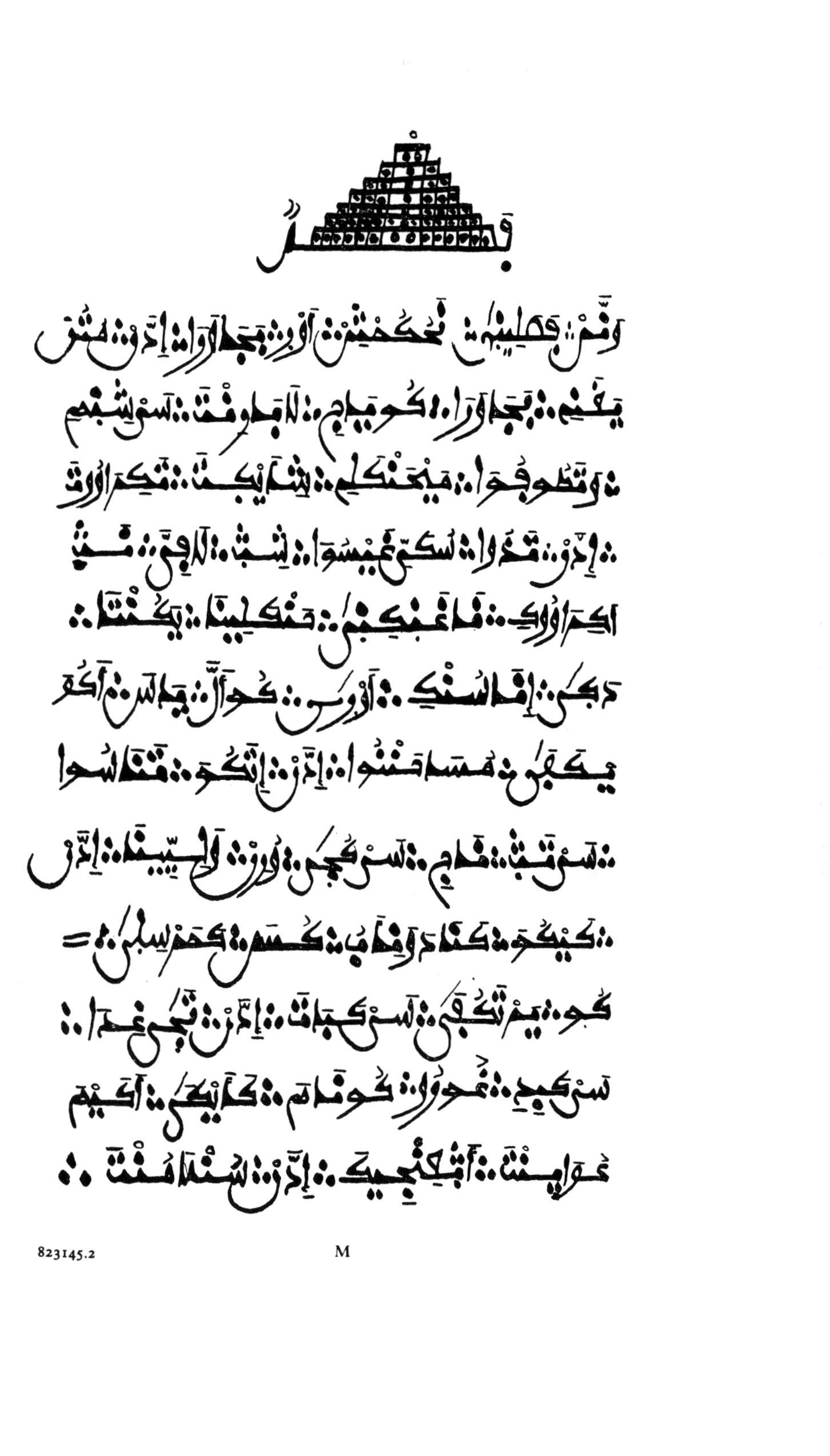

Shi ke nan. Idan ka yi surukūta kwāna bīū
sai ka aiki mutānenka, su yi rōkō aba su.
Idan aka che anba shi, sai ka bidi [5] kurdi alfin,
aje, ayi ma uwayenta adua. Saailin ka bidi
kurdi arba, da [6] gōrō hamsin, ka baiwa
mātan unguarku, su kai, kurdin gaisua
ke nan. Idan aka yi haka aka gama, sai ka bidi
zanen dauri bīū, masu-cheau, da mayāfi, asainya
chikin lefē, da kurdi zanbar gōma, su ne
ake che, kurdin tūō. Saanan ka bidi rubudīnāri,
ka zuba, akai gidan maata, da gōrō kwor-
-ia guda. Saanan, kamar gōbe za adaura
aure, ka bidi gōrō, ka raba. Su, līman

That is all. When you have wooed her for two days, then you send your people to ask that she (the woman) be given them. If they say she is to be given him (? you) then you seek two thousand cowries and they go and say a prayer over her parents. Then you seek four thousand cowries, and fifty kola nuts and give to the women of your part of the town, (and) they take it. This is (called) 'the cowries for exchanging greetings'. When this is all completed, then you seek for two fine cloths capable of being twined round a person, and coverings (for the couch), (and) they are put in a basket, with ten thousand cowries, and these are called, 'the cowries for the food.' And then you seek the cowries called 'the *rubudinari*' and pour out, and they are taken to the wife's house; also one calabash of kola nuts. Then if it be to-morrow that they are going to celebrate the marriage you seek kola nuts, (and) divide them up. They, the priests

شِيبِكَتَّنْ ؞ إِدَّنْ ؞ كَتِّ سُمْ كُوقَّا ؞ كُوَا أَقَّمْ مُوَا ؞

سَنْ كَأَيِكِ ؞ مُتَا بَقَّنْكَ ؞ سُرُو كُو ؞ أَبَا شَنْ ؞

إِدَّنْ أَكَبْ ؞ أَقْبَا شِنْ سَنْ كَبِجِ ؞ كُدِ أَلْقِنْ

؞ أَبِي أَيِ مَغُو نِقْتَ ؞ أَدْعَمِ ؞ تَسَا إِلَنْ ؞ كَبِجِ

كُنْ دِ ؞ أُوقَبَا ؞ دَمْ غُورُ ؞ تَقَفِيسَنْ ؞ كَبِنُو ؞

مَدَ قَنْغَنْغُو رُكَ ؞ سَكَنْ ؞ كُرْدِ مُغَيْسُوا ؞

بَكَّنْ ؞ إِدَّنْ ؞ أَكَنْ ؞ قَكَ ؞ أَكَغَمْ ؞ سَنْ كَبِجِ

طَبَّرْ دَرُو ؞ شِبِيُو ؞ مَدَ السَّتُو ؞ بِمَيَاقِ ؞ آسَنْتِيَ

شَكَزَ بِيْوَا ؞ دَكُرْدِ ؞ مَقْبَرْ غُومَ ؞ سُوقَمِ

؞ أَبَتْ كُرْدِ مُتُورُ ؞ تَسَقَنْ ؞ كَبِجِ رُبْغَ دِيَارُ

كَغَبَا ؞ أَكِنْ ؞ قَدِ مَقَامَقَّا ؞ دَ قُورُ ؞ كُمْ

يَاغُدَا ؞ تَسَقَنْ ؞ كَمَرْ غُوبِ ؞ دَاعِدَارْ ؞

غُورُسِ ؞ كَبِجِ غُورُ ؞ كُمْقَا ؞ سُلِيقَنْ ؞

da jamaa māsu-yawa, da mālamai, su tāru gidan
uban maatā, su zamna su damra aure. Idan
aka-gama su-ka-watse. Mātā su tāru, su tūka
tūō, su kai gidan angō, araraba ma mutāne
tūō, damri aure. Idan dare ya yi,
akai amarīa gidan angō. Saanan māta
su tāru, bābu kidi, sai wāka. Arufa [7] abuyar amar-
-īa, akai ta, dōmin wāsa. Idan zaa su kōmō,
su kōmō tāre. Ita kua akanche, 'amarīan bōkō.'

No. 34.

Faslu.

Wanan fasalī ne na dauri aure. Wada ake daura
aure. Mutāne sun tāru, līmāmi shi tanbaia
shi che, 'Wanene [1] wakīli?' Ache, 'Wāne.' Su che, 'Kāka

---

and a great number of people and the doctors of learning assemble at the house of the father of the (wife to be) and sit there, and perform the marriage ceremony. When they have finished, they disperse. The women-folk meet and stir the food (in the pot) (and) take it to the bridegroom's house (and) divide it out among the people (present). (It is called), 'the food of the marriage ceremony.' When it is night they take the bride to the bridegroom's house. When the women assemble, there is no drumming, only singing. 'The friend of the bride' (the girl who personates the bride) is covered (head to foot) (and) taken (to the husband's house), in play. When they are about to turn back, they go back with her (the pretended bride). Now she is called, 'the pretended bride.'

Descriptions.

This is a description of the marriage ceremony. What (they do) in the marriage ceremony (is this). The people are assembled and the priest asks, 'Who is the person who gives this girl away?' They say, 'So-and-so.' They ask, 'What

دِ بجعم ؞ قاسيو ؞ دقا الحم ؞ يسقاو ؞ يغد فد ؞

أبّن ما قا ؞ يسدّ فن ؞ يسد فن ؞ أورن ؞ إدّن =

أكفم ؞ يسكوابطن ؞ ما قا يسقاو ؞ يسثوك ؞

قنورن ؞ يسكن يغدرن ؞ أقغوا ؞ أر رقا مقفابن

قنورن ؞ دمير ؞ نكحو وكمن ؞ إدّن ؞ دبركس بيا تّن ؞

أكيجكم ميا ؞ يغدر أقفوا ؞ يسعقّن ؞ ما قحن

يسقاو ؞ يجاب يكد ؞ يسترواك ؞ أروق ؞ أبيم آمن

يا ؞ أكيت دو قمر والقصن ؞ إدّرن ؞ دأسن ؞ يكحموا ؞

مسكو مو قاون ؞ إنعم أكشب ؞ أمزين بجو كوا ؞

فصل

وقمن فجليبن ؞ قهد أور ؞ عخورن ؞ أد آكد ور

عورن ؞ قنا قبن ؞ يسقاو ؞ لا يقادم ؞ يشتقيا

شب ؞ وا قبن ؞ وكيدن ؞ أمثوا قبن ؞ لسبكداك

sūnan miji?' Ache, 'Sūnansa wāne.' Shi che, 'Kāka sūnan maata?' Ache, 'Sūnanta wanche.' Saanan shi tanbayi sadāki shi che, 'Sadāki nawa?' Ache, 'Kaza.' Saanan idan sun yi [2] tarālia tsakā--nin juna, sai līman shi che, 'Mu yi salātu gōma gōma ga anabi.' Saanan tārō duka su che, '[3]Alahuma swali ala sayidina Muhamadi wa Ala ali sayadina Muhamadi wasalim.' Har su yi gōma gōma. Saanan su yi shiru, sai līman shi che, '[4]Alahuma swali Ala sayidina Muhamadi wa Ala ali sayidi--na Muhamadi warham sayidina Muhamadi wa Ala ali sayidina Muhamadi wabārik, Ala sayidina Muhamadi wa Ala ali sayidina Muhamadi kama swalaita wārhinta

---

is the husband's name?' They reply, 'His name is So-and-so.' He asks, 'What is the wife's name?' They say, 'Her name is So-and-so.' Then he asks about the marriage settlement, saying, 'How much is it?' They say, 'It is such and such an amount.' Then if they (the girl's parents) have given their joint consent, then the priest says, 'Let us say prayers ten times to the prophet.' Then the whole assembly repeat, O God be gracious to our lord Mohammed and the family of our lord Mohammed and salute them,' till they have done so ten times. Then they are silent. Then the priest says, 'O God be gracious to our lord Mohammed, and the family of our lord Mohammed, and have mercy on our lord Mohammed and the family of our lord Mohammed, and then our lord Mohammed and the family of our lord Mohammed, even as he wast gracious unto and will have mercy on

شوقم مج ∴ أبجو قنسن وأفي ∴ شب عدك
سوقم ∴ هد أقتي ∴ أب سوقمت ∴ وفب ∴ سكقش
شتفبي ∴ صعافي ∴ شب هعافم ∴ قمو ∴ أب
كعا ∴ سكقم ∴ إلم زن شقني ∴ قمرايضم ∴ ظلاك
فم جوقلي ∴ سبلاييم ∴ شب ممي صمات ∴ هوم
قوتم ∴ غا قب ∴ سعقم ∴ قادوردك ∴ سب
اللهم صل على سيدنا محمد ∴ وعلى آل
سيدنا محمد وسلم ∴ قمز سبع غوم ∴
قوتم ∴ سعقم سب شمرو ∴ سبع لاهيم ∴ شب ∴
اللهم صل على سيدنا محمد وعلى آل سيدنا
محمد وارحم سيدنا محمدا ∴ وعلى آل
سيدنا محمد ∴ وبارك على سيدنا محمد
وعلى آل سيدنا محمد كما صليت ورحمت

wabarakata ala, Ibrahima wa Ala ali sayidina Ibra-
-hima inaka hamidu majidu amin. Wāne
[5] ya wakilche mu daurin aure abin walichinsa mu daura
auren wanche da wāne bisa farilan Ala sūnan
manzō Ala bisa sadāki kaza. [6] Nakadan ga
shi hanu.' Idan anbia shi ke fadi hakanan,
idan ba abia ba shi che, '[7] Ajalan, sai wata kaza
abia.' Saanan su yi fātiha uku. Idan shi-na da
kōkari, shi yi wadansu adua. Bāyan
hakanan kamar shi che, 'Ala shi bāda chi da sha, Ala
shi bāda haifua. Ala shi ba wakilai lādan sadāwa
miji da maata, Ala shi sāda hankulansu, Ala shi ba
gari lāfia. Musulmi da su-ka-mutu tun zāmanin

---

and bless Abraham and the family of our lord Abraham. Verily thou art praiseworthy. Amen. So-and-so has given us a union to bind, and the ceremony we have to perform for him is that we bind in marriage What's-her-name and What's-his-name, upon the faith of Allah, in the name of the messenger of Allah, on such and such a dower. Behold it in (my) hand.' If it has been paid (already) he speaks thus. If it has not been paid (then) he says, 'And such and such a moon they will pay.' Then they recite three verses (of the Koran). If he (the priest) is very diligent he may say some other prayers after this, as, 'May Allah give food and drink; may Allah give offspring; may Allah give the parents (of the bride and bridegroom) the reward for the union of the man and wife; may Allah complete their intelligence; may Allah give health to the town; the Mussulmans who have died since the days

أيبا وكنّ غلى أفم اهيم شو غلى آل امتج قلابرا

هيم شا إنّك قميج مجيج امين وابس

يا وكلثم دو رنغورلمن أبمز اليشسو فمدوت

أوبر فقرقث دو البلى مساقم قرأن سنفر

منغدو أآن مساصدافه بكم اقف أما غا

شعفوش إذن أفيبا شبكبق مكنّن

إدو بأ ميا فبه يشبّ أجدا سن وت عدا

أميا سعقن من سرّ قانم أك إدن لشاد

كوعم ب شي ود مسن أدعمن مبايسن

مكنّن عممشب آل شباد قمشن آل

شباد ميبقوا آل شباركيلن لادو وصاد اوا

مج دمامد آل شصاد منكلنسن آل شبا

غمر لا وجن فسلم دسعمث متراميش

anabi Ādamu har yau, maza da mātā, Ala shi jikai su, mu kūa, Ala shi sa mu wanye da alhairi, āmin.' Shi ke nan, sai mutāne su wātse, kōwa shi tafi gidansu.

---

of the prophet Adam till to-day, men and women, may Allah have mercy on them. We too may Allah cause us to die in peace. Amen.' That is it. Then the people disperse, each goes to his own home.

أَمْبَ يَمَ اَدَمُ ؞ تَمْ رِيجُو ؞ مَذَ اَدَمَ تَتَا ؞ اَلْشِيكَيْسَنْ مُو

كُو ؞ اَلْشَمْسُ مُحَمْفِيّ ؞ دَ اَلْغَيْبِ يَ اَمِينْ شِيكُنْ

تَسْ مُتَلَفِّمْ سُوَابِطَى ؞ كُوَا ؞

شِتَفِ غَدَ مُسَنْ

No. 35.

[1] Faslun.

Wanan fasalī ne zaa shi gaia muna hukumchi haifūa. Idan matanbayi [2] yā tanbaye ka, ina wada hukumchi haifua shi ke, ka che, 'Karamchi, chikin mache wata shida, mafiyawansa wata tara, saanan ta haifu. Wani chiki shēkara fudu, wanan chuta ne. Ama idan mache ta haifu, wada mu ke yi mata, sai adafa rua shi yi zāfi, adinga yi mata wanka, da ita da yārō, har kwāna bakwoi. Ranan mijinta shi sa gōrō, araba chikin gari. Idan gari ya wāye, mutāne su tāru, akāwō gōrō da kurdi, [3] azāna sūna.' Shi ke nan.

Faslun.

The Descriptions.

This description will explain to us the ceremony at the birth of a child. If a questioner has asked you what the ceremony at birth is, say, 'The shortest time (in which a woman can give birth after conception) is six months, (and) the longest nine months; then she brings forth. Some conceptions are for four years, but that is owing to some disease. But if a woman bore (a child) what is done to her is this. Water is cooked till it is hot, and she and the child are continually bathed during seven days. On that day (the seventh day) the husband sets down kola nuts (and) they are distributed in the town. When it is dawn the people all assemble, (and) kola nuts and cowries are brought, (and) the naming (of the child) performed.' That is it.

The Descriptions.

بَرْ

وَقَّنْ قَحَلِيقِّ ؞ دَاِشْ قَهِيَا مُنْ ؞ مُحَكْحِيْ قِيْنِقْوَا ؞ =

اِدَّنْ ؞ قَشْتِيبِ ؞ مِيَا قَنْجِيكِ ؞ اِقْدَارْدِ ؞ مُكَحْيْ قِيْنِقْوَا ؞

رِشْجَكِ ؞ تَكِجْ ؞ تَكِرْ قَيْشِ ؞ شِكِنْ قَجْ ؞ وَتْ يِشْعِ ؞

قَمِ ؞ بِيُوقْسَوْ ؞ وَتَ قَمَرْ ؞ اَسْعَنْمْ تُحَنِيقِ ؞ آرْ نِيكِ ؞

شْكَرْ ؞ فِدْ ؞ وَقَّنْرِ شُو قَتَابِي ؞ آقَّدْ اِدَّنْ ؞ مَحْشْ

تْحَنِيفْ وَدْ مُجَكِّيقَتْ ؞ تَسُّوْ اَمَّرْقْ ؞ زُرَّا ؞ تِيسَّرْ اِفِي ؞

آحْ قُمْ خُغْ ؞ يِهَقْتْ وَنْكِي ؞ دِرَاتْ ؞ دِيدَارُ ؞ قَرْ كُوَاقْسُ

بَكّْ ؞ رَنْمْ مِجَنْتْ ؞ مِيشَسِي ؞ غُمُوزُرْ ؞ آوُمِ تِيكِرْ غُمُرِ

اِدَّنْ ؞ غُمُرِ ؞ بِيدَارَايِي ؞ مُقَتَابِي ؞ سُتَاوُ ؞ آكَدَاوُ غُمُورُ

؞ دَكْرِدِ ؞ آدَارْ ؞ بُسُومْ ؞ يِشِبْجِسْ ؞

بَرْ

No. 36.

[1] Faslun.

Wanan fasalī ne na hukumchin sūna. Idan matanbayi ya tanbaye ka, ina wada ake zāna sūnan jinjiri ka che:— ‘Ana-zāna sūnan jinjiri da swāfe rāna da ta haifu, idan ta kēwayō, mutāne su tāru. Līman shi che, Muyi salāti gōma gōma gā anabi. Idan su ka gama shi che, [2]Alahuma swali Ala Muhamadi wa Ala. Ali Muhadin warham Muhama wa ali Muhamadin wabarik Ala Muhamadi wa Ala ali Muhamadin kama swalaita warahimta wabarakta Ala Ibrahima wa Ala ali Ibrahima filalamina inaka hamidu majīdun. Saanan shi yi fātiha uku shi che, Samaina mauludu. Idan namiji ne shi che Ibrāhīma kō Muhamadu kō wani sūna, idan mache che shi che [3] Fātimata kō Hadījatu.

The Descriptions.

This is a description of the ceremony of naming (a child). If a questio asked you what was done at the naming of an infant you say, ‘An in is named on the morning of the day she (the mother) bears it, when day comes round, the people assemble. The priest says, Let us offer prayers ten times to the prophet. When they have finished he s O God be gracious to Mohammed and the family of Mohammed and h mercy on Mohammed and the family of Mohammed and bless Mohamn and the family of Mohammed even as thou wast gracious to, merc towards, and didst bless Abraham and Abraham's family in the wo verily thou art praiseworthy and glorious. Then he repeats three ver (of the Koran) (and) says, We name the child. If it is a male child he s Abraham or Mohammed or some other name, if it is a girl he s Fatimata or Hadijatu.

فَصْلٌ

وَنَّنْ فَلَلِيْنَ تَحْخِشِنْ سُومَ إِدَنْ مُتُنْبِيِمْ

يَتَنْبِيكَ إِمَادُ أَكَرَاقُ سُونْكُنْ جِنْجِرِ تَكْبْ

أَمَادْ أَنْسُوقُنْ جِنْجِرِ دَصَالِبَ رَانَعْ تَحِيفْ

إِدَنْ تَكُو مِيُو مُتَا قَبَّ أَسْتَارْ لِيِمَعْ بِشِنْ مُتِّ

صَلَاتْ غُومْ غُومْ غَمَا قَبِ إِدَنْ اَسَكَمْ يِشْ

أَللَّهُمَّ صَلِّ عَلَى مُحَمَّدٍ وَعَلَى ءَالِ مُحَمَّدٍ وَارْحَمْ مُحَمَّدًا

وَءَالَ مُحَمَّدٍ وَبَارِكْ عَلَى مُحَمَّدٍ وَعَلَى ءَالِ مُحَمَّدٍ

كَمَا صَلَّيْتَ وَرَحِمْتَ وَبَارَكْتَ عَلَى سَيِّدِنَا إِبْرَاهِيمَ

وَعَلَى ءَالِ إِبْرَاهِيمَ فِي الْعَالَمِينَ إِنَّكَ حَمِيدٌ مَجِيدٌ

سَلَّمْنْ بِشِنْ قَدْ قَمْ أَكُ يِشْ سَمِيْنَا مُولُودْ إِدَنْ

نَجِ بَلِي يِشْ إِبْرَاهِيمْ كُو مُحَمَّدُ كُو قِبِ

سُومَنْ إِدَنْ مُتُنْبِ يِشْ قَايِمَةْ كُو قَدِيجَةْ

Saanan shi yi adua, kaman da ya sō shi che, 'Ala shi rāya shi,
Ala shi ba uwa da uba lāfia.' Shi yi adua dayawa, saanan
mutāne su wātse. Ama anyanka rāgō tun mutāne
ba su tāru ba. Saanan azāna sūna, saanan
[4] wanzāmai su tāru, māta su yi buki, idan mai-gāta
ne. Idan marēche ya yi nāman rāgō araraba
abai wa kōwa sadaka. Ita kua maata nan, ana-ba
ta abinchi mai-dādi, ta-na-chi har jinin haifūa
shi zuba duka, saanan ta sāmu lāfia.'

Shi ke nan.

Then he gives a prayer, if he wishes; he says, May Allah prolong his life; may Allah give (his) mother and father health. He prays many times and then the people disperse. Now a ram had been slaughtered before the people had assembled. After that they name the child. Then the barbers assemble (and) the women make a feast, if the man was of a wealthy family. When evening comes the ram's flesh is divided up and given as alms to any one. And as for her, this wife, she is given the choicest food to eat until all the after-birth has come away. By that time she has regained her health.' That is it.

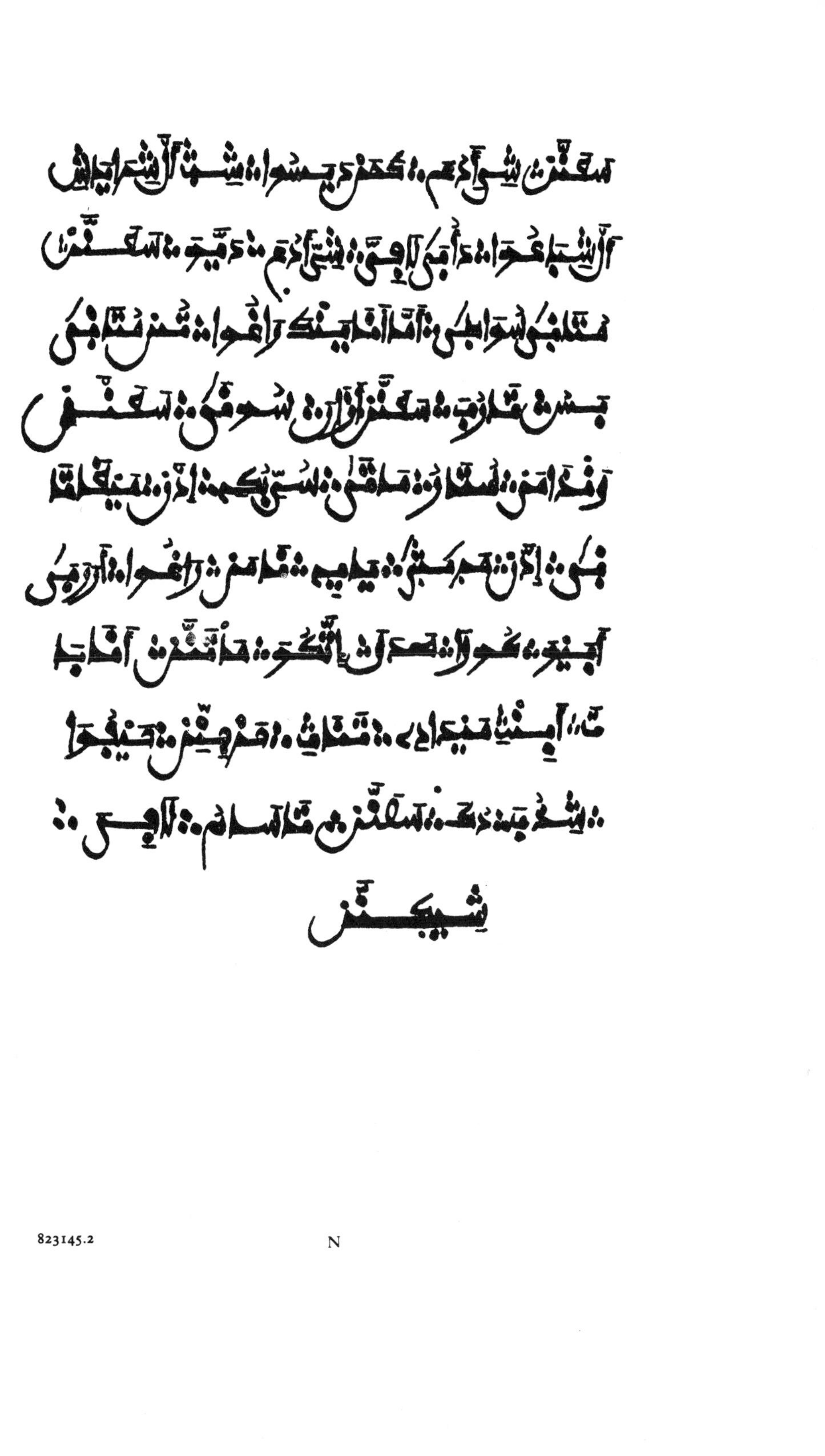

No. 37.

[1] Bābun.

Wanan bābi ne zaa shi gwoda muna wada ake yi [2] sha gaba. Idan matanbayi ya tanbaye ka, shēkara nawa ake yi ma yārō kāchia, ka che, 'Shēkara tara.' Achikin musulumchi ina wada ake kāchia ka che. 'Idan yārō ya isa kāchia, sai akirāwō wanzāmai, su tafō da asake, su yi ma yāra aski. Saanan agina [3] rāme, asaka sūma nan achikin rāme. Saanan akāmō yārō, azamna da shi bakin rāme, [4] aririke shi. Wanzāme shi hau kafāfunsa, shi zamna saanan shi kāma bākin lōba shi jāwō, shi yimte, saanan shi sake, shi fida aska daga kube. Shi kāma lōba

---

The Beginnings.

This is the opening of what we are going to be shown of what is done at circumcision. If a questioner asks you how old a boy is when he is circumcised, say, 'Ten years.' Among Mussulmans what is done at circumcision, you say (is as follows): 'When a boy has reached the age of circumcision then the barbers are summoned (and) they come with razors and shave the boy (head). Then a hole is dug in the ground and this cut off hair put in the hole. They then seize the boy, (and) sit with him over the hole and hold him tight. The barber gets across his legs (facing him) and sits down, then he takes hold of the edge of the foreskin (and) pulls it back (and) pinches it tight, then he lets it go (and) takes his razor out of the sheath. He catches the foreskin

وَفِنْ ؞ مَا بِنبن ؞ كَأَشِنْ غُدا امُرْ ؞ أَدا أَبْجِ شَدا غَبَا ؞

إِدَّنْ مَتَنْفِيِّ ؞ يَنْتَنْبِيكْ ؞ بِشُمَكَرْ فُو ؞ أَكَيِمْ بِدَارِ ؞

كَدَافِي ؞ كَبْ بِشُمَكَرْ ؞ قَمْرَ ؞ أَنْكِمْ مُسُلْمِنْشِ ؞ إِفَدا وَرِ ؞

أَبْكَرْ كَدَافِي ؞ كَبْ ؞ إِدَّنْ ؞ يَمَاوَا ؞ يَبِلِسْ ؞ كَدَافِي ؞ لَسِنْ

أَكَرَا أُوَا ؞ وَفَدَا امُنْ ؞ لَسْتَفُوا ؞ دَ أَسَكِي ؞ سُتَّمِيا رَا ؞

أَنْسَكِ ؞ لَسَفَمْ ؞ أَفْمَرْ رَامِي ؞ أَسَكْ سُومَنْقَمْ ؞

أَنْكِنْ رَامِي ؞ لَسَغَمْ ؞ أَكَدا مُوا يَدَاوُا ؞ أَذَ فَسْ

دَ شِم ؞ بَدَا كِرْ رَامِي ؞ أَرِ بَكِشِنْ ؞ وَفْدا امِي ؞ شِمَو

؞ كَبدا فُنْسَرْ ؞ شِنْدَ مَرْ ؞ لَسَغَمْ ؞ شِكَدَامْ ؞ بَايِعْ

لُوبِي ؞ شَجَاوُا ؞ شِيَمْجِي ؞ لَسَكَمْ ؞ لِشْسَكِي ؞

شَبِقِع ؞ أَسْكَنْ دَ غَمكَبِي ؞ شِكَدَامْ ؞ لُوبِي ؞

iyāka wurin da ya yimche, shi sa aska, shi yanka maza maza. Idan ya kai wurin tantāni, shi ake che "jar fāta", sai shi tsāga da hannu, saanan shi sa aska, shi yanke. Sai shi tamna bagarua shi pēsa, sai shi tāshi. Idan sun yi su dari, hakanan ake yi masu. Lōba da aka-yanka, sai ajēfa shi chikin rāme. Idan angama sai adaure da mōda, har shi kwāna uku. Saanan atafō akunche mōda, awanke asa māgani, amayar, adaure hakanan ake yi. Wanda magāninsa ke da kyeau, kāmin kwāna gōma sha fudu, [5] yā warke. Wani kūa shi-na-kai wata guda, bai warke ba, idan bai gamu da māgani mai-cheau ba. Ama wadansu ba su damrēwa,

---

at the limit of the spot where he had pinched it, he places the razor (and) quickly cuts. If when he gets to where the red flesh begins—this part is called "*jar fata*", i. e. red skin—then he tears the skin with his hand—then he inserts the razor and cuts off (the skin). Then he chews up some of the seeds of the acacia tree and spits (on the wound); then he gets up. If a hundred have to be done, this is the method. The foreskin which has been cut off is then thrown into the hole. When it (the operation) is finished then they tie up the part with the leaves of the *moda* (hemp) tree, for three days, when they come and unfasten the leaves, wash (the sore), put on medicine, put on leaves again, and tie up as before. For one who has good medicine, in about fourteen days it has healed up, but some reach a moon without healing, if it has not had good medicine put on it. But some again are not for tying up (the wound) at all,

إيّاكُ ؞ وُرفع ؞ يتّيفت ؞ أشّ أسكُ ؞ يشيفك ؞

بَ أيشيل ؞ فلتنتقّ ور ؞ عيا ؞ ن ڭّا إ ؞ ادم ؞ ن ؞

جز قداتّ ؞ اسنّ شّطا عمى ؞ ءم مشّوا ؞ اسعقّو ؞ يشس

أسكُ ؞ يشيفكو ؞ اسنّ شتفع ؞ بعكوا ؞ يشهكس

سّسن يشّتا ايش ؞ إكز ؞ سّنّي ؞ اسوكري ؞ فكشز ؞

أبهيّقس ؞ أوبكر ؞ ءاعيفك ؞ اسنّ أوهبقاش ؞

يبعُ رابو ؞ إكّز ؞ أنفحم ؞ سّوا أءزو ؤكو ؞ فوكر ؞

هم يشكوا ارش أكُ ؞ قسعقّز ؞ اتبوا ؞ اغفب فوكر ؞

أوفكي ؞ أسحا غفي ؞ أقيم ؞ أم ؤوكو ؞ فكشّز ؞

أكتي ؞ ؤفّع قا عفيس ؞ بكءعكخو ؞ قلامز ؞

كرا قكُ ؞ عُوتم ؞ شّا فجُ ؞ يا ورزكي ؞ أركو

يشّنا عو ؞ ورتّ ءغدا ؞ بيّورك ؞ جب ؞ أكّ زن ؞ بيقم

ءما غفي ؞ فيشّا ؤوت ؞ أمّا ؤد قّمس ؞ جا سّع قبر كلا

sai su sa kara, su na turārāwa da hayāki. Da a-
-subāhin idan ya bushe, su jika achikin
sabō kaskō. Sai shi banbare, asa
māgani kuma. Hakanan wadansu ke yi
har shi warke ama ba su kwanchi bisa tābarma,
kō būzū, kō dan sarki ne, sai bisa
rai rai, idan wurin rai rai ne. Idan bābu
rai rai agarin, sai adēbō gainye dayawa,
azuba chikin dāki, su-na-kwāna bisansa
har su warke. Ba su sa riga, ba su damra
bante, kō zane, ama ana-kashe masu
gārā dayawa su chi. Idan sun ji kai kai

---

but set down straw (and set fire to it) and smoke the wound. Early next morning if it (the wound) is dry they soak it (the penis) (in water and medicine) in a new clay pot. When (the water) loses its medicinal properties, some more medicine is put in. Thus some do, till (the wound) heals. Now they (the ones operated on) never lie on a mat or on a skin, even if he be the son of a chief, but on sand, if there is sand about. If there be no sand in the town, they then pluck many leaves, (and) spread them in the room (and) they sleep on them till they recover. They wear no cloak, they fasten on no loin covering, or cloth, but are given all kinds of luxuries to eat. If they have felt any irritation

لسع لسسر كرا ⁖ سنا قمر او او ⁖ كر قيا كي ⁖ كر أ

لعبا جن ⁖ إدن قيا بو بشي ⁖ سجك ⁖ أثكن

تصا بجوا ⁖ كنسكوا ⁖ أسن بشتبتبر بن ⁖ أسد

قما غيم كتم ⁖ قتكتن ⁖ وكر فمسن بكن ⁖

قمر شقو ربكي ⁖ أما بدا سكنث ⁖ بمسر قدا بمرتا

كجو بوتر وا ⁖ كجو فمسر كيشي ⁖ أسن ببس

وبير بن ⁖ إدن ⁖ وفر بير بيم بني ⁖ إدن ⁖ قلب

وبير بيم ⁖ أغير ف ⁖ نسن أجر مجوا ⁖ غشبي كر قيجوا

أدب ⁖ ثكمر دا كي ⁖ سنا كجوا أمي ⁖ بمستنس

قدر سجو وبكي ⁖ بدا سستا ويخلي ⁖ بدا سحر قمر ⁖

بنبشي ⁖ كجو قبكي ⁖ أما أقدا كبشمسن ⁖

قداوا ⁖ د قيو ⁖ سثي ⁖ إدن ⁖ سنجم كبكي

ba su sōsāwa. Ana sainya karta su yi jira-
-nsu dōmin mūgun kwāna kar su fāma
miakunsu. Dōmin hakanan akwai wani abu
ana-che da shi " Aka-chi ", su kan rika bugāwa su-na-
-che: " Aka-chi, aka-sha, aka-kwāna kasa, kō dan sar-
-ki, a-shi-kwāna kasa, kō dan malām, a-shi-kwāna
kasa, kō atājir, a-shi-kwāna kasa, bale
talaka, wōfin banza, a-shi-kwāna kasa, aka-chi
aka-sha, aka-kwāna kasa, kō dan wāne, a-shi-kwāna
kasa." Ama mache ba ta zūa
6 wurin, dōmin kar su gane ta,
kwodainsu shi je
garēta.'
Shi ke nan.

---

they must not scratch. Big powerful men are set to watch them in order that they (the patients) may not hurt their sores by tossing about in their sleep. Because of this there is a kind of (musical) instrument they call the "*Akachi*", which they beat while at the same time say (sing): " They eat, they drink, they lie on the ground, be he the son of a chief, he must lie on the ground; or be he the son of a doctor of learning, he must lie on the ground; or a wealthy man, he must lie on the ground; how much more the poor man, the useless vagabond, must he lie on the ground. They eat, they drink, they lie on the ground, but he the son of So-and-so, he must lie on the ground." Now no woman comes there lest they behold her and desire go out towards her.' That is it.

بدا سنو لسا ورا ؞ أقد السنتو ؞ قم قد ؞ لسو جم
قشن ؞ د وقمن ؞ مو غمن ؞ كوامي ؞ كم سقام
ميد كوشن ؞ دومن ؞ مكتن ؞ أكومن ؞ ونا ب
أمد قم لشم ؞ أكش ؞ السكنري ؞ بعدوا ؞ سقا
ب ؞ أكش أكشن أككوان ؞ كسن كود قسم
كم أشكوان ؞ كسن كود قمداه ؞ أشكوان
كسن كو أمد جمر ؞ أشكوان ؞ كسن مل
قلك ؞ ورقمن بغدا ؞ أشكوان ؞ كسن أكش
أكسن أككوان ؞ كسن كود قوابم ؞ الشكوان

؞ كسن أمد ؞ مش بد تدو ؞
ورن ؞ د ومن ؞ عم سغنة
كد يشن شيمي
غم مدة ؞
شيكمن

No. 38.

[1] Faslun.

Wanan fasalī ne na [2] kāchiar [3] māta. Idan matanbayi ya tanbaye ka, 'Ana wada ake-yi kāchiar māta?' ka che wada ake-yi: 'Idan za afārawa sai ache su tafi su kāma rua. Idan sun kāma rua, sai su zo, su kwanta, su mīke kafāfunsu. Wani shi zamna bākin rāme bisa chikinsu. Saanan wata mache (mch) da ta iya ta zō, ta zamna tsakānin kafāfunta, wadansu su kan kāma kafāfunta. Saanan [4] maatar nan ta sa hannu, ta [5] kāmō dan tsakanta. Ta sa aska daga karkashin abin, ta [6] shārō shi har bisa, ta kwalfe shi duka, ta jefa rāme. Saanan ta tāshi, ta je, ta tsuguna. Wata kuma ta zō

The Descriptions.

This is a description of the removal of the clitoris of a woman. If a questioner asks you (saying), 'But how do they perform the operation of removing the clitoris of a woman?' say what is done is as follows: 'When they are about to begin, then they (the girls) are told to go and take water (and wash). When they have washed, then they come (and) lie down (and) stretch out their legs. Some one sits, near the edge of the hole (they have already dug), on their bellies. Then a certain woman who is skilled (in the work) comes and sits between her legs, others seize hold of her feet. Then this woman (who is operating) puts her hand and draws out the clitoris. She places the razor under the thing, (and) draws it up to the top (and) cuts it all out (and) casts it into the hole. Then she (the girl) rises (and) goes (and) sits down. Another also comes

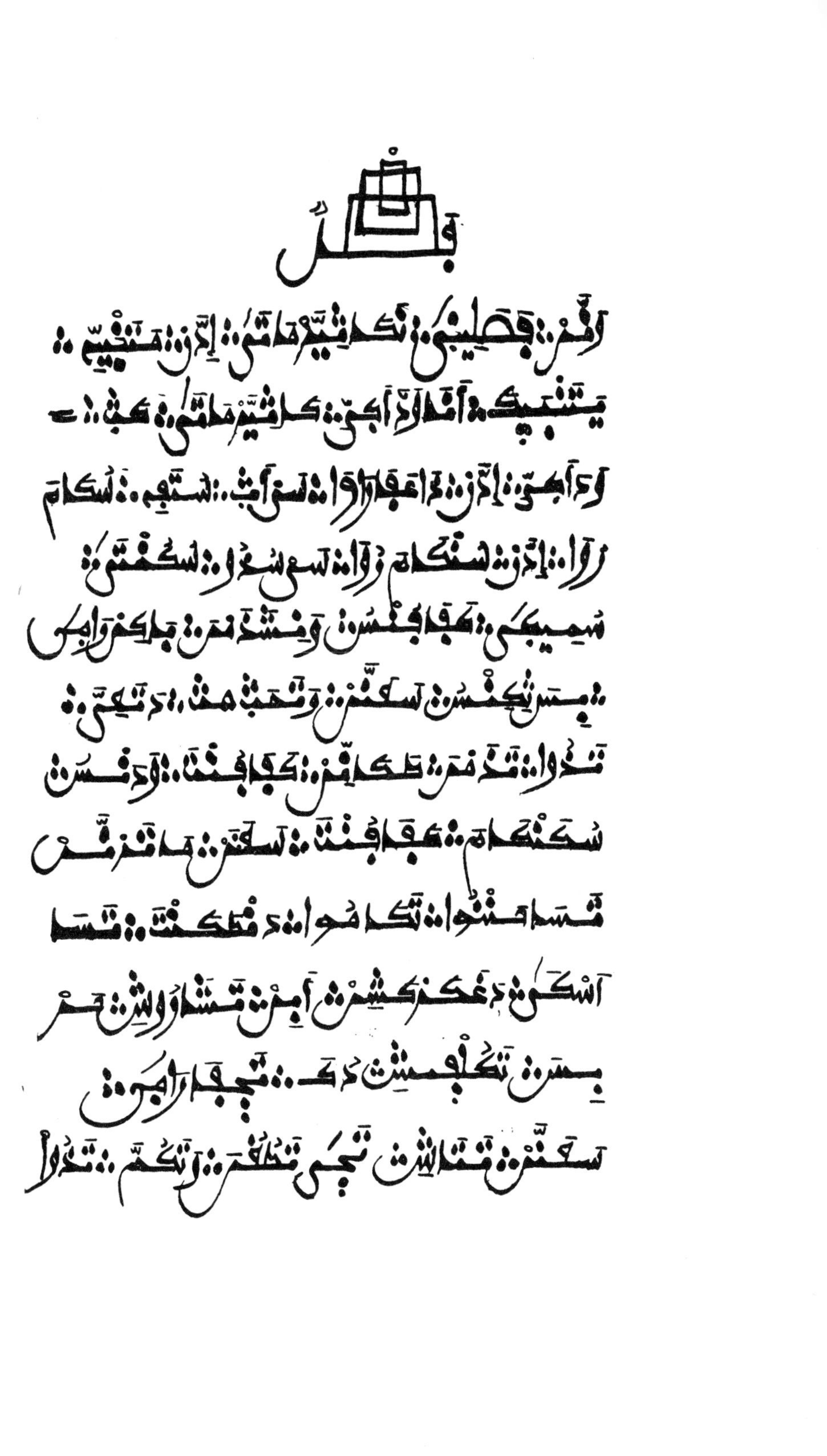

[illegible]

[illegible]
[illegible]
[illegible]
[illegible]
[illegible]
[illegible]
[illegible]
[illegible]
[illegible]
[illegible]
[illegible]
[illegible]
[illegible]

ayi mata hakanan, kō sun kai nawa hakanan ake yi masu. Idan jini ya kāre tsiyāya, sai anarka mai kadainya, asainya masu, ayi masu kirshe. Idan gari ya wāye awanke, asainya mai kade, wadansu [7] sābōni, hakanan ake yi, har shi kāre.' Shi ke nan.

---

and the same is done to her, and so on whatever number there have been. When the blood ceases to flow then shea butter is melted and put on them (on the place cut) and a cloth is tied between the legs. Next day they bathe, (and) put on (more) shea butter, some (put on) soap, and this is what they do, till the place is healed up.' That is it.

أَيِّمَّتْ ؞ تَكَّنْ يُكُوسْنْكَنْ قُوّ ؞ تَكْقَسْ

أَبْتِّيقَّسْنْ إِدَّرْ ؞ جِنِي فِيدَا كَدْ وُرْ طِيدَا تْنْ ؞ قَسِّي

أَقْرْكْ ؞ فِيبْكَجْ قُمِّي ؞ أَسْنْبِيَا قَسْنْ ؞ أَيِّقَّسْ ؞

يِكْرْشْكِي ؞ إِدَّرْ ؞ غْمْ فِيدَا الِّيبِي ؞ أُرْنْبكْمْ أَسْفِيْرْ =

فِيبْكَجْ بِرْ ؞ وَرْدْ قْسْرْ ؞ قَسَا بُجُورْ ؞ تَكَّنْ أَكْبِّي

تَنْرْشْكَدْ وُرْ ؞ شِيبْكَنْتْ

No. 39.

[1] Bābun.

Wanan bābi ne na matache. Idan matanbayi
ya tanbaye ka, 'Idan mutun ya mutu, ana wada ake ma gāwa
tasa?' Ka che:—'Idan mutun ya mutu dafārin, sai adi-
-bi rua, ashāfa ga idānunsa, dōmin idānunsa
shi rufe. Saanan, idan mai-gāta ne, sai
adēbō rua, ayi masa wanka. Saanan adauke shi
bisa tābarma, aaje shi akasa, afuskanta
da shi zua [2]Alkibla, arufa masa farin zane.
Saanan afita, agaia ma mutāne, dōmin
kōwa shi sani. Azo wurin bisō, saanan
ache, Ana wurin [3] kabri? Idan angwoda wurin kabri ache, Abidō

The Beginnings.

This is the commencement of a (description) about the dead. a questioner asked you (saying), 'If a man died what is done to h corpse?' you (can) say, 'When a man dies, then, first of all, wat is drawn (and) his eyes are bathed in order that his eyes may clos Then, if (the deceased) was a man of means, water is drawn and he bathed (all over). Then he is lifted on a mat, (and) placed on th ground (and) set with his face turned to the East (and) covered wi a new cloth. They then come out and tell the people in order th every one may know (he is dead). They go to the burying-groun and they say, Where is the place for the grave? When show where the grave is to be, they say, Let a stalk of corn be sought

وَتَنْ تَبَا بِيْنْ : تَهَتَبْشِ : إِدَّنْ تَتَشْبِيمِ : ب

يَتَفْبِكْ : إِدَّنْ مُشْرِيَّتْ : أَمَا وَدْ أَكَمَغَوَا

تَسَنْ كَبْ إِدَّنْ مُشْرِيَّتْ : دَ قَدَرُنْ اَسُوَا

يَبْ رُوَا : أَشَا قَدَا : عُمْدَا اَمُنْسَنْ دُ وُقَدْ إِدَا مُنْسَ

شُرُوفِى : تَسَغَنْ : إِدَّنْ مَيَنْغَا قَدَا فُنْ : تَسَ

أَدَ مُبُوُوَا : أَبِّحَسَنْ رُفْكَن : تَسَغَّنْ : أَدَ وُبَكْشِ

يَسَرْ قَدَا بَرْ مُنْ : أَعَجِيشِنْ أَكَسَنْ أَفُسَرْ كَنْتَ

دَيْشِ : دُوَا : أَلْفُبَنْ أَرُقَدَا مُسَنْ وَمَرْ ظَلْقُ

تَسَغَّنْ أَبَتَ : أَغْمُيَا مُهَتَا فَبُنْ : دُ وُقَسَنْ

تَكُوَا : تَشَسَنْ اَدُوَا وُ وُفُبُسُوَا : تَسَغَّنْ

أَبْ أَمَا وُ نُفُبُمْ : إِدَّنْ أَتَقُدُ وُ وُفُبُمْ : أَبْ أَمِدَ لَا

kara agwoda. Idan aka-sāmu kara, sai
aje wurin gāwa nan, adaidaita tsawō kara nan
da tsawon gāwa. Saanan, idan aka zō da karan,
sai agwoda da kushēwan adaidaita, agina.
Saanan ana-gina, masu-gāwa su kōmō
wurinsa, su dēbō rua adāma da magarīa,
ayi masa wanka. Akoma, aajiye shi.
Su zō wurin jamaa, ache, Ana likafani? Saanan
asāmū fari, azō, adumka likafani
da shi, ana-yi ma gāwa likafani. Idan mai-gā-
-ta ne, da abu bīar, wadansu shida, wada-
-nsu bakwoi, da kworzalē da fūla

---

and (the corpse) measured. When a stalk has been found, then they go to where the body is, (and) compare the length of the stalk with the length of the corpse. Then when they come with the stalk, they lay it on the grave (and) measure it out (and) dig. While (the grave) is being dug the people who have been attending to the corpse go back to where it is. Water is drawn and mixed with (the leaves) of the lotus, (and) they wash it (the body). He is once more set back (on the mat). (Then) they come to the people and ask, Where is the shroud? Then the white (sheet) is procured and they come and sew a shroud of it and make a winding-sheet for the corpse. If he was a man with rich relations, as many as five (robes) things, in some cases six, in others seven, and a waist-cloth and cap

كَمْرَا ∴ أَغْمُد ∴ إِدَّرْنْ أَكْسَا مُوا كَمْرَا ∴ سَّنْ

أَجْرْ وُرْ فْغَا وَقّنْ أَدْفِيدِيتْ ∴ طُورْكَرْقّْنْ

دْطُورْنْ ∴ غْمَاوَ ∴ لْسَغْقّنْ ∴ إِدّرْنْ أَكْغْ وُدْ كْتَرْنْ

لْسَزْ أَغْدَا ∴ دْكْشْمُوْنْ ∴ إِعْ ئْجِي مِيتْدَا أَغْنْ

∴ لْسَغْقّنْ ∴ أَمَا غْقْنِي ∴ مَدْ لْسَغْدَاوَا ∴ لْسْكُومُوا

وُ وْفْسَنْ سُبْ مَبُوا وْ وَا ∴ أَدَامْ ∴ دْمَقْمْرِيَا

أَيْمَسْ ∴ وُنْكْمْ ∴ أَكْمْ ∴ أَعْجِيبْشْ ∴ دْ

سْدْ وْرُنْ جْمَعْ ∴ أَبْ أَمَّا لْكَقْبِنّْ ∴ لْسَغْقّنْ

أَسَا مُوا قْبِرِي ∴ أَعْرَا ∴ أَدْ مْكْ ∴ لْكَقْبِنّْ

دْلِيشِي ∴ أَمَا يْمْقَا وَا ∴ لْكَقْبِنّْ ∴ إِدّرْنْ قِيقَا

تْدَابْنّْ ∴ دْ أَبْ مِيئْرْ وَدْ فْسْنْ ∴ لِيشْدْ ∴ وْدْمْ

فْسَنْ ∴ بْكُورْنْ دْكْمْ لْبِنْ ∴ دْ فُولْسْ

da rawani, da rīga, da uwan likafani. Idan ankā-
-re, saanan aturāra shi da kāfur, kō da jā-
-wul. Wadansu mālamai sun kia. Idan za ayin
turāre, sai abidō rua, amurza turāre chikin
rua, saanan adibi azuba ga likafani,
ayāfa masa. Saanan asāmu rua tsaltsalka,
aje, ayi ma gāwa wankan farila. Saanan asa
masa likafani, aajie shi, aje adūba ma-
-su-ginan kushēwa sun kāre. Idan sun kāre
adauki gāwa, akāwō wurin, sarari mai-chau,
aajie, akirāwō mālamai su zō, su yi masa
sala. Idan sun kāre, adauki, aje, abisna,

---

and turban, and cloak and the mother shroud (i.e. large) (are put on the corpse). When they have finished they anoint him with camphor or spices. Some learned men have not permitted this. If they are going to perfume the body then water is sought and the scents mixed in the water, then it is taken (and) sprinkled on the shroud (and) rubbed over him (the corpse). Next they take some of the purest water and come and wash the corpse according to the religious custom. Then the shroud is put on (and) (the body) set down. They go and see if those digging the grave have finished. If they have finished the body is lifted up and taken to some clear open space, (and) set down, (and) the learned men are called to come and say prayers over it. When they have ended they lift it (and) go (and) bury it,

دْرُوفِي : دْوِيفِي : دْغُو قْلِكَبْنِي :: إِدَّنْ : أَنْكَدْ

وَمَنْ : لسَّغْفَّنْ : أَمْرْ أَوْرَاشْ : دْكَا بْقِيرْ : كُوجْبَطْ

وُرْنْ : وَدْ قْمُسْ مَعَ الْحَمْ : لسَّنْفِي : إِدَّنْ : دْ أَعْمِيتْ

تْمْرَابْرِيْنْ لسَّرْ أَمْدْ وَأْ :: زُوَّا :: أَمْرْ دْ تْمْرَاوِيْنْ تْكْسْ

زُوَّا : لسَّغْفَّنْ : أَدِيبْ :: أَدْ أَبْرْغَلْكَبْنِي :: هَمَّ

أَيَّا قَبْ أَمْسَنْ لسَّغْفَّنْ : أَسَاضْ زُوَّا : طْلَحَالْكْسْ

أَجْرَ أَيَّمْغَا وَا : وُنْكْرْ قِيرْضَنْ : لسَّغْفَّنْ : أَسَدْ

مَسَنْ لْكَبْقِيمْ :: أَعْجِيشْنْ : أَجْرْ أَدْوَبْ :: قَدْ

سُرْغَمْنَرْكْ بْشْوَا : لسَّنْكَابْرِي :: إِدَّنْ : لسَّنْكَابْرِي

أَدْرُكْ غَدْ أَوَا : أَكَاوَرْ : أُرْفَسْتْرُوِي :: فِيْنْتُوا ::

أَعْجِيبِيْنْ : أَكْرَاوْ وَا : مَدْ الْقَمْ :: لسَّذْوَا : لسَّيَّحَسْ

صَلَّوْ : إِدَّنْ لسَّنْكَابْرِي :: أَوُكْ :: أَجْرْ أَمْلَسْ

Idan anbisna, asāmu kurdi kadan
akāwō, abai wa malāmai, su yi adua. Akāwō na mai-
-wanka daban, da na mai-sala, da na māsu-ginan kushēwa.
Idan aka-kāre, sai kōwa su wātse. Mai-kū-
-ka na-kūka, mai-murna na-murna, har kwāna
bakwoi, saanan akirāwō mālamai. Su tārū, su yi
adua, su wātse. Bābu mai-zakūa kuma. Māta
su shiga takaba. Idan mai-mutua ya kai kwāna
arbain, akirāwō mālamai, su yi adua. Idan
shi-na da dūkīa, shi-na da yāya, araba masu
gādō. Idan ba shi da yāya, akai dūkīasa
gidan sarki, ya zama na talakāwa da marāyū.

When he has been buried, a small amount of cowries are brought, (and) given to the malamai (learned men), and they offer prayers. Those who washed the body, and those who prayed, and those who dug the grave are each given some separately. When it is all finished, every one disperses. The mourners mourn, (and) they who are glad rejoice, till seven days pass; then the malamai are summoned. They assemble and pray (and) disperse (again). There is no further coming (of friends and relations). The wives of the deceased enter upon the period of retreat for the dead. When the deceased has been dead for forty days the malamai are called (and) they pray. If he (the dead man) had property and if he had children the inheritance is divided up among them. If he had no children his property is taken to the chief's house and becomes (the possession) of the poor and orphans.

إِدْرْ ∴ أَفِبِلْسَقْ ∴ أَسَاسُوا ∴ كُمْرْدِ ∴ تَكَدَّنْ ∴

أَكَدَاوْرْ ∴ أَبْنِيوْ مَدَالْقَمْ ∴ لْسَّ أُدْعْ ∴ أَكَاوْرْ ∴ نَحَمْ

وْنْكُمْ ∴ دْمْ بَّمْرْ ∴ دْ تَفِيْجِمَلْ ∴ دْ لْقَدْ اسِفْنَّرْ ∴ كُبْشُوا

إِدْرْ ∴ أَعَكَدَارْ ∴ لْسَيْبْكُوَرَا ∴ لْسُوَاجِمْ ∴ فَيْكُو

كُمْ نَاكُرْ ∴ فَيْفِعْرْ ∴ قَدْ امْرْرْ ∴ فِعْرْكُوَا قَمْ ∴ كُمْ

بْكُوْنْ ∴ لْسَفَنَّرْ أَكِمْ اوْرْ قَدْ الْقَمْ ∴ لْسْتَارْ ∴ لْسِ

أَدْعْ ∴ لْسُوَاجِلْ ∴ بَدَافْ فَيْغْ كُوَاكُمّْ ∴ قَدْ اقْشْ

∴ لْسْشِغْ تَعَبْ ∴ إِدّْرْ ∴ فَيْفِمَتُوْ ∴ يَجْمْ كُوَاتْشْ

أَرْوْجِمْرْ ∴ أَكِمْ اوْرْ ∴ قَدْ الْقَمْ ∴ لْسَّ أَدْعْ ∴ إِدّْرْ ∴

يِشْنَا دْوْكِيَا ∴ يِشْنَا دْ يَدَايِي ∴ أَوّْجِي فَسْ

غَدْوَا ∴ إِدّْرْ ∴ قِدَايْشْ دْيَايِي ∴ أَكْمْ دْوْكِيسْ

فِدْ فَسْرْكِمْ ∴ يَادْمْ ∴ تَلْكَدْ اوَادْقَمْرَا يُوا ∴

Ama mātansa su-na-zamnāwa dāki [4] wāta fudu
da kwāna gōma, su-na-kukya kukye, saanan
su fita su yi aure. Idan su-na-kukya kukye
namiji ba shi magana da su. Su kuma ba su magana
da namiji har su kārē. Wanan alaada che ta Muhamadīa.
Idan namiji shi-na-son wata chikinsu, ba shi magana,
sai sun kārē. Idan ya yi magana da su tun ba su
kārē ba, kō sun yi aure, idan mahukumta sun
gani hakanan, sai araba su. Shi ke nan.

But his wives remain in the house for four months and ten days (and) they mourn; after that they come forth and (can) marry again. During this time when they are mourning a man does not hold conversation with them, and they too do not converse with a man until (this period) is over. This is Mohammedan custom. If a man wants one from among them (for a wife) he does not speak until (the time of retreat) is completed. If he hold converse with them before they have completed this period or if they have married, if the lawgivers have seen that this has been done then they separate them. That is it.

أَمَّا مَا تَنْفُسَنْ سُنَنَ مَنْدَاوَا ؞ دَاكِ ؞ وَتَ فَدُ ؞

دُكُوا نَمُ غُوتَمْ ؞ سُنَا كُجُمُكُجِي ؞ سَعَنَّ

سُبِتَ ؞ سَنَّ أَوْ وَرْ ؞ إِدَّوْ ؞ سُنَا كُجُمُكُجَ ؞

نَمِجِ ؞ مَبَاشِ مَعَمَ ؞ دُسُو ؞ سُوكُمَّ ؞ مَبَاسَ مَعَمَ

دُ نَمِجِ ؞ حَمْ سُكَاوَرْ ؞ وَقَّمْ أَلْعَادَ ابْ ؞ تَمُحَمَّدِ مَنَّ

إِدَّوْ ؞ نَمِجِ ؞ شِنَا سُنُوفَ ؞ شُكُنْسَ ؞ مَبَاشِ مَعَمَ

؞ لَسَنْ سُنْكَاوَرْ ؞ إِدَّوْ ؞ مَيْلَسَّ مَعَمَ ؞ دُسُو ؞ فَنْ فِسَنْ ؞

كَاوَمَبِ ؞ كُوسُنَّ أَوْرَسِنْ إِدَّوْ ؞ مُحَمَّدُ فَتَا ؞ سَنْ

قَمِنْ ؞ فَكَنَّنْ ؞ لَسَنَّ أَوْمَاسُنْ ؞ شُبِجُمَّنْ

No. 40.

[1] Faslun.

Wanan fasalī ne zaa shi gwoda muna wada ake ginan
kushēwa da wada ake bisō. Idan matanbayi
ya tanbaye ka, 'Ana wada ake ginan kabri?' Ka che: 'Idan
mutun ya mutu, sai abidō kara agwoda da shi. Saanan
atafi wurin da ake ginan, anōme wuri da chau.
Saanan agina kadan. Saanan agwoda kara, idan
ya yi daidai. Saanan agina. Idan kara ya fi
tsawō, sai akara gina da tsawō. Idan aka gina,
ya kai ga kwobri, sai [2] agina wata karama chiki. Saanan
agiyāra da chau. Abidō itāche [3] asasāre.
Saanan idan angama, sai adaukō gāwa atūra shi

The Descriptions.

This description will show us how the grave is dug and the burial conducted. If a questioner asked you how the grave is dug you say, 'If a man dies, then a corn stalk is sought (and) the corpse measured with it. Then they go to where they are digging. A place is well cleared of bush; then they dig a little; next they measure with the stalk (to see) if it is the proper length; then they dig. If the stalk is longer than (the place) they have dug, then they increase the length. When they have dug a trench about the depth of a leg bone, then they dig a smaller (trench) inside (this one). Next all is neatly prepared. Sticks are sought and cut (the proper length). Then if they have finished, the corpse is lifted and laid

ومن فحليبني . دأشغد امن . ودأكن غمن .
كبشلوا . دادأكي مسوا . إأدن . مقتبيم . ب
يتشتبيك . أمدادت . أكي غمن . وقبم . اكتب إأدن
منزيهت . اسن أمد وكرا . أمد دشم . اسعن
أمبم ورش دأكي غمن . أمحوبين . اوري . د ثمو
سعقن أغمر كدن . سعقن . أغد كرا . إأدن .
بيامن . دنردن . سعقنم أغمن . إأدن . كمرا . بياو
طحون . اسن أكدو . غتادم طون . إأدن . أكغن
يكن غكبر . اسن أغمرومة . كمرمات . تكم . اسعن
أغيا ورن . دثمو . أمدوا . إقامتن . أاسسا برن
سعمن . إأدن . أقفحم . اسن أدوكوا غدا . أتواالله

chiki, sannu. Aajiye shi da sauki; ba akāma shi
da [4]karfī. Idan aka-ajiye shi chikin kushēwa, [5]amaida gabansa
gabas. Sai ayi adua ashāfa masa ga gōshi. Saanan
asa itāche. Saanan asa gaiṅye kō haki.
Ama wadansu ba su sāwar itāche sai tubali,
kō katangū. Saanan asainya dainyar kasa
ayābe. Saanan amaida busasa aturbudē.
Mutāne su wātse. [6]Yā kārē.' Shi ke nan.

---

inside very gently. It is set down with care, (and) not laid hold of violently. When the body has been set down in the grave its front is turned towards the East. Then prayers are said and the hair on the corpse's forehead is gently brushed back. Then the sticks are laid across and leaves or grass put (on top). But some do not put sticks but mud or potsherds. Then they put on wet earth and plaster over, and the dry earth (dug out) is replaced and (all) covered over. The people disperse. It is finished.' That is it.

ثِكَمْ لَسْنُوا :. أَعْجِيشْ :. دَ سُوكَمْ :. بَدْ أَكْدَ مَدَاشْ

دَكَمْ رَجِمْ :. إِدَّرْ :. أَكَعْجِيشْ :. ثِكَمْ :. كُشُوا :. أَمِيدْ غَبْنُسْ

غَبِسْ :. سَرْ أَمْرْ أَدْعَمْ :. أَشَا قَدَامَسْ :. غَعُوشِمْ :. سَعَقَّنْ

أَسَرْ :. إِقَّاقِي :. سَعَقَّنْ :. أَسَدْ غَنْيِيرْ :. كُوقِكْ :.

أَقَّدْ أَوْدِ فُسَنْ :. بَدْأُسْ :. سَدْ أَوْرْ :. إِقَّدْ أَقْبْ :. أَسَرْ قُومِلْ

كُوكَنْدْ قُوا :. سَعَقَّنْ :. أَسْنَرْ دَنْيِيرْ كَسَسَ :.

أَيْدَابِي :. سَعَقَّنْ :. أَمِيدْ بُوسَسْدَ :. أَقَّرْ بِجِرْ :.

فَتَّابِي :. لُسُوا بُكَنْ :. بِيدْ كَدْ بَرْ :. شِيكَقَّنْ

No. 41.

Faslu.

Wanan fasali ne zaa shi gwoda muna wada ake wankan gāwa. Idan za awankan gāwa, idan ankāwō rua mai-chau. Sai akirāwō wani mālami shi yi wankan. Idan zaa shi fārāwa, sai shi dauki wata jika, shi sainya ga hannu, dada shi dēbi rua, shi kurkure ma gāwa bāki; shi wanke hanuansa bīū. Saanan shi kāma masa rua shi wanki marēmara--insa. Saanan shi sa masa rua ga hanchi. Saanan shi wanke masa idānu, shi yi masa alwala. Saanan shi yi masa wanka, shi wanke kai(n)sa. Saanan shi wanke kafada tasa ta dāma har kasa. Saanan shi wanke kafada tasa ta hagu har kasa. Saanan shi wanke bāyansa. Saanan shi wanke kirjinsa

---

Description.

This description will show us how the corpse is washed. If they are about to wash a corpse, when they have brought some clear water, then they will call some malam to do the washing. When he is about to begin he takes a kind of bag and puts it on his hand. Then he takes the water and washes the corpse's mouth; he washes its two hands, he washes all the private parts. Then he puts water up the nose. Then the eyes are washed and ablutions performed for it (the body). Next he washes it all over; he bathes its head; then he washes the right shoulder right down, then he washes the left shoulder down to the bottom; then he washes its back; then he washes from its breast

قـــر

وَقَّرْشِ قَصِيبِنِ ؞ دَاشِ نِمْدَ امْرَ ؞ وِدَ آبِجُو نَكْنِغَلْوَا ؞

اِدَّرِ ؞ دَاعُو نَكْنِغَلْوَا ؞ اِدَّرِ ؞ اَنْكَدَاوُرِ ؞ وَرَّا ؞ مِيثْوُ ؞

سَرَ اَكَرَاوُرِ ؞ وَرَنْمَدَ اَلِيمِ ؞ شِيوُنْكَرِ ؞ اِدَّرِ ؞ دَ اَشِقَدَاوَرَا ؞

سَعِشِدَّرِكِ ؞ رَتَ جِكَرِ ؞ شِسَنْيَا غِمْشُوا ؞ دَدَرِ شِجَمِ

وَرَا ؞ شِكَرِكُمِ مَغَدَاوَرَا بَاكِمِ ؞ شِوُنْكَرِ ؞ قَمُونْسَ

مِيوَا ؞ سَعَفَّرِ ؞ شِغَدَا مَدَمْسَرِ ؞ وَرَا ؞ شِوُنْكَمِ مَرَ مَكَرَ

يِسَرِ ؞ سَعَفَّرِ ؞ شِسَدَامْسَرِ ؞ وَرَا ؞ غِمْشِغِ ؞ سَعَفَّرِ ؞

شِوُنْكَرِ ؞ مَسَرِ ؞ اِدَامْفُوا ؞ شِيمْسَرِ ؞ اَلْوَلِرِ ؞ =

سَعَفَّرِ ؞ شِيَّمْسَرِ ؞ وَنْكَرِ ؞ شِوُنْكَمِ كِيمْسَرِ ؞ سَعَفَّرِ

شِوُنْكَرِ كَدَا اَمْسَرِ ؞ فَدَ امْ ؞ قَعَ كِمْسَرِ ؞ سَعَفَّرِ ؞

شِوُنْكَرِ كَدَا قَدَا امْسَرِ ؞ تِحَعْ ؞ حَرَ كِمْسَرِ ؞ سَعَفَّرِ

شِوُنْكَرِ ؞ بَدَا مِنْسَرِ ؞ سَعَفَّرِ ؞ شِوُنْكَرِ كِرْ بِنْسَ

har ga māra. Dada wanka [1] yā kārē. Sai asumkē shi chikin likafani. Ama ana-yi ma gāwa wanka ba da sō-
-sō ba, ba da sābuni ba, da rua tsartaka.
Ana-yi ma wani daga zamne, ana-yi ma wani daga kwanche.
Duka nan ana yi, da adua ake yi, har agama. Ama
ba awanka kasashe fagin fāma, ba ayi masa
sala, hakanan ṣaryayē. Shi ke nan.

---

to below the navel. Then the washing is completed and (the body) is put in a shroud. But a corpse is never washed with a sponge and soap, (but) with pure water (only). Some are bathed (while) held in a sitting position, some from a lying position. All this is performed with prayers, (and) they are offered till all is finished. But those who fall in battle have not this done to them, nor prayers said; and so it is also in the case of a person executed. That is it.

قَرْ غَمَادَوْ ؞ دْ وَنْكْ يَاكَارِيْ اسْرْ اُصْحْكْمْشِ

ثِيكْرْ لِكْ قِبْنِمْ ؞ أَمَّا أَمَّا يِسْغْدَاوْرَا ؞ وُنْكْمْ ؞ بَادْصُو

صُوَابْ ؞ بَادْ تَصَابُ وِفِيبْ ؞ دْ زُوَّا الطَّطْرْكِكْ

أَمَّا يِمُوْرِيْ ؞ دْ غَحْنْثْ ؞ أَمَّا يِمُوْرِيْ غَنْدْ قْبِنْ

دْكَنَّنْ أَقَّلْيْ ؞ دَادْعْ ؞ أَجِنَّ ؞ فَرْ أَغْمْ ؞ أَمَّا

بَاوْنْكْلْ ؞ كَسْبْشْ وَجْنْقْبَامِيْ ؞ بَا أَيِسْ ؞

صَلِّ ؞ تَحْكُمْ ؞ اسْرْ بِيمْ ؞ نْشِيكْنْسْ

No. 42.

[1] Bābun.

Wanan bābi ne na [2] chiniki. Ala taala [3] yā halalta chiniki ama ya hana riba, shi ne [4] chin kūra. Idan ka-na-sō ka saya, idan ka je [5] kausuwa, kō dōki, kō jāki, kō sānia, kō rā-kumi, kō rāgō, kō akwia, kō kāza, kō zā-bō, kō jimina, kō alfadari, kō dangōgi daga tufa, kō alkeba, kō rīga, gāre, kō gir-kē, kō tagō, kō jaba, kō [6] sha jiki, kō fūla, kō wandō, kō balar, kō zane, kō alkila, kō wadansu kāyan aiki, kō sirdi, kō likāfa, kō bauji, kō kāfu, kō linzāmē, kō kāmāzūrū, kō

The Beginnings.

This is the beginning of (a description) of how people trade. Allah the exalted has made trade lawful, but he forbade unjust profits, that is (known as) the eating of the hyena. If you want to buy a thing when you come to the market, whether a horse, or an ass, or cow, or camel, or ram, or goat, or hen, or guinea-fowl, or ostrich, or mule, or of the nature of clothes, or a burnous, or cloak, or tobe, with ornamental hems, or strips of cloth, or a short shirt without sleeves, or a jacket, or a second-hand shirt, or a cap, or trousers, or wide-legged trousers, or cloth, or a striped shawl, or any implement of work, or a saddle, or stirrup, or girth, or saddle-cloth, or bit, or reins, or

وقش بابينش فتنكم ⁖ آزتعالي ياقلت
ثنكم ⁖ آمابا حمربا ⁖ شيني ثركورا ⁖ إدرش
كنداسوا ⁖ كسبا ⁖ إدون كدابش ⁖ كوسوا
⁖ كودرك ⁖ كوباكم ⁖ كوسافيا ⁖ كورا
فيم ⁖ كوراغوا ⁖ كوأكش ⁖ كوكدا ⁖ كودا
بوا ⁖ كوبينا ⁖ كوأقدري ⁖ كودنفوغم
دغنق ⁖ كوألكب ⁖ كوريفو ⁖ غابرش كوغم
بكش ⁖ كوتفوا ⁖ كوبب ⁖ كوشابكم ⁖
كوفولش ⁖ كوفدوا ⁖ كوبلم ⁖ كوقلبش
كوألكلا ⁖ كوردفسش كدينذأنيك ⁖
كوسردي ⁖ كولكاقش ⁖ كوبوجم ⁖ كو
كدفو ⁖ كولترابش كوكداماذوورش كو

kayāmai, kō wani abu ka ke sō ka saya,
idan kā je sai ka che, 'Nawa?' Ache, 'Nawa ka saya,
nawa ka bari?' '[7] Zanbar dari.' 'Albarka.' 'Nā rage
alfin.' 'Albarka.' '[8] Nā rage alfin kuma.' Ka che,
'Albarka, naa saye zanbar arbain.' Shi kuma
shi che, 'Albarka.' Kai kuma ka che, 'Nā kāra hamsa.'
Shi che, 'Albarka.' Ka che, 'Nawa ne gaskīa tasa?' Shi che,
'Gaskīa tasa, zanbar tamānin.' Sai ka che, 'Naa
saya zanbar hamsin.' Shi che, 'Albarka.' Kai kūa,
idan ba ka sō ka bari, idan ka-na-sō ka kāra.
Idan yā game shi, shi bar maka, idan bai game shi ba
shi che, 'Albarka.' Sai ka wuche gaba. Idan kā gani

---

spurs, or some thing you wish to buy, if you have come (to the market) then you say, 'How much?' You are asked, 'How much will you buy it for, how much will you allow me. One hundred thousand (cowries)?' (Buyer) 'No, thank you.' (Seller) 'I have reduced it by two thousand.' You say, 'No, thank you.' (Seller) 'I have reduced it by two thousand again.' You say, 'No thank you, I will buy it for forty thousand.' He too (the seller) now says, 'No, thank you.' You again say, 'I have added five thousand.' He says, 'No, thank you.' You say, 'How much is the real price?' He says, 'The true price is eighty thousand.' Then you say, 'I buy for fifty thousand.' He says, 'No, thank you.' You, for your part, if you do not wish (the thing at that price) you leave off; if you want you increase your offer. If it has come up to what he expects, he lets you have (the thing); if not, he says, 'No, thank you.' Then you pass on. If you have seen

كَيَ اَمِنْ كُو رِنَا اَبْ ∴ تَجَكِ كُسُوا ∴ كَلَسِيَ

اِدَنْ تَدَابِي شَسِيكَشْ ∴ مَوَّ ∴ آمْشْ مُوَّ كَلَسِيَ

قُوَّكَبْ ∴ دَفِبْمُرِي ∴ اَلْبَرْكَ ∴ قَدَا رَغْمِ

اَلْعِيمْ ∴ اَلْبَرْكَ ∴ قَدَا رَغْمْ اَلْعِيمْ كَحَّمْ ∴ كَشْ

اَلْبَرْكَ ∴ قَدَا سَبِيْ ∴ دَفِبْرَا اَوْ بَعِيْ ∴ شِيكَحَّمْ

شِبْ اَلْبَرْكَ ∴ كَنْيَكُحَّمْ ∴ كَشْ قَدَا كَدَا رَفَمْسَ

شِبْ اَلْبَرْكَ ∴ كَشْ مَوَّبَرْ ∴ غَمْسِكِيَا قَسْ ∴ شِشْ

غَمْسِكِيَا قَسْ ∴ دَفِبْرَ قَحَدَا فِنْ ∴ اَسِرْ كَشْ مَدْ

سَبِيْ ∴ دَفِبْرَ خَمْسِنْ ∴ وَشِبْ اَلْبَرْكَ ∴ كَيْكُحَّوْ

اِدَنْ ∴ بَا كَسُوا كَبِرْ ∴ اِدَّنْ ∴ كَنْدَ سُوا ∴ كَكَدَارَ

∴ اِدَّنْ ∴ بَا غَشِّشْ ∴ شِبْرْ مَكَ ∴ اِدَّنْ زَبِيْ فَجَلِشِّبْ

نَفْنْ اَلْبَرْكَ ∴ اَسِعْ كَوْفْ غَمْبْ ∴ اِدَّنْ ∴ كَدَا غَمْنِي

wani ka saya. Idan ba ka gani ba, idan ka-na-kārāwa
ka kōma, ka kāra. Idan ya game shi shi salama,
idan bai game shi, ba ka bar masa. Ama wada alaada
ta Muhamadīa ta ke. Idan kā sai dōki,
sai ahau, ayi sukūa, ku gani idan ba shi gar-
-dama, shi-na da gudu kworai, ba shi tabarīa, ba
shi tūtsū. Saanan ache, 'Ansaya, ama [9] muu
kai gida mu dūbi kāmun hakinsa da shan rua-
-nsa kwāna uku.' Idan masu-shi sun
lāmunta ka kama, ku kai gida, ku daure.
Idan kun gani abinda ku ke sō, ba shi da
alāfa, ba shi da ruāye, ba shi da kasa, ba shi da
kilmisō, ba shi da wani aibi, saanan

---

another you buy (from him). If you do not see another (and) if you are going to increase your offer you come back (to the first seller). If he agrees to (your offer) he says you can take it, if not you leave (the thing) with him. Now there is another custom among the followers of Mohammed. If it is a horse you have bought then it is mounted and galloped. You see that it is not stubborn, (if) it has great speed, it does not rear up and does not buck, then it is said, 'It has been bought, but we will take it home and see how it feeds and drinks for three days.' If the owners of it have granted permission you catch (it) and take it home and tie it up. When you have seen what you wish, (i. e.) that it has no hoof disease, or hock disease, or eye disease, or sickness of the legs (or) other blemish, then

أَوْ كَسِيَا : إِدَوْ يَكْغَنِيبْ : إِدَوْ كَنَا كَدَا وَاوَ :

كُوكُومْ : كَكَدَوْ : إِدَوْ يَيَا غَجِشْ نَفْ سَلَمْ :

إِدَوْ يَيكَجَشَبْ : كَبَرْ مَسَرْ : أَمَا وَدَا أَفَادَ :

تَمُمَدَ نَ تَجَكُ : إِدَوْ كَاسَنْ : دَوَكِ :

سَا أَدَوْ : أَيْسَكُوَا : كَغَنِمْ : إِدَوْ يَدَا شَغَمْ

دَمْ : أَشَادَ غَمَدَ : كَمَرْ نَوْ مَدَا شَنَبَرْ يَدَا : بَا

شَرْ تُوطُو : سَعَنْ : أَبْ أَفْسَيَا : أَمَا : مُوْ

كَيْ غَدَا : فُدَاوِ : كَدَا مَرْ فَكَفْسَنْ دَمْشَنَرْوَ

فَسَرْ كُوَا قُمْ : أَكَ : إِدَوْ مَدَا شَشَيْمْ : شَوْ

أَلَا فْنَتْ : كَكَدَامْ : كَكَنْ غَمَدَا : كَدَ وُرَسْ

إِدَوْ نْكَنْغَنِمْ : أَمَغْمْ : كَكَبَسُوَا : بَدَاشَدْ

أَلَا قَبَيْ : بَدَاشَدْ رَوَابِيْ : بَدَاشَدْ كَسَرْ : بَدَاشَدْ

كَلْمِسُوَا : بَدَاشَدْ وَفَكَيْبْ : سَعَنْ

ku bia. Idan kā sai bāwa, sai ayi masa wanka, adūbi jikinsa duka. Idan ba shi da albaras, kō kuturta, kō [10] idānu guda daia, kō wani aibi mabayani, saanan ku che adakata muku kwāna uku, kō bakwai, dōmin ku gani, kō shi-na da aiki. Idan ba shi da kyuya, saanan ku bia. Idan kun gani wani aibi garēshi, ku mayar, ama da chi, da sha, ku ke ba shi. Idan ya yi maku [11] murgu ba nāku ba ne na ubangijinsa ne. Shi ke nan.

You pay (for it). If you have bought a slave he is washed, (and) his whole body examined. If he has not white leprosy or leprosy or one eye only or other blemish apparent then you say he must wait on you for three, or perhaps seven days, in order that you may see if he is a worker. If he is not a lazy man then you pay (the price). If you have found any blemish in him you give him back, but food and drink you are the one to supply. If he has done any work for you (the proceeds) are not yours but his master's. That is it.

كُبِسَّن ؞ إِدَّرْن ؞ كَدْ اسْنْ ؞ بدَاوَن ؞ لسْنْ أَيِّمسن ؞ وَفْكي ؞

آدْ وَبْ جكِفْسَنْ ؞ دْ كْ ؞ إِدَّرْن ؞ بدَاشْدْ أَبْرَضْ ؞ كُو

كُشْرْقَ ؞ كُوَا إِدَافْوا اغْدا إِدَّرْن ؞ كُو وَفْلَكيب ؞

قَبَيِّنم ؞ تسقنْرْ كُش ؞ أم أكتا مُكُ ؞ كُوَامُل

أبْكُ ؞ كُو بكُومْ ؞ دُرْوِقْم كُكَفْنِم ؞ كُوشِنَدَام

أبْكِ ؞ إِدَّرْن بدَاشْدْ كِوبِيَا ؞ تسقنْر كُبِسَّ ؞ إِدَّرْن

كُنْفْنم ؞ وَفْلَحِيبِ ؞ غْمْرَ بَكشن ؞ كُحَيِّرْ ؞ أَمَّدْ

دُفِم دُكُشْرْ ؞ كُو كْبَدَاشِنْ إِدَّرْن ؞ بَيْأَيُكُ ؞ مُرْعُ ؞

بَدَاقْدَا كُبْنَبُو ؞ قْدَا أَبْنَغْجْ فْسْبُنْ ؞ شِيَيُكُنْرْ ؞

No. 43.

Faslu.

Wanan fasalī ne zaa shi gwoda muna wada ake chinikin tufāfi. Idan kaa sai kōrē, sai arāre ta, ka dūba da chau gaban dilāli. Idan [1]tā game ka, ka bia, idan ba ta game ka ba, ka bari, ka bidi wata. Hakanan, kō rīga, kō wandō, kō alkeba, sai ka dūba da chau wurin masayi. Ba ka zūa da shi gida. Idan dare ya yi, ba achinikin tufa kō wani abu. Idan rīga sāki ka saya, sai ka dūba da chau gaban masayi. Idan ka-na da abōkin shāwara, ka yi shāwara da shi nan kausuwa, ba ka zūa gida. Saanan idan kā saye aje gida akirga kurdi. Idan ka-na da dirhami nan kō miskāli, ka bia, ka dauki abinka, ka tafi gida.

Description.

This description will tell us what is done when buying clothes. If you are going to buy a black tobe, it is opened out that you may see it well, in front of the trader. If it is what you want you pay for it; if it does not please you, leave it and look for another. And so with a gown or trousers or a burnous, until you have examined it well in the presence of the vender, you do not take it home. If darkness comes on there is no further trading in clothes or other things. If it is a blue striped tobe you are buying, then you examine it well before the one who is selling. If you have some friend to advise you (about the purchase) get his advice here at the market-place; you must not go home. Then if you have bought, lay it aside in the house and let the money be counted out. If you have silver or gold with you here pay (and) lift your purchase (and) go home.

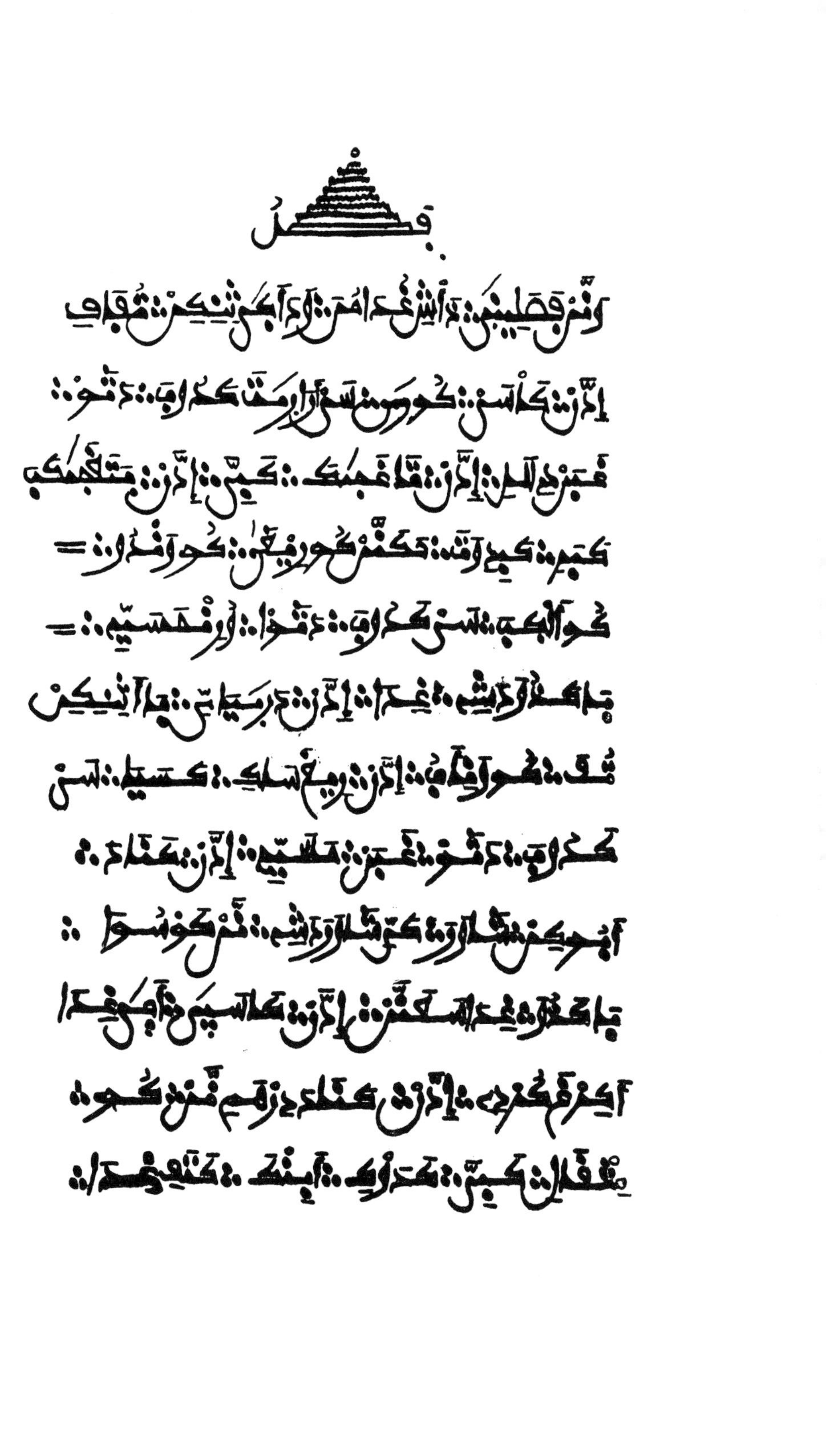

فَصْلٌ

[illegible]
[illegible]
[illegible]
[illegible]
[illegible]
[illegible]
[illegible]
[illegible]
[illegible]
[illegible]
[illegible]
[illegible]
[illegible]

Achikin sharaa ta Muhamadīa bābu rikichi,
dōmin Ala taala [2] yā fadi chikin Alkorāni:—
'Idan ku ka yi alkawāli, ku chika, dōmin
alkawāli abin tanbaya ne.' Shi ke nan.

In the laws of the Mohammedan faith there is no deceit. Allah the Exalted has said in the Koran, 'If you made a promise fulfil it, for a promise is something to be accounted for.' That is it.

أَتِكِنْ شَرَعَ تَمُحَمَّدِ مِنْ بَامُبَرِكِثِمْ

دُوِمِّنْ أَلَّ تَعَالَى ثِيَاقِدِ تِكِنْ أَلْفُرْءَانِ

إِمَّنْ كُكَّنْ أَلْكُوَلِمْ كُثِكَ دُ وَقَّسْ

أَلْكُوَلِمْ أَ بِسْتَنْبِيَا بِمْ ثِيبِكَ قَّنْ

No. 44.

[1] Bismi alāhi alrahmani alrahīmi.

Wanan fasalī ne zaa shi gwoda muna kaman da ake kēra [2] mutun mutun
Alāmarin nan shi-na da bai māmāki, Ama ana-yin dabāra nan
da yinbū, da dankō, da jan [3] karfē, da sinādari,
da dalma, da wuta. Fārin, idan za ayin mutun mutumi,
sai abidō yinbū, agiyāra shi da chau, afida tsākuwa
da ke chiki, aludē shi da chau. Saanan agina
panpama, saanan agina haba, ama na ga panpamar.
Saanan ayi hanchi da idānu. Agerta dunbārun bāki.
Saanan asainya wani itāche da aka-gerta kaman wuka.
Adinga shāfe shi. Ana-sa rua kadan kadan ana-shāfe shi

In the name of Allah the Compassionate, the Merciful. This accou will show how the (Benin) figures are made. This work is one cause wonder. Now this kind of work is done with clay, and wax, a red metal (copper), and solder (zinc), and lead, and fire. The first thi to be done if one of the figures is to be made, is to get clay and wo it most thoroughly, and get the little stones which are in it work out. It is well worked in the hands. Next the shape of the top of a he is constructed (from the clay), and then the jaws on the same piece as t top of the head. Then the nose is shaped, and the eyes and the lips ma Then a certain stick which has been shaped like a knife is put (agair the model) and it is smoothed (with this). A very little water is put when it is being thus smoothed

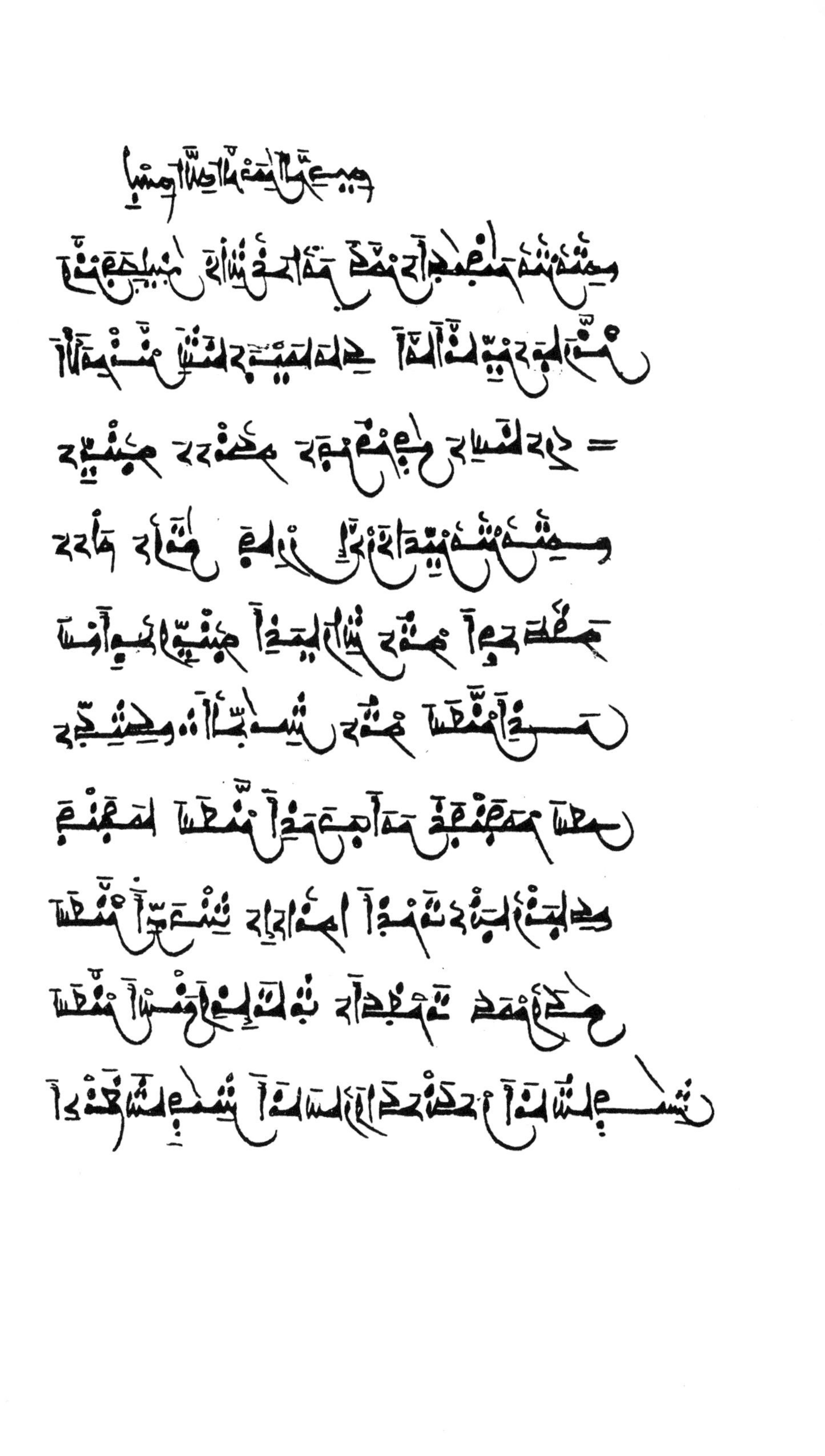

[illegible]

[illegible]

[illegible]

[illegible]

[illegible]

[illegible]

[illegible]

[illegible]

[illegible]

[illegible]

[illegible]

har shi yi chau saanan [4] ashainya rāna shi būshē. Saanan anarka dankō, azuba bisansa. Saanan asainya wuka. Idan ya yi karfī, ana-karchewa. Akarche da chau. Saanan afūra wuta, ana-sa wuka chikin wutan. Shi yi zāfi kadan, adauki ana-mana ma dankō, dōmin shi damparu da chau. Agerta idānu, da gira, da bāki, da haba, da gēmē. Saanan abidō itāche nan, mai-kaman wuka, ana-tsōmāwa chikin rua, ana-mana ga dankō, ana-shā-fē shi. Ashāfē shi da chau, [5] shi-na-walkīa. Idan mache che, saanan ayi mata zankāye. Wada shi ke yi [6] zankāyen, shi-na-murza dankō kamar-igia, da rua, shi yi tsawō. Saanan (s)

---

until it is perfect; then it is set in the sun to dry. Next wax is melted and poured over it (the clay model), (and) then it is gone over (again) with the knife. As it (the wax) hardens it is smoothed over. When it has been well done, then a fire is kindled, (and) a knife put in the fire. When it is slightly warm it is taken up and pressed over the wax in order that it may adhere well (to the clay foundation). The eyes get the finishing touches, (and) the eyebrows, and mouth and chin and beard. Then this stick like a knife is got out (and) dipped in water (and) pressed against the wax, (and) passed over it—it is well smoothed (and) shines (all over). If the model is of a woman's head then the hair adornment is put on. How the adornment of the hair is made, is as follows. Wax is rolled out till it is like a string—water is used; it forms a long piece. Then

صَرْ شِينْتُو سَعَنَّ أَشَفِيَا وَاقَى شِجُوبْشِي سَعَنَّ

آمَرْ كَدْ نْكُوَا أَدُبْ بَسَغْسْ سَعَنَّ أَسَنِي وُكَسْ

إِدَّرْ بَيَا يِكَرْ وِمِ آمَا كَرْ بْشُوَا آكَرْ بْدْ قُمُو سَعَنَّ

آبْجُورُ وُتَسْ آمَا سَرُ كَكِي ڤْكِيمُرُ وُقَمْ شِيَّدَ اِبِمِ

كَدَّنْ آدُوكِ أَمَّا مَرْ مَدْ فْكُودُ وُمِّرْ شِعِي نْبَجْمُ

دَقُمُو أَبَغْرَقَا إِدَا فُودْ دِمْرَا دُبَا كِمِ دَقَبَّ

دَبْغَكُبَسْ سَعَنَّ أَمِدِ وُاِمَّا بْشَنَّ مِيكَمَرُ وُكَسْ

آمَا دُطُو مَاوَا بْكِيمَرْ وُا آمَا مَعْقِدْ نْكُوا آمَا بْشَا

بَسَقْسْ آشَا بْجَمَشْ دَمْحُو شَنَا وُافِيَا إِدَّرْ وَقْتِبْ

سَعَنَّ أَيَمَتَ دَنْكَا بِيمِي وَدْ شْبَعِي دَنْكَا بِيمْ شَنَا

مُرْ دَ دَنْكُو كَمَرْ إِغَنِي دَرْوَا شِيَّطُورْ سَعَنَّ سْ

shi yanyanke shi mana bisa kai. Saanan shi sa aska shi tsatsāge. Saanan shi yanka wani dankō gajejērū, shi kakafa bisa kai. Saanan shi murza wani dankō da rua, shi yi tsawō kamar igia. Shi ribia bīū, shi daidaita, shi aza bisa zankāyen, shi mana. Abinda ya saura shi yanke, shi yas. Saanan shi gerta wani dankō da fādi, shi yi kunnuwa da shi, shi mana. Ama kōwane zaa shi manāwa, sai ya sainya wuka chikin wuta, shi mana ga dankō. Saanan shi zamna, wanan [7] yā kāre. Sauran zubin karfē. Idan [8] yā gama wanan sai shi dēbi yinbū, shi rufe pampamar duka da yimbū, shi bar kafa kadan shi shainya shi būshē. Wanan yā kāre, sauran zubin karfē.

---

he (the smith) cuts it into pieces (and) fastens them on top of the head. Then he takes a razor (and) cuts (them the required length). Next he cuts off other short pieces of wax (and) sticks them along the head. Then he rolls out another bit of wax with water, making it long like a rope. He divides it in two (down the middle, not across), lays them side by side, and puts them on the top of the first upright pieces and sticks (the whole) on. The part left over he cuts off (and) casts aside. Then he prepares a certain broad piece of wax and makes ears out of it (and) fixes them on. But whenever he is about to stick any piece on, first he puts the knife in the fire and presses it against the wax. Then he sits down—this (part of the work) is completed. There remains the pouring in of the metal. When he has finished (the part just described) he takes up mud (and) covers the whole head with it; leaving only a small hole. He puts it in the sun to dry—this part is finished. There remains the pouring in of the metal.

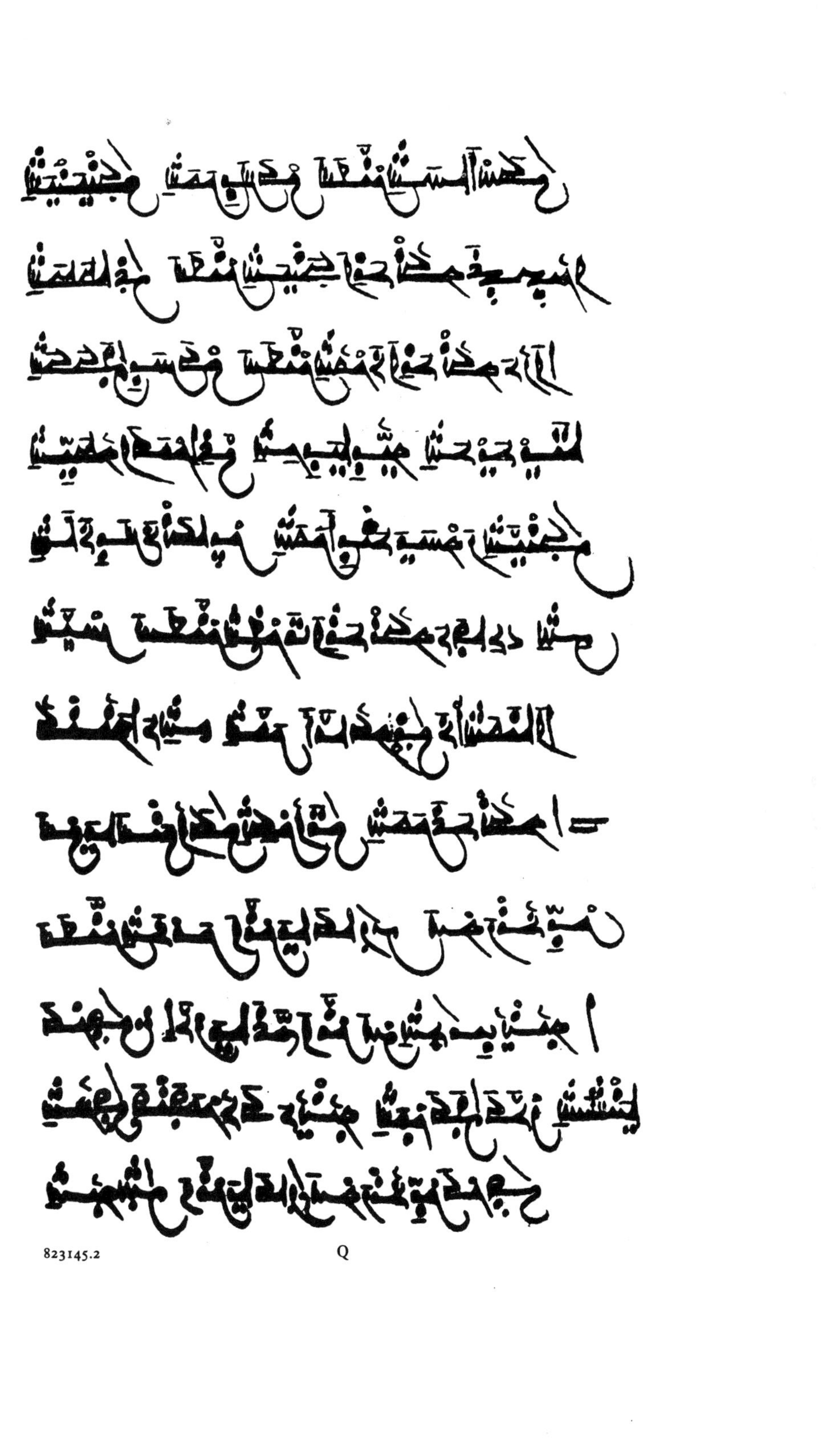

Wanan fasalī ne na zubin karfē.

Wada ake zubin karfē. Idan aka-dēbō wuta, azuba chikin murfu kīra, asainya zuga zugi, ana-fūra wuta azuba gawayi. Saanan adauki [9] mutun mutumin, adōra bisan wuta, azuba rua ach kaskō kō tasa. Idan mutun mutumi nan yā yi zāfi, sai dankō da ke chiki shi narkē. Sai adaukō shi, adōrō awartaki bisa kaskō(n) ruan, kō wadansu, itāche, adōra mutun mutumin bisansu dankō shi rika tsiyāyewa. Hakanan ake yi har dankō shi narkē duka atsiyāye shi chikin rua. Saanan azuba gawayi dayawa. Adora mutun mutumin bisa wuta. Adaukō sandar karfē adinga sārāwa da muntalaga, asāra dayawa azuba chikin tukuniar kīra. Saanan atōna gawayi asa chiki, amaida gawaye arufe, akāwō mutun mutumi, adōra.

This description is of the pouring in of the metal. The way metal is poured in is (as follows). When the fire has been broug is poured into the melting-furnace, (and) the bellows are set to w (and) the fire blown (and) charcoal poured in. Then the mod lifted (and) placed on the fire. Water is poured into a pot or When the model has become heated then the wax inside m Then it is taken up, the tongs, or some (take) a stick, are pl across the pot (of water), and the figure put on top, and the keeps dropping out. And it is held so till all the wax has melted dropped into the water. Then a great quantity of charcoal is pou (into the furnace). The figure (in clay) is set on the fire. Bar metal are continually being cut with a hammer; many pieces broken up in this way, (and) put in the smelting-pot. Then t scrape out a hole in the charcoal and put the smelting-pot in, rep the charcoal again, (and) cover up. The (mud) figure is brou and set.

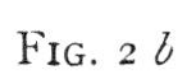

FIG. 2 *b*

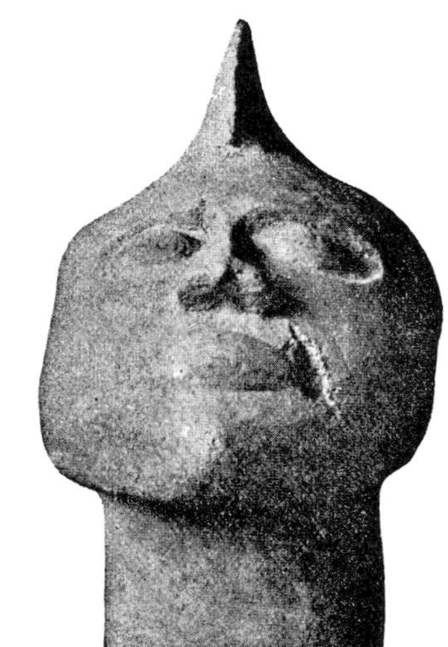

FIG. 1 *b*

FIG. 3 *b*

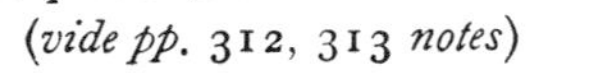

HEADS, SHOWING *cire perdu* METHOD OF CASTING. (FRONT VIEW)
(*vide pp.* 312, 313 *notes*)

ومّن قصليبنل فذمّن محم قبي

ودابه ذبن محم قبل اذو اعجه مبو وقتل اذ ب شكن مرقن

فيبر اسنتن ذغا ذغبه انا فجو روقتن اذ ب غموبيّه

سعنن اذوك متن متجوهن اذ وربسن وقتل اذ مبر ا اثبهن

تحسكو تحوتاس اذن مثن متيمثن بهاتي ذ اجبه سن

ذنكو ذ بثيكي شتن بكي اسن اذ و كوشن اذ و ر اورتبك

بسن تحسكو وران تحو وذ فسن اثاث اذ ور مثن متيثن

بسنثن ذنكو شيرك حيتا ييو ؛ تحكمن ابحي

تمن ذنكو شتمن بكي ذك اطيتا بيمثن نكن ورا =

سعنن اذ ب غموبيّه ذبيو اذ ور مثن متمن بسر وقتي

اذ و كو سند وكمن قبي اذ نغ سذ وراو ذ منتلغ اسار

ذبيو اذ ب نكن تكفنبر فيبر سعنن اثبو غموبيّه =

اسا ثبكي امبذ غموبي ا ورقبي اكا او ومثن متمه اذ ور ؛

adōra bisa wutan. Adinga zuga, ana-jujuya kasar nan ta mutun mutumi har shi yi jā. Saanan karfē yā narkē, sai adaukō mutun mutumi, atōna rāme, akafa shi chiki, dōmin shi tsaya da chau. Abūde kafar, azuba narkaken karfē chiki. Idan ya chika, tō, ya yi chau ke nan. Idan bai chika ba, sai akāra dōmin shi chika. Idan ya chika, yā kārē ke nan. Sai aaje har shi yi sainyi, saanan aparpashe. Sai ka gani mutun mutumi mai-chau. Shi ke nan. Aikin Ali yā̆ kārē.

[it is set] on the fire. They keep blowing the bellows, and this clay lump is turned till red hot. Then the metal has melted, then the figure is taken up, a hole is dug, (and) it is placed in it so that it is firmly set. The hole left in the clay is cleared out and the melted metal poured in. If it is filled, that is well; if not, more is added to fill it. If full then (the work) is finished. Next it is set aside to cool, then (the outside covering of clay) is broken off. Then you see a beautiful figure. That is it. The work of Ali is completed.

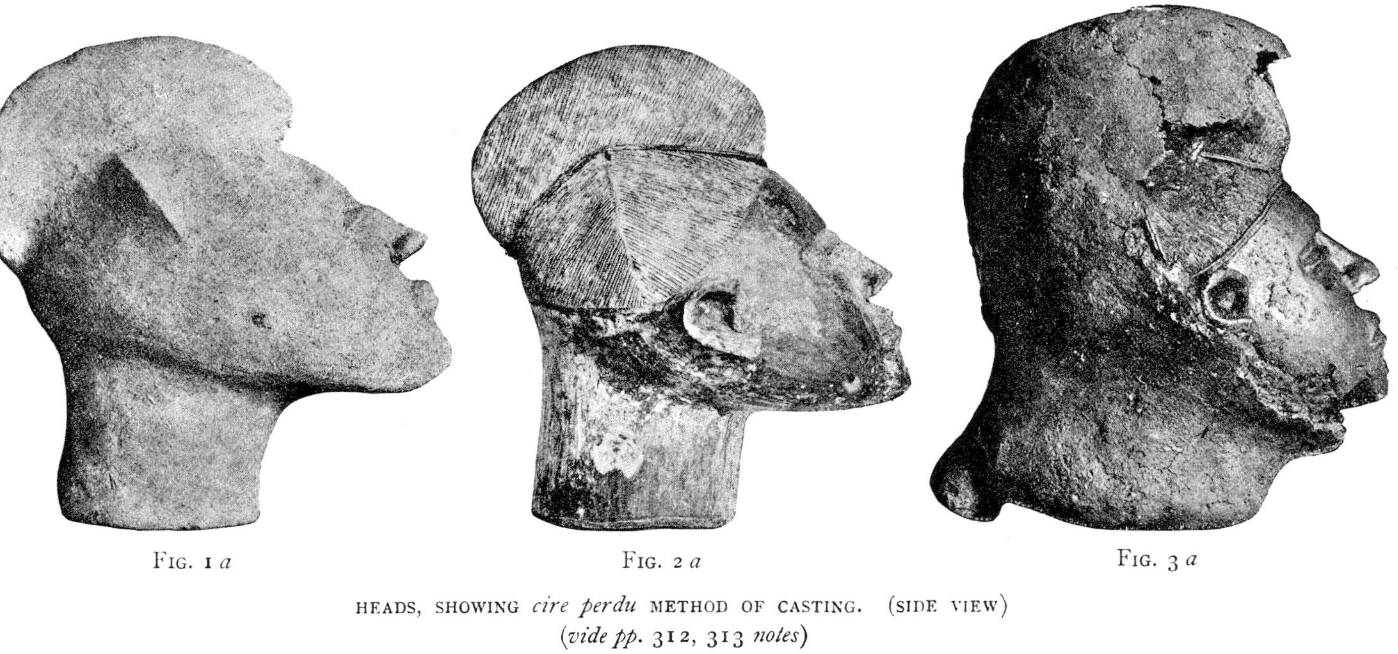

FIG. 1 *a*　　FIG. 2 *a*　　FIG. 3 *a*

HEADS, SHOWING *cire perdu* METHOD OF CASTING. (SIDE VIEW)
(*vide pp.* 312, 313 *notes*)

أَدُورُ وَبِسَرْ وُتَمْ أَدِفْعَ دُغَمْ أَمَاجِجُوجِجُومَ كَسَرْفَنْ

تَهُشَرْ مُتُمِي حَرْشِيجَ سَقَمْ كَرْفِي يَا نَمْرْ بِجِي

تَسَرْ أَدُوكُو مُتَرْ تُمِي أَثُورَ ابِي أَعَجَابِشَ تَكِي

دُ وَمَرْ شَطُو دَقُو أَبُوبُرْ كَجَمْ ۞ أَدْبَ قَمْرْ كَكَجَنْ

كَجَبُ تَكِي ۞ إِدُرْ بِيتَكَ ثُو وَيَا اِيَّ ثُو بَجَنَّ إِدُنْ

بِتْشِكَبْ تَسَرْ أَكَادَرْ دُومَرْ شَتَكَ إِدُو بِيتَمَكَ يَا

كَدَرْ مَكَتُمْ تَسَرْ أَقَجَنْ حَرْشَتِي سَفِيِي = سَقَمْ

أَقَمْ وَقَشُو تَسَرْ كَكَنْمْ مُتُرْ فُتَهِي مِيتُو ۞ يِشِيكَمْ

٤١ أَيِّكِسَرْ أَلِي بِيَا كَطُوبِرْ

No. 45.

[1] Bābun.

Wanan bābi ne na jīmar fāta. Ana jīmar fāta iri bīar, da jar fāta, da baka, da fara, da gangamō, da kōrinō. Ama wada ake jīmar jar fāta. Idan aka-sāmu buzun rāgō, kō na akwia, sai abidō tōka da gainye gwanda, asāba, azuba chikin tōka, saanan asainya fāta achiki. Ta kwāna bīū achiki, saanan afitas, akwāre [2] gashin, awanke. Saanan abidō bagarua, adaka, ajikata da rua, saanan asainya fāta chiki. Ta kwāna bīū achiki afitas awanke ashainya. Ta būshe saanan ashāfa mata mai(n) shānū kō alayadi.

The Beginnings.

This is the commencement of (a description) of tanning skins. There are five ways of tanning skins (so that they become) red skins, and black, and white, and cream coloured, and green. Now how red leather is tanned (thus:—) When a ram's or goat's skin has been procured, then ashes and pawpaw leaves are sought. They (the leaves) are rubbed down and poured among the ashes (and) then the skin is put in. It is left two days in the mixture (and) then removed, (and) the hairs rubbed off (and) washed. Then the seeds of the acacia are procured (and) pounded (and) moistened with water, (and) then the skin put in. It lies in it two days, is taken out, washed, spread in the sun. It dries, (and) then the fat of a cow is rubbed on it, or palm oil.

وَقْرْشْ بَلِيبِّينْ فِجِيمَرْ قَادَاتْ ؞ أَمَّا جِيمَرْ ؞

قَادَاتْ ؞ إِرْوِيِّزْ ؞ دْ جَمْ قَادَاتْ ؞ دْ بَكَّشْ ؞ دْ قَمْرَا ؞

دْ غَنْغَنْمُوا ؞ دْ كُووْفُوا ؞ أَقَّاوْدْ أَبْكِي جِيمَرْ ؞

جَرْ قَادَاتْ ؞ إِدُّوْ ؞ أَكْسَامُوا ؞ بُوُرْشْ وَاغْمُوا

كُونْدَأَكْسَمْ ؞ لَسْقْ أَمْدُوَا ؞ قُوكَسْ ؞ دْ غَنْيِسْ

غُنْدْ ؞ أَصَاحْ ؞ أَدْبْ ؞ ثْكَمْ قُوكَسْ ؞ سَقْنْ

أَسْنْ قَادَاتْ ؞ أَثْكِمْ ؞ ثْكُوَارِ مِيُوا ؞ أَثْكِمْ ؞

سَقْنْ ؞ أَجْتَسْ أَكُوَا رِمْ غَدْ إِشْتِنْ ؞ أَوْنْكَسْ

سَقْنْ أَبِدُو وِمْغَارْ وَا ؞ أَدْكْ ؞ أَجِقَادَاتْ ؞ دْ زْوَا

سَقْنْ ؞ أَسْنْسَ ؞ قَادَاتْ ثْكِمْ ؞ تْكُوَارْ ؞ مِيُوا

أَثْكِمْ ؞ أَجِتَّسْ أَوْنْكَسْ ؞ أَشْنْيَا تَجُوشْبَرْ ؞

سَقْنْ ؞ أَشَدْ قَامَتْ ؞ مِينْشَا قُوا ؞ كُوأَلَيْجِ ؞

Achudē ta da shi. Saanan adaka karan dafi
da kanwa, asainya chikin rua, asainya fātar achiki.
Achudeta asainya ta chikin ruan zāfi azazage ta.
Saanan ayanyanka laimu, asainya ta achiki, amurza ta,
Saanan afitas, ashainya chikin inua, sai ta yi chau.
Haka ake yin jar fāta. Ama baka, idan aka sainya
būzū achikin tōka aka-jeme, sai asainya
ta chikin bagārua, achude ta, abar ta, ta yi kwāna
bīū chiki, saanan afitas, ashainya.
Idan ta sha iska sai asa kulōkō. Shi ke nan.

It is rubbed well with it. Next stalks of dafi (?) and natron are pounded and put in water, and the skin put in. It is worked soft (and) then put into hot water and shaken out. Then limes are cut up (and) it (the skin) is put among them (and) rolled about (in them). Then it is taken out and dried in the shade, until it is as desired. This is how red leather is made. As for black, when the skin has been put among the ashes (and) the hair rubbed off, then it is put among the acacia (seeds) and worked with the hands, and then left in for two days. Then it is taken out (and) spread out. When it has been aired (lit. drunk the air) then the 'kuloko' is put on. That is it.

أَقُوبَمَتَ دَ ايشَم ∴ أَسَغَقَن ∴ أَدَك ∴ يكَم فَعرفي ∴ =

دَكَفُوا ∴ أَسَنيَا ∴ ثيكَم زَوَا ∴ أَسَنقَ دَامَقَر ∴ أَثِكَم ∴

أَقُوبَمَتَ ∴ أَسَقِيَا مَ ثيكَم ∴ زَوَرَدَا فِي ∴ أَزَرْبَعَمَتَ

سَغَقَن ∴ أَيِنيشَك لَيمُوا ∴ أَسَنيَامَتَ ∴ أَثِكَم ∴ أَمَقَرَاتَ

سَغَقَن ∴ أَفِتَنَس ∴ أَشَفيَا ∴ ثِيكَم إِقُوَ ∴ تَسَ قَتَم قُوَ ∴

تَكَ أَبِتَن بَدَرقَدَامَتَ ∴ أَقَدَ بَكَمُ ∴ نِيَا دَرَن ∴ أَكَسَنتَم

بُوزُوَ ∴ أَيِكَم قُوكُو ∴ أَكَجِجَن ∴ تَسَر أَسَنيَا

مَ ∴ ثِيكَم بَيَقَدُورَا ∴ أَقِوبَمَتَ ∴ أَبَرقَ ∴ قَتَم كُوَ أَمَر

بِيُّوا ∴ ثِيكَم ∴ سَغَقَن أَفِتَنَس ∴ أَشَنيَا ۞

إِدَرَن ∴ قَدَا شَدَا إِلَسَك ∴ تَسَر أَسَدَا كُلُوكُو ∴ شِيبَكَنَس

No. 46.

Faslu.

Wanan fasalī ne na kulōkō. Wada ake yin kulō-
-kō. Ana-bida kāshin makēra, idan ba-
-bu, asāmu guntāyen karufa. Asainya
achikin kaskō, kō tukunīa. Azuba rua,
da zumuwa, ko sikiri, ko giar hatsi, ko
ruan fura, azuba chiki. Shi tsima, ya zama kulō-
-kō ke nan. Kōmē ka ke sō ka mayar baki,
kō da [1] yā yi fari kamar takarda. Idan ka dībi,
ka zuba akai(n)sa sai shi zama baki. Shi ke nan.
[2] Nā chi, nā bia, ban hadie ba,
kā ga bākina.

Descriptions.

This is a description of 'kuloko'. The way 'kuloko' is made (is as follows). Iron filings are sought, or if not to be had, pieces of iron. They are put into a clay pot or iron vessel (and) water poured in, also honey, or sugar, or beer made of corn, or water of porridge, is poured in. It stands (for about three days). This becomes 'kuloko'. Whatever you wish you can change it black, though it has been as white as paper. If you take it, the 'kuloko', and pour it on the top then it becomes black. That is it.

I have eaten, I have paid, I have not swallowed, you have seen my mouth (i. e. I have taken your pay, I have finished your work, I have not refused to tell you all, behold my work).

فصل

وفن ؞ فصلين ؞ نكلوكوا ؞ ودّ ابيين نكلوا
كو ؞ آندمد ؞ نكدشن ؞ مجمرا ؞ ادن مبا
ب ؞ آسدصوا ؞ غنتامن كرق ؞ آسنيا ؞ =
آشكن ؞ كنسكوا ؞ كوتكنيا ؞ آدقبرا ؞ =
دن موا ؞ كوسكرى ؞ كوغنير قطنم ؞ كو
ور مقبرا ؞ آد مبا شكم ؞ شيطن ؞ ببادرق ؞ كلو
كوا ؞ بكنن كومن ؞ كجسوا ؞ كميّز بكم
كود ميابقمرى ؞ ككمن تكدا ؞ ادن كدميب
كدب ؞ آكميسن ؞ بسن لنغم بكم ؞ شيبكمن

تمّت ؞ نقامين ؞ منجي مب
كدغ ؞ مباكنند ؞

PART V

PROVERBS

Bābun.

Wanan bābi ne na sherbāchen magana
shi akan che, 'habaichi.' Mun fāra anan.

The Beginnings.

This is the beginning of words which are taken and jumbled up (that a man may not know their meaning), and such is called a '*habaichi*', proverb. We have here begun.

1. Bakin jini na [1] muzūrū, mai-kāza zāgi, maras kāza zāgi.
2. Hanunrua ba gōrō ba, agulu ba nāma ba.
3. Kafar agulu bāta mīa.
4. Idan ka gani akwia makwanchin zāki, sai aji tsōrōnta.
5. Idan ka gani zōmō shi na [2] baje [3] bunga kare, ya gōyō dāmisa ne.
6. [4] Agwāgwa ba ruanki da tsāfi.
7. Hanchi bai san dādin gishiri ba.
8. Abinda ke giwayan bāyan gida, zaa shi shiga gida ne.
9. [5] Wa masani? Wa ya ki nasa, sai wāwa?
10. Idan [6] kā kōri yārō shi-na-gudu, ka-na-binsa zaa shi shiga zaure ya kōmō, ya tsaya, ba banza ba, akwai ubansa ne.

---

1. The tom cat is a bad character, the owner of a fowl curses him, and he who has no fowl curses him.

2. The hanunrua (nut) is not a real kola nut, (though like it), the vulture is not meat (i.e. you do not eat it).

3. The vulture's foot spoils the soup.

4. If you see a goat at the lion's sleeping-place, you fear her.

5. If you see a hare dancing on the dog's earth mound, you may be sure he is carrying a leopard on his back.

6. Duck, you have nothing to do with the sacrifice.

7. The nose does not know the flavour of the salt.

8. The thing (you see) going round the back of the house, it intends to enter the house.

9. Who knows best? Who hates his own relations, except a fool?

10. If you have chased a boy, (and) he runs off, (and) you follow him, (and) when he is just about to enter the porch leading to his house, he comes back (and) stands (waiting for you), he does not do that for nothing, his father is there.

بكنجين نمد وزو قنيكا اذا اداغ قرسكا اذا اداغ

قنز زو با غوز زوت أغمز بد نا قاب

كفز اغمز با اتيمز

إدز كفين أكز مكو اتينز د اك سز أجطو زونت

إدز كفين دمو شنا بيل بنغ كبز با غو بو ادا امسا بل

أغو اغو بازونك د طاڢ

حنث بيس دا إدز غشريب

أبنذ كجڢو بز با بزغم اذا أيش شڢا غذ ابنل

وا مسني وا بك نا سز وا وا

إدز كا كوز بيزوا شنا غد كنا بنس دا شيشڢا د وري

يكوم يطز با بند اب آكو بي بنسبز

11. Dāmanā mai-ban sāmu.

12. Rashin farin wata, tāmrārō ke haske.

13. Rashin uwa, akan yi uwar dāki.

14. Kūsu ne ba shi gida, dōmin hakanan su ke ajia barkatai.

15. [7]Kinwa che ba ta gida, dōmin hakanan bēra ke gāda.

16. Ai wāne kīfin rījīa ne.

17. Nāma mai-wāri shi-ka-kāma kūra.

18. Sānia ashāfanta ake-yi, tun ba afāra twātsanta ba.

19. Gātari da wuta, mai-wiar rātaya.

20. Lizāme da wuta māganin tsayayan dōki.

21. Kāza mai-yāya, ita ke tsōrō shirwa.

---

11. It is the rainy season that gives wealth.

12. When the moon is not full, the stars are bright.

13. If one has not a mother of one's own, one makes one whom one calls one's 'house-mother'.

14. There is not a rat in the house, that is why the things are left scattered about just anyhow.

15. The cat is not at home, because of that the mice are playing.

16. No, So-and-so is a fish from a well. (A shy man.)

17. It is the stinking bit of meat that catches the hyena.

18. They pat the cow before they begin to milk her.

19. A (red)-hot axe is difficult to carry on the shoulder.

20. A hot bit is the cure for a stubborn horse.

21. It is the hen with chickens that fears the hawk.

دامفا ميبي سلام

رشن قبر نوت تمرارو بجمسكو

رشن عوا اكنب عوزداك

كوس بن باشفدا ادو من تكن سكن اجي بن كنش

كنواب با انفد دو من تكن برا اجعادا

اءوا ابن كيفي ريجيا بنو

نلام ميوار شيككام كورا

نرنيا اشا قبنت اكي نربا قارنوا طنسب

غما اير دوتا من وبيرز انتي

بزامود وتبا ما غني طيبين دم وك

كاذا امن يابا اتكطورو نشرو

22. Tsōrō na dāji, kumya ta-na gida.

23. [8] Akwia taa yi wāyō da yankaken kunne.

24. Idan mūgun mutun ya shibka zanba, kai ka sa lauje ka yanke.

25. Tantabara dūkīa sama, idan kin tāshi, Ala ka kāwō ki gida.

26. Idan da kamar nika, kwādō ya fi kwāgūa.

27. [9] Gātari ga nāma, nāma ga wuta.

28. A shekara sāran rua, sai tanbatse.

29. Gumāgumai ka kwāna da wuta, kirārua sai tōka.

30. Rīmi tsakar gida, rānan sāra mutānen gida na kuka, na waje na mur

31. Yārō ya so aure, [10] gidansu bābu gōdīa.

32. [11] Adāwa ba ta hana sāmu ba.

---

22. Terror is a thing of the wilds, shame of the home (the abode of me

23. The goat will learn sense by having its ears slit.

24. If a bad man has sown evil, do you set your sickle to it and cu down.

25. Pigeon, your riches (food) are in the sky; when you have risen al Allah it is who brings you back home.

26. If it is a matter of grinding corn (between two stones) the fr should be better at it than the crab.

27. Axe, there is the meat; meat, there is the fire.

28. Though one were to spend a year hacking at water (one wo make no impression on it) it only splashes up (and is still again).

29. (If you have) a big log you have a fire beside you all night, if a sti then ashes only.

30. The silk cotton tree in the middle of the compound, on the day it cut down the people of the house grieve, outsiders rejoice.

31. The boy wants to marry, but at their (his) house there is no ma (he has no money).

32. Because a person hates you, that does not prevent you getting wh you want.

طورو نادا ج كموتنا نجدا

آكوتالي وايوادِ ينككبي كنبل

ادر مو نمر مثر يا تشبك د نب كركسا لو بر كينجل

تنشبرا دوكيو سم اد نكنشا شرآ ككاوو ك نجدا

ادر د كمر نك كوا دوايا ف كوا غوا

غا تكر غا نام نام غاو تنى

آشبكر سا زنروا سو تنبطل

غا غمر ككوا نرد ونا كرا زو سو نوكل

ربيع طكر نجدا زا نرسارا مثا بر نجدا نا كوكر نو جو نا مرن

يا زو يا سو عو ري نجد تسر يا ب نمو د يا

غدا و بتمر سا موب

33. Jia Ka raba yau aka-ba mu.

34. Zaman dūnia hakuri, mai-kīa sun fi ma-sōya.

35. Domin [12] dan karamin tsuguni nan, ba shi yi mani kōmi.

36. Aki marada, azamna da wa?

37. Ma-aikata da 'wai', zunubinku ka dadu.

38. [13] Lalē mai-saurin kāmu.

39. Gingidin kunāma, kōwa ya taba, shi sha kāshi.

40. Mai-hali, mai-sābō.

41. Ala ke da rabō, daa mutun ke da rabō, daa wani bai sāmu ba.

42. Ala ya gīāra rīmi, chīdia ta bar fushi

43. Harāra bai māri ba.

44. [14] Idānun da ya gani sarki ba shi tsōrō gāladīma.

---

33. Yesterday You (Allah) portioned out (good and evil fortune), to-day we shall be given (our share).

34. Live patiently in the world; (know that) those who hate you are more numerous than they who love you.

35. Because of these few people (shall I desist)? they cannot harm me.

36. If you refuse to live with the slanderer, whom are you going to live with?

37. You who condemn on hear-say evidence alone, your sins increase.

38. Henna stains quickly.

39. The snoozing scorpion, whoever touches it (quickly) gets a blow

40. He who is naturally gifted in anything becomes expert in it.

41. Allah has the portioning out (of blessings), if it was man who had the distribution of them, some would go without.

42. Allah made the (great) silk cotton tree beautiful, let the (little) chidia tree cease being angry (discontented).

43. A frown is not a slap, (it does not hurt).

44. The eyes that beheld the chief do not fear the *galadima* (a court official).

جِتِ كُرَبَ يَوْ أَكَبَامْ

ذُ مَنْدُ وَنْيَا تَكُرِ مَكِيَا سَنْفِ مَسُوِيَا

دُ وُمَرْ دَ نْكَرَمِ طُفُرَ نَرْبَا شِيمَرْ كُومِ

أَكِمَرْ دَا أَذُ مَرْ دَ وَ

مَا أَيْكَتَا دَ وَنْ ذُنْبِكْ كَا دَ دُ

لَلْبُو مَيْبِسُوْرِ نْكَامْ

نَمْنْغِدِ نْكُنَامْ كُوَوَا اَيْبَ شِشْشَ، كَا شِمْ

مَرْحَلِ مَيْسَا بُو

أَرْكُبُدُ رَبُوا دَ أُمَتَرْكُبُدُ رَبُوا دَ أَوَنْبَيْسَا مُوبَ

أَرْيَا غِيَارَ رِبِجِ ثِمِ يَا أَنْبَرْفُبِشِ

حَرَارَا بَا قَارِبِبَ

إِدَ انْرُ دَ بِغِنْم سَرْكِمِ بَاشِطُو رُو غَلَادِيم

45. Mai-chiniki chikin dufu, kai dai jimri ɬalabe.

46. Dainyan kaskō wanda ba shi kai rua bai' dāki.

47. Murfu uku ba shi kāsa wa yārō rīga.

48. Tūō tūlū mai-wīar kwāshēwa da [15] māra.

49. Munduwar wīa, ana-sō zārēwa, ana tsōrō jin chīwo.

50. Wanda bai sha kāshi ba, ba shi jin bari.

51. Mai-lāmuni, shi ne ma-bachi.

52. Mai-dādin kai shi-na-fitō daga Ala.

53. Wanda ya bi ki, ya bi iska.

54. Gangara kōgi, mu je Zāria.

55. Har shi mutu ba shi kula kaba.

---

45. The man who works at his business in the dark must always be feeling about with his hands.

46. An unburned earthen pot is not one to bring water in behind the house.

47. The three cooking-stones (i.e. the family) do not fail to give the boy a coat.

48. The food in the pot with the narrow neck is difficult to take out with the 'māra' (spoon) (a flat bit of a broken calabash).

49. The ornamental metal rings round the neck, when one wants to take them off, one cannot, for fear of hurting the person.

50. One who has never had a flogging will not pay any attention when you merely tell him to stop.

51. He who goes surety is (often) the one who has to pay.

52. The truly contented man comes from Allah.

53. He who follows you (the advice given) follows the wind.

54. Here is the river bank, let us slide down and go to Zāria.

55. Till he dies he will not twist a 'kaba' palm-leaf even. (He is good for nothing.)

مِنِيكِي نِكِنْدُ فُ كِيدَنْ جِمُرْ لَلَبُو

دُنِيُو كَسَكُو وَنْدَ بَاشِرْ كَيْ رُوَا بِيْدَ اِكِ

مُرْدَ اُكُ بَاشِرْ كَاسَ وَبَارُو رِيغُو

تُؤُدْ رِتُولُوا مَنِيُو يِرْكُوا شُبُوا دَمَارَا

فَنْدَ وَرْوِ تَوَ اَنَا سُوْدَ اِرِعُوا اَنَا طُورُ وَجِنْ نِيُو

وَنْدَ بِنِيشَا كَرْ شِيبَ بَاشِجِنْ بَرِ

مِيلَا مُنِي شِيمْبَرْ مَتِّي

مِيَدَا دِنْكَنْ شِنَا فِتُووَا دَ غَمَاَلَّ

وَنْدَ بِيسِكِ يَابِ اِسْلَكْ

غَنْقَرْ كُونِي مُجِنْدَ اِرِي

حَرْ شِمُثْ بَاشِرْ فَرَكِبْ

56. Idan ba ka shan fūra, bari dāma ta.
57. Māgani yā kāre ana-[16]gudin jan jika.
58. Dūtsi afar maka bābu dādi, ka far ma mutun bābu dādi.
59. Makwanchin zāki dāmisa na haushi.
60. Suturan Ala tā yi gaba, ama mazambachi ya bi ya gaji.
61. Mutun ba shi sani wada laifi dūnia shi ke ba, kō bāba da bābānai.
62. Kuyenga yi magana, che ba ki kāra kai tāki bākin marmarō.
63. Harāra da ya tsuna ba shi tāda gofna shi na bākin mashāya.
64. Kumurchi yai hadīa, bai hadi ba, anmātse bāki, ya tudas.
65. Kō dawuri nā fadi dārīa 'ga ta yi yawa, barna achiki.
66. Wanda bai yi tāra kāshi ba ya chiji shākiraka, kar ka ji tāra mājina chiji hanchi

---

56. If you are not going to drink the pap, stop stirring it.

57. When the medicine (in the medicine bag) is finished, (the doct runs away for fear they snatch the bag from him.

58. You, O stone, if a man falls on you, it is not pleasant, if you fall a man, it is not pleasant (for him).

59. The leopard envies the lion's resting-place.

60. The blessing of Allah goes before, but the evildoer follows it vain till he is weary.

61. A man does not know what evil there is in the world be he (yc father or father's brother (i.e. old and full of experience).

62. Slave girl, speak; say you will not carry the sweepings of the ho to the spring, any more. (Meaning obscure.)

63. A scowling look will not cause the 'gofna (?)' to rise up from drinking-place.

64. When the python is swallowing (anything), but has not yet finis swallowing, and they squeeze its mouth, it vomits it up.

65. From the first I maintained that this excessive laughter had evil its cause.

66. He who is not averse to eating excrement, and therefore bites y on the anus, as for you, do not be squeamish about mucus, but bite him the nose.

إدن يا كشن فرابرد امات

ما غني يا كرابر انا غم نجنجكن

دوط اقبر مك باب دادي كقبر مقش بابدادي

مكو نشر داك دامسنا حوشي

سشرز ازنلي غب اما مد نبشي ياب يا غج

مشر با شيسرو دليجي دونن شيكب كوباب د با بانس

خنفو يمغرنبا ككار كوناك باكز مر مرو

حراردي يا طن باشن نا د غجر شنا باكز مشاري

كغرنم يرحد تر بنجديب انقاطر باكم يا ند س

كود ورنا قد داريغ تار يوبرنر انكم

ونبيون تار كاشيبا ننيم شا كرك كو كركج نار ما جنا ثيم خنتنسر

67. Ala ba Ka ɗa kēta, gōnar māye rua Ka-ke-yi.

68. Ai Hausa ba dabō ba che.

69. Baban kai ba kāya ba ne.

70. Namiji tankwa ne, sai antamna akan-san mai-yāji.

71. Haba yi hankali, ai ba dukan tafasa ta ke nuna da nāman kai ba.

72. Tūō na iyāli, nāma na mai-gida.

73. Kad alūra ta tōnō galma.

74. Sankara bātā gōrīa.

75. Gorīa mai-tankwa sankara ba ta chi ba.

76. Uwar dīa da dīa tata, du' ka san ba ka gama su ka aure ba.

77. Shi wanda ke jiran kabaki baba, kā san ba ya tsaya jira ta da lōma

---

67. Allah, You have no evil, You make the rain to fall even on t wizard's garden.

68. Oh, no, Hausa is not a conjuring trick (it is easy to learn).

69. A big head is not a big load (a conceited man not necessar a wealthy one).

70. A man is like a pepper, till you have chewed it, you do not kn how hot it is.

71. Come, be patient, not all the boiling will cook the meat on a head.

72. The 'tūō' (food made of grain) is for the household, the meat (a grea delicacy) is for the master of the house.

73. Do not let a needle turn up a hoe (a mountain out of a mole-hill).

74. The 'sankara' insect spoils the big kola nut.

75. The big kola nut, sprinkled with ground pepper, the 'sankara' ins does not eat.

76. The girl's mother, and her daughter, both you know you can join together and marry.

77. He who is waiting for a huge helping, you have known is not goi to stand and wait for a handful.

أَزْنَكَرَ كَبَسَتْ غُونَزْقَابِلِ زْوَاكَكَبِيِ

أَءْ حَوْسْ بَادْبُوبَثْ

بَنْزْكَنْزْبَاكَايَابَنْبُ

نَفْجِ تَنَكُوَانْبُ سَوْاْ مُتَفْرَاكَنْسَرْقَنُوبَاجِ

حَبْ يِعَنْكَلِيمْ أَءْ يَاءْ كَرْبَفْسَرْ تَكُونْدَ نَامْرْكَبِيَب

تَوُوْ وُنْيَ يَارْ نَامْ تَقْيِغَدَا

كَدَ الْوَرْ تَسُونُو غَلْمِي

سَنْكَرَ ابَاتُو غُورِي

غُورِيَ مَيْنَكُوا سَنْكَرَابَا ثَيَب

غُوزْدِي دَدِ يَا نَتْ دُو كَا سَنْرْبَكَا غَمَاسْ كَاوْرِلَب

شَيْوِنْدِ بَجْرْزْكَبِكِي بَبْ كَالَّنْ بِيَاطَلِي جِرَاتْ دَلُومَاب

78. Aja mu akai mu, anba uwar makāfo kāshi.

79. Mazō gaba yā yi kō, na bāya sai lābāri.

80. Kututure dabīnō ba kamar kututure kirya ba.

81. Farfarū likāfū kō afāda, sai yan sarki.

82. Kōmi chau tafarnūa, ba ta yi kamar albasa ba.

83. Matanbayi ba shi rasa huja ba, sai ya ki jin abinda ka nūna mai.

84. Me kare gōma ke yi da kūra?

85. Wanda bai bata dare ba, bai abata da rāna ba.

86. Bakin būnū bāta baibaia.

87. Rugurugu baban dafūa.

---

78. Let them pull me, let them take me there, (that is what) the blind man (says) when (he hears) his mother is being beaten.

79. The one in front has reached there, the one behind only hears about it.

80. The date-tree stump is not like the stump of the kirya-tree.

81. Silver stirrups even (when you see them) at the chief's courtyard, it is the chief's son who has them. (There are plenty of rich and powerful people about, but none of them have the privilege of having silver stirrups.)

82. However fine the garlic may be, it is never like the onion.

83. The questioner does not inquire without good cause unless he refuses to hear what you tell him.

84. What can ten dogs do with a hyena?

85. He who does not get lost by night, will not get lost by day.

86. Old grass spoils a roof.

87. Thunder is a mighty (pot) boiling.

أَجَامْ أَكَيْمْ أَنْبَا غُوَرْ مَكَا فُوا كَاشْ

مَدُ وَغُبَ يَا يِبِكُو نَبَا تَ سَنْ لَا بَارِ

كُشُبْرِ دِيِشُوا ابَا كَمَرْ كُشُبْرِ كِرْيَابَ

فِرْقَبْرُ وِيَكَا فُوا كُوا قَبَا دَ سَوْ يَنْ تَشِرْكِ

كُوِمِ نُوْ نَغَبْرُ نُوَا بَتَوْ كَمَرْ أَلْبَسَابَ

مَنْتَبِي بِيشِ رَسَفِجَابَ سَوْيَاكِ جِرْأَيِنْدَ كَنُوْ نُوْ مَ

مُبْكَبْرِ غُوَمْ كَايِدَ كُوْرَا

وَنْدَ بُوْنَتَ دَزِيَتَ بِيَابَتَ دَرَاتَبَ

بِكِنْبُو نُوَا ابَاتَ بَنْ بِيَ

رُغْرُغْ بَتَنْدَ فُوَا

88. Mu kwankwanbishi ne ba yāda gātari.

89. Mai-shanyayen gindi ke da kwatana tasa bābu mai-kwāche masa.

90. Mun san juna, kai mu yā yi dai dai.

91. Mahasada ku bar gajia, yārō yā geterē.

92. Tābarman kashi, madājin karfē, machi awazain kāto.

93. Kīfin fadama ba shi gāsa da na gulbi.

94. Wāne ya haye tudu ya bar na gangare sai lēkē.

95. Idan kun sō mun yi kō, idan ba ku sō ba mun yi ko sarautar ala tā iss

96. Tudun mahasada abi shi da sūnan Ala.

97. Fada ma kia, Ala yā fi su.

98. [17] Wīar nika pashi, idan anpasa wīar nika tā kārē.

---

88. We are (like) the little biting ants (on trees) that (when you go cut a tree down fall on you) and make you throw away the axe.

89. No one can pull off the girdle from another, even if he has buttocks. (One has a right to what is one's own.)

90. We know one another, our heads have made one.

91. Slanderer, cease tiring yourself out, the boy has crossed (i.e. I a beyond your reach and power now).

92. A mat made of bones, edged with metal, is the thing to eat into th shoulders of even a huge man.

93. The fish from the well does not make itself the equal of that fro the river.

94. So-and-so has climbed the hill and left the one on the slope peerir up at him.

95. If you wished us to prosper, even so we have prospered, if you d not wish it, even so we have prospered, the kingdom of Allah has bee sufficient (for us).

96. The hill of the slanderer, (when you take that way) follow it wi the name of Allah (on your lips).

97. Say to them who hate you, Allah is more powerful than they.

98. The hard part of grinding is the first grinding, when that is do the rest is easy.

مُو كُنْكُنْشِيبِنِي بَايَا دَغَدَا آتِيرَه

مَيْشِنْشِيوُ غَنِدَ كَبْدَ كُنْتَا تَسَرْ بَا بَمَيْكُوَا انَبِقَسَ

مُسْنْجِمُو نُو كُنِّيمْ يَابِرْ دُ نِيَدَ مِنْ

مُحَمَّدُ اكْبَرْ مَجِتُو يَا زُو تَا غَبْتَرَلِ

تَا بَرْ مَنْكَنْشِي مَدَا اجِرْ كَرْ فَبُو مَشِيَا وَزَرْكَا اللَّهُ

كَيْفِي قَدَمْ بَاشِمْ غَدَا سُنْ دُ نَغَلْبِي

وَانْبُو يَا اجِيرْ لَدُ يَا بَرْ نَقْنْقَرْ بَرْ لِسَنْ لَبِجُو

اِدَ رْكُنْسُوا فَيْكُوا اِدَرْ بَكْسُو بَا فَيْنْكُوا اسَرُونَرْ اَلْلاَاِلسِ

لَدُ نَمُحَمَّدُ اَبِيشِرْ دُسُونَرْ اَرْ

قَدْ مَكَيَا آزِيَا فِيشْ

وُنِيرِنْكَ بِشِرَ اِدَ زَانْقِسَرْ وُنِيرِنْكَ تَا كَرِيرِي

99. Daga kan fāko kōma kan dabe.
100. Iyāka kurji, iyāka ruansa.
101. Kai ba shi wuche wīa, wīa kūa ba shi wuchi kai.
102. Idan da kamar nika, kwādō ya fi kusa da kasa
103. Tsānin tsāni ke nan kuwar kuwa.
104. Duba shi, shi-na-sumumu kamar tūsa achikin gōra.
105. Idan kīfi ya fitō rua, ya che, idānun kada guda ne wa ke musu
106. Wāne mai-karangīar hanū ne.
107. Yau wāne ya fāda fako.
108. Garwāshin wāne ya hababaka.
109. Wāne daga tafō na tafō shii zama zumunta?

---

99. From a hard bare piece of ground, to come to a hard beat floor (six and half a dozen).

100. The limit of a sore is the limit to which the matter from the so spreads.

101. The head does not go on and leave the neck behind, nor t neck the head.

102. If it was a matter of grinding grain (between two stones) t frog should be the best at it, it is so close to the ground (but it is not).

103. A ladder above a ladder, a friend's friend.

104. Look at him, he is as sulky as a 'tusa' circulating rou a calabash.

105. If the fish comes out of the water, and says the eyes of t crocodile are one in number, who is going to argue with him?

106. So-and-so is like the 'karangiar' thorn (he clutches hold everything).

107. To-day So-and-so has fallen on a hard place. (Met with a greec person.)

108. So-and-so's cinders are flaring up. (He is in a rage.)

109. So-and-so has come (from far away), I have come (we have me does that make us relations?

دَغَ كَنبَقكُوا كُوقَا كَنْدَ بُي

إِيَا نَكَا فُرْجِي إِيَا كَارُوَ نسَس

كُوبِ شَ وُثْبُ وُتَّ تِكُوَا بَا شِرُوتِ كَوْ

إِدُرَدَ كَمَرْنِكَ كُوَا دُو بَا بِهِمِ كُسَرَ دَكَسَا

طَانِ طَارِ كَبَنِس كُوُرْكُوَا

دُ بَا تِرِ شِنَا صُمُ كَمَرْ لُو سَرَ إِنِكَرْ غُورَا

إِدُرْ كِبِهِ بَا فُلُو رُوَا بِتِ إِدَ أُنْرَكَدَ نُمُدَ ابْرُوَا كُبُفَس

وَابُو قَبِكَرِ نَغِبِرْ حَسُو بُل

بِيُوَا بْرِيَا قَبَادَ قَكُو

عُمَرُوا تِشَرُوَا بُلِ بَا حَتَبَك

وَابُو حَ نُمُتَبْوُا اُنَ تَبُوا شِعْدَمَ دُمُتَا

110. Mai-kāza ba shi jimrim as!

111. Ala shi sa akwia ta sha kunu sanbiru.

112. Ala shi tsarīmu da mai-kai-kōmō.

113. Da wīa ni kidan ganga da lauje.

114. Idan kā ji ganga ta-na-zāki, ta kusa pashēwa.

115. Bāko ba bāwa ba sai ya sō.

116. Chin bāshi da dādi, rānan bia da wīa.

117. Abu ne mutun, idan ba ka da abu, bābu mai-sō ka.

118. Inuan bagārūa, ga sainyi, ga kaya.

119. Talaka ba shi abōki.

120. Me gara ka yi da dūtsi sai ta kwāna gewaya?

---

110. The owner of a fowl is sure to be angry with any one who says shu! (though it may not be his fowl that is being chased).

111. Allah causes the goat to drink the 'sanbiru' (poison) pap.

112. Allah protect us from the tell-tale.

113. It is difficult to beat a drum with a sickle.

114. If you hear the drum sounds sweet, (you can be sure) it is near to the time it will split.

115. A stranger is not a slave, unless he voluntarily becomes one.

116. To borrow is sweet (easy), the day of payment is hard.

117. Things (wealth) is the man (so it seems); if you have nothing no one loves you.

118. Shade of the 'bagarua' tree, behold coolness, behold thorns.

119. A poor man has no friend.

120. What has the ant to do with a stone (it cannot eat it) (they) it can only lie round it?

مَيْكَاذَا ابَاشِيجِيرْ زَأَسْ

أَرْ شِسَرْ أَكُرْ تَنْشَا كُنُوا سَنْبِرُوا

أَرْ شِطِرِيمْ دَمُرْكَيْنِكُومُوا

دُوَيَا بُرِكَدْ نَقْنَقَا دَ تَوْجُو

إِدْرْكَابِي غَمْنَفُو تَنَّا زَاكِي تَا كُسَرْ قَشِيلُوَا

بَاكُوا تَبَا تَا وَاتَسَرْ يَا سُوا

نِيِنْبَاشِرْ دَ دَاءِ رَاتَرْبِيَو دُويَا

أيُونْبُمَشُرْ إِدِ زْبَاكَدَ آبُ بَابُ مَيْسُوكَ

إِنُونْبَقَارُوَا إِنْغَدْ سَنْبِي غَاكَوْ

تَلَكَ بَا شِيَأبُوكِي

مَيْقَرَا كَابِرَدَ دُوطِ سَرْتَكْوَانْ غَجُوَتِي

121. Māganin kōmi Ala.

122. Abu duka shi-na ga wa? Shi-na ga Ala.

123. Ba reshi ga Ala.

124. [18] Dākin kasa da kasa, gōbara tai kumya.

125. Ba aure ke da wīa ba, bidan kurdi.

126. Ai sama ba ta kōmō kasa harabadi, tudu ba shi kōmōwa gangar

127. Dutsi ba shi zama rua.

128. Akwia ba ta gāsā da kura.

129. Bāwa ba shi gāsā da yāya.

130. Bawan [19] Māku dai dai da Māku.

131. Idan sarki ya che, kōwa shi yi kūka shi chika masaki da hawāye, kai mai-idānū guda dai, fāra tun dawuri.

---

121. Allah is the cure for all (ills).

122. To whom does everything belong? to Allah.

123. There is no not getting a thing if you seek it from Allah.

124. A house of nothing but mud, the conflagration (turns away) shame.

125. It is not the act of marrying that is difficult, it is getting t money (to marry).

126. No, the heavens do not ever come down to the earth, the hills not come down to the valleys.

127. A stone does not become water.

128. A goat does not make itself the equal of the hyena.

129. A slave does not make himself the equal of a free man.

130. The slave of Māku is one with Māku.

131. If the chief commands that every one is to weep and a calabash with tears, do you, who have only one eye, begin from t very first.

فَانْغِنِي كُومِي آلْ

أَبُدْ كَ شِنَا غَوَا شِنَا غَاآلْ

بَارِشْ غَاآلْ

دَاكِزْ كَسَا دَ كَسَا غُوبَرَا أَنْسُو كُفِيَا

بَاغَوْرُمُو كَبْتَ وُتِيَابَ بِأَنْكُرْدِي

أَدْ سَمَ بَا أَنْكُومْ كَسَرْ تَرْ أَبِدْ نَدْ بَا شِكُومْ وَاغَمْنْغَبْرِي

دُ وِطِ بَا شِنْدْ مَرْوَا

أَ كُتُو بَا تَغَا سَا دَ كُورَا

بَاوَا بَا شِغَا سَا دَ يَانِيَا

بَاوَ نْقَا كَ دَ نِيَدْ نِدْ مَكْ

إِدْ رَسَرْكِي بِنْتْ كُولَوَا شِي كُو كَوْ شِنْكِي قَسِكِي

دَ حَوَايِبُو كُوَاِدَ انُوَا غُدَ ادَ تَرْ قَارَا انْتَدْ وِرْ

132. Rabon kunkuru ba shi chikin wuta.

133. Kurtun zuma, gama da madāchi.

[20] Tamat.

---

132. The share of the turtle is not found in the fire.

133. A pot of honey mixed with bitter herbs.

Finis.

رَبُو كُنْكُرُو بَاشِّا تِكِرُو تَا

كَتَرُ دُمَ غَمِ دَ مَدَا تِي

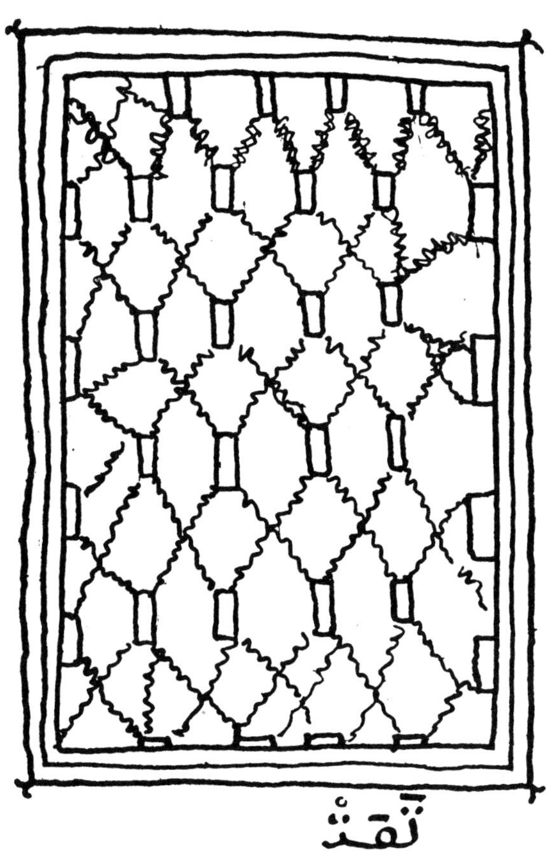

تَقَذْ

NOTES

PART I. HISTORICAL

No. 1

[1] *Bismi alahi* .... Arabic; a common opening. Used in manuscripts even where the remainder of the text may be in Hausa. Note the *alif da tabi* (آ) in *alahi* and *alrahmani*, &c., which causes these words to be pronounced *'lahi*, *'rahmani*, &c.

[2] *Karbōwa.* The termination of the verb (or, as here, the verbal noun) in *o* signifies motion towards or advantage to the subject. *Tafi* means 'to go', but *tafō* means 'to come' to the speaker, and is equivalent to *zō*.

[3] *Mai-chāu.* Also written and pronounced *mai-kyeau*; better thus.

[4] *Barebari.* The name for the inhabitants of the country round Lake Chad, the Bornu people. Their tattoo marks are easily recognizable. One, or sometimes two, lines down the forehead and along the bridge of the nose, seven longitudinal cuts on the right cheek, six on the left. Three on the upper and fore-arm, three on each side of the body. Three on the thighs, legs, and instep. These people are also sometimes known as Kukāwa.

[5] *Arewāwa.* Lit. 'the northerners'; *wa* termination denoting 'people', 'nation'. *Hausāwa*, *Turāwa*, *Tonāwa.*

[6] *Barnō.* The district of Bornu, bordering on Lake Chad.

[7] *Dōkin nan.* Here we have the first example in this book of the Hausa definite article. Canon Robinson in his *Hausa Grammar*, chap. i, p. 9 (new edition), states, 'There is no *article* in Hausa.'

One has here an instance of the value of a thorough acquaintance with Hausa in the written characters. In colloquial Hausa it would be impossible, or at least very difficult, to detect the presence of the final (ں) *nun*, or (ر) *ra*, which is undoubtedly the equivalent of the English definite article. A double *wasali* or double *rufua* sometimes takes the place of the *nun*.

The definite article in Hausa is rendered by affixing *n* or *r* to the noun, according to the gender, masculine or feminine.

It is often replaced by the demonstrative adjective (here curiously enough it is found coupled with it).

Sometimes again it will be omitted in Hausa where one would expect to find it in English. This may be due to carelessness in writing or to a certain laxness in the use of it in Hausa. The writer believes the honour of first finding the long-lost definite article belongs to Professor Mischlich, who in the course of a conversation with the writer in 1908 stated he had come across it. Professor Mischlich, however, did not inform him what form it took in Hausa, and it was not till some months later that a careful perusal of Hausa manuscripts revealed it to the present writer.

[8] *Aka-bōye.* Passive voice past tense (*ka*). Note the *object* of the verb, *shi.* The pronoun is in the objective case governed by the verb. Here, which is rarely the case in Hausa, the verb is *a true verb* and governs a pronoun in the accusative, instead of being qualified by a possessive adjective, or in other words not being a verb at all, but at best *a verbal noun.* So much of a noun often that it has a gender. This is seen in the passive voice in the present tense. Here the verb seems to lose any true verbal form it ever possessed, and becomes a noun, the *na* alone retaining the function of a verb. E.g. *ana-bōye-n-sa,* lit. 'There is (*ana*) a hiding (*bōye*) of (*na* or *n*) him (*sa*).' Here *bōye* is a masculine noun as is seen by the *na.*

[9] *Sarkin.* Definite article, '*the* chief'. Vide note above on *dōkin nan.*

[10] *Dinga,* 'to do anything repeatedly.' Also expressed by *kan.* The latter perhaps expresses the idea more. 'To be accustomed' to do a thing.

[11] *Tasa.* The so-called Hausa 'possessive pronoun' always appears to present some difficulty to students. This difficulty will disappear if one realizes that there is no exact equivalent in Hausa of the English possessive pronoun.

In Hausa the possessive pronoun is simply the personal pronoun (inflected for gender as in English) and a connective particle (one can hardly term it a preposition as it has an inflexion for gender) which can be readily translated by the English 'of'.

Thus in English where we say 'mine', 'thine', 'his', in Hausa they say 'of me', 'of thou', 'of him'.

The only thing to remember is that the particle corresponding to 'of' in English must in Hausa agree with its antecedent noun in gender. Once remember this and the rest is easy.

In English we say 'his mare'. In Hausa they say 'the mare of him'.

Now 'mare', or rather the word for mare, is feminine in Hausa, therefore the connective particle 'of' must be feminine too. Hence we have

gōdīa, fem. noun;

ta, 'of', fem. agreeing with *gōdīa*;

sa, 'him', masc. pronoun as in English.

Note the 1st person sing. has the peculiar form *wa*, and the form *sa* is generally used instead of *shi*.

[12] *Ranan*, 'one day'. Note the vowel lengths in the following words: رَانَا, *rānā*, 'the sun';

رَاْنَا, *raanā*, 'the day' as opposed to 'the night'.

[13] *Bāye*. Used of horses only; of persons, *tāra*, *chi*, &c.; of cattle, goats, *barbara*.

[14] *Sarki*. One would expect the definite article, *sarkin*, omitted in the Hausa.

[15] *Rigāyi*. To do anything previously, first, before another person.

[16] *Aka-gani*. The verb governs *kowa*, the object, which here precedes the verb, in the accusative. Vide note above on [8] *aka-bōye*.

[17] *Ranan*. Vide note above on [12] *ranan*.

[18] *Akāwō*. Vide note on [2] *karbōwa* above.

[19] *Su-ka-wātsu*. Middle voice.

[20] *Tafō*, 'come'. Vide note above on [2] *karbōwa*.

[21] *Mutun bīū*. Note this idiom is as correct if not better Hausa than *mutāne bīū*.

[22] *Wātsē*, 'were scattered'. Cf. [19] *wātsu* above.

[23] *Akāmō*, 'seize and bring back to'. These two ideas are expressed in one verb, the first by the verb itself, the second by the final *o*. Vide note above on [2] *karbōwa*.

[24] *Tafīa tasa*. For *tasa* vide note above on [11] *tasa*. *Tafia* here a feminine verbal noun. *Yi* or *yin* is probably understood.

[25] *Ahawa*. This should be *hau*, having a *rufua bisa*, not a *wasali bisa*.

[26] *Daura*. An Emirate about 60 miles north of Kano and 40 east of Katsina.

[27] *Garin*, '*the* town'. Definite article seen in the final *n*.

[28] *Ta-na-sonsa*. *Sō* here a noun. Vide note above on [8] *aka-bōye*. *'nsa* is for *nasa*, the former Katsina, the latter Kano Hausa.

[29] *Yāyē*, 'to wean'.

[30] *Mafārin fitar*. Two verbal nouns, the first masc., the second fem., as seen in the connective particles *n* and *r*.

[31] *Barnō*, Bornu. Vide note above on [6] *Barnō*.

[32] *Fasara*. Arabic, 'interpretation', 'meaning'.

[33] *Maabōchin* = *Mai-shi*.

[34] *Rinjāya* = *Iko*.

[35] *Abūbakari-Sidīku*. This name serves to show more or less exactly when this history of the conversion of Hausaland to Mohammedanism purports to begin, for it is undoubtedly that of the first of the four Califs or Halifs. *Abūbakari-Sidīku* ('the father of the maiden', as the Arabic word means) was the father of *Aishatu*, one of Mohammed's wives. His successors, also mentioned in this history, were *Omar*, *Osman*, and *Ali*, here called *Umaru*, *Usmanu*, and *Aliu*.

How long previous to this the supposed flight of the son of the king of Bornu, and the founding of the Hausa race took place, it is of course impossible to say. In this history we have undoubtedly historical facts interwoven with mythology, as is common in most histories or traditions of barbaric and savage peoples; nor are the historical facts of less value, or to be rejected, because the historian has sought to fill up the gaps he finds in authentic records, by resorting to his own imagination or to myths and traditions common among his people.

[36] *Wanchānanka*. *Wanchan*, *wanchāna*, and *'nka* = *naka*, lit. 'that person of yours I have told you about'. Plural *wanchānanku*.

[37] *Mazōwan tāwāye*. *Mazōwa* = *maabochi* = *mai-shi*. *Tāwāye*, 'twins', a way of saying 'the father of the twins'. The writer does not know to whom this refers.

[38] *Umaru Ibunuhutābi*. Omar, the second of the four Califs. Vide note above on [35] *Abūbakari-Sidīku*.

[39] *Sahabai*. Arabic, 'friends'.

[40] *Kasausawa* = *Māshi*.

[41] *Garkūa*. Generic name for all shields. *Kunkele*, 'a round shield', *kwangwara*, 'oval', the latter introduced from Asben into Hausaland.

[42] *Fūlar sarauta*. A red fez; a turban is bound round it.

[43] *Kasanashe.* *Sanashe*, 'to instruct'. *Ka*, meaning and use here obscure. One would expect the personal pronoun *ya* before the verb. *Ka* may stand for *kan* or be an unusual use of the *ka* of the past tense, plural. Probably though an error in the script.

[44] *Sābunta*, 'to establish' or 'confirm', here, his right to the kingship.

[45] *Matukan.* *Matuka* = *iyāka.*

[46] *Shigifū.* Singular *shigifa*, the flat roof of a house.

[47] *Mutānen.* Perhaps for *mutun.*

[48] *Garin.* Note the definite article.

[49] *Kabi*, north-east of Kano.

[50] *Mainamugabadi.* *Maina* = *sarki* in the language of Bornu.

[51] *Alfahari.* Arabic, 'boasting'.

[52] *Alkunia.* A sobriquet.

[53] *Suna.* Note the short *u*. *Sūna* is a different word.

[54] *Fa che.* Translate by, 'only that . . . not'.

[55] *Kāchia.* Of a woman, better *maskasche.* For a description of these operations vide nos. 37, 38, and pp. 258–63.

[56] *Gīla.* Also *zamba.* To kill a man from behind. Punishable by death in the Mohammedan law.

[57] *Yankake.* Past part. passive, from *yanka.*

[58] *Sashe*, 'caṣt out', perhaps from *sa.* Cf. *fādade* from *fādi*, 'to fall'.

[59] *Sananīa.* As above, *yankake.* The participle is here feminine to agree with *kushewa.* Masculine form is *sanane.*

[60] *Mai-kalgō.* A kalgō-tree (*Bauhinia reticulata*) grows on the grave, which is thus known as 'the Kalgō man's grave'.

This tree has aromatic leaves. These leaves, when they first open, are semicircular in shape, but later on one side of the leaf folds back, when the whole leaf becomes a circle. A decoction is made from the leaves and used as a cough medicine.

[61] *Gwoboron dūtsi*, 'the single rock'. A hill near Kano.

[62] *Usmānu dan Fōdio.* The Fulani conqueror of Hausaland.

[63] *Sāsan.* *Sāsan* = *wajen.*

[64] *Gōbir.* A district in Hausaland. The chief town in it was Alkalawa, from which Shefu drove out the king of Gobir.

[65] *Kinkumu.* Used of lifting a very heavy load with great difficulty.

[66] *Dawama.* *Dawama* = *tabata*, Arabic.

[67] *Bōka.* A wizard, a quack doctor. The word is used by a *mālam* to describe any person, not a recognized *mālam*, who practises medicine.

[68] *Kidāyuwa.* The termination *uwa* signifies 'able to be done'. Some other examples are *iyuwa, foruwa, geteruwa.*

[69] *Marādi.* A town on the borders of Hausaland and the French Soudan.

[70] *Bida.* Arabic. Certain prohibited conduct, e.g. drinking, card-playing.

[71] *Bāwa-jan-gwarzō.* The opposite of *rago.* A brave man, warrior.

[72] *Takaita.* To stop doing any work before you have quite finished it.

PART II. STORIES ABOUT PEOPLE

No. 1

[1] *Bismi alahi....* Note the *alif da tabi* (آ) in *alahi, alrahmani, alrahimi, alahu*, causing these words to be pronounced *'lahi, 'rahmani, 'rahimi, 'lahu.*

[2] *Bābi. Bābi*, Arabic, lit. 'gateway'. Here metaphorically, 'the entrance', 'the commencement of the story'.

[3] *Gātanan, gātanan, ta je, ta kōmō.* 'A story, a story. Let it go, let it come.' *Gātanan* is used for 'story', as *tātsūnīa*, but is really not a noun but a sentence. *Gā ta nan*, i.e. 'See it there', *ta* being feminine to agree probably with the noun *tāstūnīar.* A story-teller always commences thus, his hearers replying *Ta je, ta kōmō*, 'Let it (the story) go, let it come (to us)'; the *o* form, motion to the speaker. Vide note on [2] *karbōwa* (Part I).

The form *ta je, ta kōmō* is sometimes varied to *ta je ta dawō.*

[4] *Maatansa.* Mistake for *maatarsa.* Note the following words differently spelt, differently pronounced, and with different meanings:

1. *Maata*, مَاتَا, 'a wife', sing.
2. *Māta*, مَاتَا, 'wives', plur.
3. *Mātā*, مَاتَا, 'women', plur. of *mache.*

[5] *Bai zaka ba. Zaka* here equal to *zō.* Not to be confused with *zaa ka*, future, 'above'.

[6] *Maatar, 'the* wife'. Note the definite article. Vide note on [7] *dōkin nan* (Part I. Historical).

[7] *Galādīman.* Note the *wasali bisa bīū*, giving the nasal ending in place of a (ں) *nun.*

[8] *Baubawa.* Used of a foreigner who does not speak Hausa properly; possibly an onomatopoetic word.

[9] *Galādīman.* Vide note above on *galādīman.* Here the nasal ending is the definite article.

[10] *Gadō.* Note the two words differing only in the length of the vowel sounds, but with totally different meanings:

gadō, قَدُو, 'a bed'.

gādo, قَاڽ, 'inheritance'.

[11] *Galādīman.* The *galadima.* Definite article.

[12] *Zamnē.* Present participle. The author of *Hausa Notes* thinks there is no present participle in Hausa (vide p. 56, chap. xvi, *Hausa Notes*), but we have here an example of it. *Zamnē* is from the verb *zamna.* The past participle is, masc. *zamnanē,* fem. *zamnania*, plur. *zamnanū.* Cf. [6] *tsugunē* (No. 21, Part II).

[13] *Yā zō.* Perfect (or aorist) tense.

Previous writers on the Hausa language appear either to have overlooked the fact that the Hausa verb has a distinct form for the perfect and past tenses in the singular as it has for these tenses in the plural, or to have come to the conclusion that *there is no inflexion of the pronoun for the first three persons of the singular in the past tense* (*Hausa Notes*, p. 38, chap. x).

The present writer is convinced that distinct forms do exist for the singular as for the plural in the past and aorist tenses. This distinction is seen *in the length of the vowels.*

The full forms for the aorist and past tenses are as follows:

Perfect or Aorist.		Past.	
In English writing.	In Hausa characters.	In English writing.	In Hausa characters.
Singular.			
1st person. *Nā*	نَا	*Na*	نَ
2nd „ *Kā* (fem. *kin*)	كَا, كِن	*Ka* (fem. *ki*)	كَ, كِ
3rd „ *Yā* (fem. *tā*)	يَا, تَا	*Ya* (fem. *ta*)	يَ, تَ
Plural.			
1st person. *Mun*	مُنْ	*Mu ka*	مُكَ
2nd „ *Kun*	كُن	*Ku ka*	كُكَ
3rd „ *Sun*	سُنْ	*Su ka*	سُكَ

It is seen that in the plural the well-known forms *mun, kun, sun*; *mu ka, ku ka, su ka,* for the perfect and past tenses are found, but that in the singular number the only difference is in the length of the vowel *a*, which is *short* in all the persons of the past tense, but *long* in the corresponding persons of the perfect.

That such (to the English idea) apparent slight variation should be sufficient to alter the tense of a verb is not surprising when one comes to understand the great influence of lengths of vowels in Hausa, for the entire meaning of a word can be altered by the omission or addition of an accent on a vowel.

The present tense is too well known to require special remark. It is worth while to note perhaps that in the present tense (*ina, ka na,* &c. and *ni ke, ka ke,* &c.) the pronouns are real pronouns and do not suffer any inflexion.

In the use of the past and aorist tenses one should note that, except in certain well-defined instances, the use of the past for the aorist and vice versa seems permissible, or at least they would often appear to be interchangeable. In cases where one finds a past where an aorist would have been expected in written Hausa, the fault probably lies in the writing.

Some examples are now given to show how these tenses (the past and aorist) are used. In the instances the plural forms which are in these tenses impossible of confusion are given, and then the corresponding tense in the singular.

Kun gama aikin? Have you (plur.) finished the work?

Kā gama aikin? Have you (sing.) finished the work?

Mun gama. We have finished.

Nā gama. I have finished.

A. *Tun ku na samāri na yi muku alhēri, ama ku ka yi mini munā futshi.*

Here both the verbs *na yi* and *ku ka yi* are past tense.

If made perfect the sentence would read

B. *Tun ku na samāri nā yi . . . kun yi . . .*

The meaning is only slightly different; the point to notice is that *na yi* in A is not the same tense as *nā yi* in B.

Da mu ka tafi . . . When we went . . . (past tense).

Da na tafi . . . When I went . . . " "

Mun diba rua, mun kāwō chiāwa, mun zō wurinka dōmin . . .

Nā diba rua, nā kāwō chiāwa, nā zō wurinka dōmin . . .

Here the verbs are aorist tense.

We have seen the two distinct verbal pronominal forms, the long *ā* for the aorist, the short *a* for the past. There is still a third vowel sound for the future singular. In this the *a* is not so much a long *a*, as most writers seem to have rendered it, as a double *a* sound—two distinct *a*'s—and it is thus the sound has been written in this work. This is more akin to the Hausa than its transliteration by *ā*. In the plural the writer has repeatedly found this reduplication of the last vowel (in the plural a *u* not an *a*), and has not met with the *mua*, *kua*, &c., which are generally given. This tense therefore stands:

Future Tense.

In English writing.		In Hausa characters.
	Singular.	
1st person.	*Naa*	نَاْ
2nd ,,	*Kaa* (fem. *kii* or *kya*)	كَاْ، كِيَاْ
3rd ,,	*Yaa** (fem. *taa*)	يَاْ، تَاْ
	Plural.	
1st person.	*Muu*	مُوْ
2nd ,,	*Kuu*	كُوْ
3rd ,,	*Suu*	سُوْ

The other form of the future the writer also prefers to transliterate *zaa ni*, *zaa ka*, &c. instead of the usual *za ni*, *za ka*, &c.

[14] *Ke wācheche anan.* Imitating the bad grammar the slave spoke.

[15] *Ki.* As above; for *ka.*

[16] *Shi-na-kunche. Kunche*, pronounce *kwanche.*

[17] *Gaza. Gaza* as *kāsa*, 'to take no notice'.

[18] *Mātasa.* Should be *maata tasa.*

[19] *Ke ya dulin . . . kin lena Dūnia.* The bad grammar is to imitate the slave's speech as above.

[20] *Maida magana.* 'To state a case' (in Court).

[21] *Kungurus kan kūsu. Kungurus*, an onomatopoetic word supposed to represent the sound of an object falling on the ground (here a rat's head). All Hausa tales end thus. The meaning seems to be that the story is ended, the rat's head is off, that is the end of him. Sometimes the phrase is enlarged on by the story-teller saying, 'The rat will not eat my head, rather shall I eat his head, the son of a worthless fellow.'

* Sometimes *shii.*

No. 2

[1] *Gātanan, gātanan.* Vide note on [3]*gātanan* (No. 1, Part II).

[2] *Machen,* 'the female'. Note the definite article; vide note on [7] *dōkin nan* (Part I). *Matche* appears to be treated as masculine.

[3] *Baban wansu.* *Wa* = elder brother; *kane* = younger brother. The fem. of these being *ya* and *kanwa* respectively.

[4] *Tā batche.* *Tā,* aorist tense. Vide note on [13]*yā zō* (No. 1, Part II).

[5] *Unguan.* *Ungua,* a small hamlet composed of only one or two huts.

[6] *Shii je.* Future tense. Oratio recta would be *naa je.* Vide note on [13]*yā zō* (No. 1, Part II).

[7] *Daure.* Present participle. More correct *daurania,* the perfect participle.

[8] *Mādugun.* Note the definite article.

[9] *Bigire.* *Wuri.*

[10] *Sa . . . zane.* *Sa zane,* a euphemistic phrase for consummating a marriage.

[11] *Uba yā kōmō.* *Yā* and following verbs aorist tense. Vide note on [13]*yā zō* (No. 1, Part II).

Kōmō here equal to *zama,* 'to become', 'turn out to be'.

[12] *Ta-na-kunche.* Pronounce *kwanche.*

[13] *Jārīriya.* Feminine. Masculine, *jārīri.*

[14] *Uban,* 'the father'. Note the definite article.

[15] *Bakā.* Here fem., generally masc.

[16] *Yan uba.* The children of one father by different mothers; half-brothers and sisters.

[17] *Kungurus kan kūsu.* Vide note on [21] *kungurus* (No. 1, Part II).

No. 3

[1] *Gātanan.* Vide note on [3]*gātanan* (No. 1, Part II).

[2] *Yā sa . . . yā gani.* Note aorist tense. Vide note on [13]*yā zō* (No. 1, Part II).

[3] *Kaa gani.* Vide future tense note on [13]*yā zō* (No. 1, Part II).

[4] *Sai yārō ya . . . ta . . . ta . . . sai ya halbe ta.* Note all the verbs past tense. Vide note on [13]*yā zō* (No. 1, Part II).

[5] *Tsara.* Perhaps for *tsakar.*

[6] *Kungurus.* Vide note on [21] *kungurus* (No. 1, Part II).

No. 4

[1] *Gaya.* An alliance generally for some work such as hoeing, gathering grass for roofing, &c.

Derivation probably *gaya,* 'to tell', 'to inform'. *Gaya wāne da wāne,* 'tell so and so and so and so that.'

[2] *Gātanan.* Vide note on [3] *gātanan* (No. 1, Part II).

[3] *Shi-ka-aure.* Perhaps for *shi ke aure.*

[4] *Maatā,* 'a wife'. Vide note on [4] *maatansa* (No. 1, Part II).

[5] *Kunya,* 'a furrow'.

[6] *Gumki.* Pronounce *gwamki.* Here evidently from the context 'a hartebeest', not *gumki,* 'a fetish'.

[7] *Tanpasua.* As *alura,* 'a needle'.

[8] *Kungurus.* Vide note on [21] *kungurus* (No. 1, Part II).

No. 5

[1] *Shasharbō.* An onomatopoetic word, the sound of a stick beating an object, *sharb! sharb!*

[2] *Mātansa.* Vide note on [4] *maatansa* (No. 1, Part II).

[3] *Sai ta dauki . . . ta je, ta . . . ta.* Note all these verbs past tense. Vide note on [13] *yā zō* (No. 1, Part II).

[4] *Su-ka-chi.* Note the past tense as continued from the preceding sentence.

[5] *Ta je, ta . . . ta . . .* As above, vide note on [3] *sai ta dauki.*

[6] *Talga.* To stir with the *murchia,* of a fluid; of a thicker substance, *tūka.*

[7] *Farutanka.* Sing. *farehe,* of persons only. Of animals, cat tribe, *akaifa, kumba*; of cattle, horses, &c., *kofatō.*

[8] *Zaa ni.* Vide note on future tense under [13] *yā zō* (No. 1, Part II).

[9] *Walki.* A skin loin-cloth.

[10] *Nā tsōma,* 'I have put in'. Here *na tsōma* would be quite wrong and would never be used by a Hausa. Vide note on [13] *yā zō* (No. 1, Part II).

[11] *Kai ka ji da abin fadi. Ka* should be future. This sentence is peculiar and difficult to translate in English. It seems to mean 'you will regret this', 'I shall pay you back for this'.

[12] *Kyale.* Spelt *kelē,* but pronounced *kyale.*

[13] *Māra.* A broken bit of calabash used as a spoon to serve out food from a pot. Roughly shaped round.

[14] *Sannū.* Note this is one of the few words in Hausa spelt with a double consonant. The effect is to make each syllable pronounced distinctly *san-nū.*

[15] *In gwiya.* Better *in gwaiya.* In answer to the salutation *sannū* (Sokoto Hausa).

[16] *Maatar nan.* Cf. [7] *dōkin nan* (No. 1, Part I).

[17] *Shibshibtō.* *Shibtō* = *debō*, 'to serve', 'to help food'.

[18] *Tūka.* Vide note above on [6] *talga.*

[19] *Ta daukō, ta . . . ta . . . ta . . ., su-ka-kōshi.* Note the past tense throughout; *tā* aorist would be quite wrong here. Vide note [13] *yā zō* (No. 1, Part II).

[20] *Maatar.* Note the definite article.

[21] *Rufēwa.* A storehouse for corn, &c. Also *rumbū* and *runbū.*

[22] *Mātan.* Plural. Vide note on [4] *maatansa* (No. 1, Part II).

[23] *Abuya.* Feminine of *abōki.* *Abuya* = *kawa.*

[24] *Nā tūba*, 'I have repented'. Note long *ā.* Aorist tense *na tūba* would be quite incorrect here.

[25] *Ta je . . . ta . . . ta . . . ta che.* Note the past tense.

[26] *Kā gani, nā sāmu.* Aorist tense.

[27] *Kunche.* Pronounce *kwanche.*

[28] *Kunta.* Pronounce *kwanta.*

[29] *Kungurus.* Vide note on [21] *kungurus* (No. 1, Part II).

No. 6

[1] *Gātanan.* Vide note on [3] *gātanan* (No. 1, Part II).

[2] *Naa mutu.* Vide note on future tense under [13] *yā zō* (No. 1, Part II).

[3] *Kā mutu.* Aorist tense. Vide note on [13] *yā zō* (No. 1, Part II).

[4] *Kūra*, 'the hyena', feminine. *Kūre*, masculine. The personification in Hausa folk-lore of all that is greedy and treacherous. Quite a different character from that ascribed to the *gizō gizō* for instance, whose cunning and plausibility are rather admired than otherwise. *Chin kūra*, 'to eat as a hyena', that is, to charge exorbitant prices or interest.

[5] *Chintō.* Also *tsintua.*

[6] *Sānia.* Note spelt (in error?) *chānia* throughout.

[7] *Kafāhu.* Plural. Sing. *kafa.* Note *kafō, kafōni*, 'horn'.

[8] *Watanda. Yi watanda,* 'to buy food on credit', more especially of meat. When an ox is killed the meat is divided up, and people are allowed to buy on credit.

[9] *Kabarin.* Arabic. Hausa is *kushēwa.*

[10] *Kafa. Kōfa.*

[11] *Dawō.* Also *Fūra* (Kano), made with maize or guinea-corn.

[12] *Asha.* Note also exclamation *ashe!* 'indeed!' a different word.

[13] *Idānu gudā.* Cf. expression *mutun bīū.* Here perhaps the idea is 'eyes, one in number'.

[14] *Nāman.* Note the definite article. Vide note on [7] *dōkin nan* (No. 1, Part I).

[15] *Ka tafia(r)ka.* Cf. [24] *tafia tasa* (No. 1, Part I).

[16] *Su-nā-dūka.* Note length of vowel, *dūka,* 'to beat'; *duka,* 'all', a different word.

[17] *Sāmō,* 'find and bring back'. Both these ideas expressed in the one Hausa word. Vide note on [2] *karbōwa* (No. 1, Part I).

[18] *Ya sāmu ... ya kāwō. Su-ka ...* Note the past tense in the verb throughout. Vide note on [13] *yā zō* (No. 1, Part II).

[19] *Nāman.* Definite article.

[20] *Galabaita,* 'to become insensible'.

[21] *Shi-na-kīra.* Note *kira,* 'to call'; *kīra,* 'to forge'.

[22] *Danfara,* 'to plaster', 'to stick on'.

[23] *Kyale.* Spelt *kelē.*

[24] *Rāgada,* 'to work up and down'.

[25] *Gizō gizō,* 'the spider', also called *tau tau.* The spider is the hero of many Hausa animal stories. The same is the case among the Ashanti. In fact the Ashanti name for a story, even when the spider does not appear in the narrative at all, is *anansesem,* i.e. *ananse asem,* lit. 'words about the spider'. The Hausas call the praying mantis the spider's wife (*kōki*).

The character given to the spider in West African fables is not unlike that ascribed to the rabbit (*kalulu*) and the tortoise (*kamba*) in the stories of the Bantu Mang'anja in British Central Africa (Nyassaland). Vide also note above on [4] *kūra.*

[26] *Kungurus.* Vide note on [21] *kungurus* (No. 1, Part II).

No. 7

[1] *Gātanan.* Vide note on [3] *gātanan* (No. 1, Part II).

[2] *Mātansa.* Vide note on [4] *maatansa* (No. 1, Part II).

[3] *Nā bar.* Aorist. Vide note on [13]*yā zō* (No. 1, Part II).

[4] *Kunche.* Pronounce *kwanche.*

[5] *Kīshia uwa tata.* Lit. 'the hater of her mother', or 'the one who was jealous of her mother'. This phrase has been translated freely throughout by 'stepmother' to avoid the clumsy Hausa idiom. When a man has more than one wife, then each is called the *kīshiar* of the other, this even should they be the best of friends.

[6] *Ta tāshi . . . ta . . . ta . . . ta che.* Note the past tense throughout. Vide note on [13]*yā zō* (No. 1, Part II).

[7] *Uma.* Arabic. Hausa *uwa.*

[8] *Daka.* The process of pounding (in a wooden mortar with pestle, just such as is used on the East Coast) is as follows:

The first pounding is called *susuka* (*surfe*). The corn is taken out and winnowed (*bakāche*) and the husks thereby removed. The result of this process is put in the mortar and pounded again (*daka*), then winnowed again (*tankade*). The grain is again put in the mortar and pounded a little, water being sprinkled. This third pounding is called *ribidi.* Next the grain is washed and rolled into balls (*dunkula*). The balls are put in boiling water, boiled, taken out again, pounded (*kirbi*), rolled into balls again (*dunkula*), and are ready for eating. *Chāse* is to pound rice.

[9] *Nasa.* As *jefa.*

[10] *Tsinbire.* To get burned by sticking to the pot.

[11] *Tsāme.* To lift out with a spoon.

[12] *Sāsanwa.* As *girki,* to set a pot on the three stones (*murfu*) which form the fire-place. 'To take off the fire', *shīde.*

[13] *Jarabi.* Arabic. Hausa *dūba.*

[14] *Naa tafi.* Vide note on future tense under [13]*yā zō* (No. 1, Part II).

[15] *Angarmu,* 'a big horse'. A pony is *kūru.*

[16] *Kyale.* Pronounced thus; spelt *kelē.*

[17] *Kashēdi.* An exclamation, 'Have a care!'

[18] *Nasa.* Better *tasa.* Vide note [11] *tasa* (No. 1, Part I).

[19] *Kungurus.* Vide note [21] *kungurus* (No. 1, Part II).

No. 8

[1] *Mayā,* 'a witch'. Masc. *maye*; plur. *mayu.*

[2] *Gātanan.* Vide note on [3]*gātanan* (No. 1, Part II).

[3] *Ta je.* Past tense. Vide note on [13]*yā zō* (No. 1, Part II).

[4] *Wakatin.* Arabic. Hausa *lōkachī.*

[5] *Ya tāshi, ya . . . ya . . . ya . . .* Note past tense throughout. *Yā* would here be quite incorrect.

[6] *Kunche.* Pronounce *kwanche.*

[7] *Mazan.* Note the definite article. Vide note on [7] *dōkin nan* (No. 1, Part I).

[8] *Mātan.* Vide note on [4] *maatansa* (No. 1, Part II), and for the definite article vide note on [7] *dōkin nan* (No. 1, Part I).

[9] *Dākin.* Definite article.

[10] *Yankaki.* Perfect participle. Error for *yankakū.*

[11] *Zaa ta.* For future tense vide note on [13] *yā zō* (No. 1, Part II).

[12] *Kyale.* Spelt *kelē.*

[13] *Magarīa.* The zizyphus lotus.

[14] *Naa.* Vide note on future tense under [13] *yā zō* (No. 1, Part II).

[15] *Maraki.* Better here *maraka* (fem.).

[16] *Muu rāma.* Vide note on the future tense under [13] *yā zō* (No. 1, Part II).

[17] *Nā kāwō.* Aorist tense. Vide note on [13] *yā zō* (No. 1, Part II).

[18] *Uma.* Arabic. Hausa *uwa.*

[19] *La ila'.* The complete sentence is *La ilaha ila alahu,* 'there is no god but Allah'.

[20] *Hannu(n)ki.* Note the double consonant *n.* Vide note on [14] *sannū* (No. 5, Part II).

[21] *Shii gani.* Vide note on future tense under [13] *yā zō* (No. 1. Part II).

[22] *Sasāre.* Note the reduplication, not uncommon in Hausa. Cf. the reduplication in Greek verb.

[23] *Ya tāshi, su-ka-gudu.* Note the past tense. Vide note on [13] *yā zō* (No. 1, Part II).

[24] *Ya che yā yāda.* Here we have a good example of the past tense *ya,* with the aorist *yā.* In oratio recta it would stand *nā yāda.* One could use the past tense in both verbs here in Hausa, as in English.

[25] *Daukō.* The idea of 'lift' and 'return with' expressed by the *o* termination. Vide note on [2] *karbōwa* (No. 1, Part I).

[26] *Ya che, yaa kōma.* Here again we have an example side by side of the two tenses, the past *ya,* the future *yaa*; cf. note above *ya che, yā yāda.* For both vide note on [13] *yā zō* (No. 1, Part II).

[27] *Tunka.* Pronounce *tankwa,* as *berkōnō.*

[28] *Kyaure*, 'a wooden door'. A grass door, *tufania*; of iron, *gambō*, in wall of a town.

[29] *Kuble*, 'to close a door'.

[30] *Ya che yā ba shi . . . ya che yā baiwa.* Vide note above on [24] *ya che yā yāda.*

[31] *Tsari*, 'a protection', 'something to ward off'.

[32] *Kungurus.* Vide note on [21] *kungurus* (No. 1, Part II).

No. 9

[1] *Mālami.* Also *mālam*; plur. *mālamai.* There would seem to be a slight distinction in the use of the words *mālami* and *mālam*, the former being used when speaking about the person or in his absence, the latter in addressing him or using his name, e.g. *Mālam Manzō*, not *mālami Manzō*. Derivation perhaps Arabic, *mualami.*

[2] *Kūra.* Vide note on [4] *kūra* (No. 6, Part II).

[3] *Gōdīar.* Note the definite article. Vide note on [7] *dōkin nan* (No. 1, Part I).

[4] *Zaa ka.* Vide note on [13] *yā zō* (No. 1, Part II).

[5] *Asha.* Vide note on [12] *asha* (No. 6, Part II).

[6] *Nā gani.* Vide note on [13] *yā zō* (No. 1, Part II).

[7] *Ta kāma, ta . . . ta . . . ta . . . gida.* Note the past tense. Vide note on [13] *yā zō* (No. 1, Part II).

[8] *Karen buki.* Also *dilā*, 'the jackal'. The personification of cunning.

[9] *Nā tasō.* Note aorist tense. Vide note on [13] *yā zō* (No. 1, Part II).

[10] *Karfī.* Note the two different words *karfī*, 'strength', and *karfē*, 'metal'.

[11] *Kyale.* Written *kelē.*

[12] *Naa.* Future tense. Vide note on future under [13] *yā zō* (No. 1, Part II).

[13] *Mamāya.* Fem. to agree with *sānia.*

[14] *Nā zō.* As above, [9] *nā tasō.*

[15] *La ila'.* Vide note on [19] *la ila'* (No. 8, Part II).

[16] *Nāman.* The definite article. Vide note on [7] *dōkin nan* (No. 1, Part I).

[17] *Nā ji.* Aorist *na ji* would be quite incorrect here. Vide note on [13] *yā zō* (No. 1, Part II).

[18] *Tafianta.* Better *tafiarta.* Vide note on [24] *tafia tasa* (No. 1, Part I).

[19] *Kungurus.* Vide note on [21] *kungurus* (No. 1, Part II).

No. 10

[1] *Garnakaki.* As *gwarzō*, 'a very powerful man', 'a warrior'.

[2] *Karfī.* Vide note on [10] *karfī* (No. 9, Part II).

[3] *Ya fida.* *Ya* past tense. Vide note on [13] *yā zō* (No. 1, Part II).

[4] *Maatansa.* Better *maatarsa.* Vide note on [4] *maatansa* (No. 1, Part II).

[5] *Ta-na-sō(n)sa.* Vide note on [8] *aka-bōye* (No. 1, Part I).

[6] *Aka-kāwō shi.* Vide note on [8] *aka-bōye* (No. 1, Part I).

[7] *Naa.* Future tense. Vide note on [13] *yā zō* (No. 1, Part II).

[8] *Maatar nan.* Note the definite article. Vide note on [9] *dōkin nan* (No. 1, Part I).

[9] *Tānadi.* Arabic. Hausa *zanba.*

[10] *Kungurus.* Vide note on [21] *kungurus* (No. 1, Part II).

No. 11

[1] *Ya yi . . . ya . . . ya . . .* Note the past tense throughout. Vide note on [13] *yā zō* (No. 1, Part II).

[2] *Kori.* Pronounce *kwori.*

[3] *Kungurus.* Vide note on [21] *kungurus* (No. 1, Part II).

No. 12

[1] *Gātanan.* Vide note on [3] *gātanan* (No. 1, Part II).

[2] *Ya fitō.* Past tense. Vide note on [13] *yā zō* (No. 1, Part II).

[3] *Maatarsa.* Vide note on [4] *maatansa* (No. 1, Part II).

[4] *Kaa.* Future tense. Vide note under [13] *yā zō* (No. 1, Part II).

[5] *Yā kāwō.* Aorist tense. Vide [13] *yā zō* (No. 1, Part II).

[6] *Maatar.* Note the definite article. Vide note on [7] *dōkin nan* (No. 1, Part I).

[7] *Kā.* Aorist. Vide note above, [5] *yā kāwō.*

[8] *Wasaki.* A skin gathered up all round the edge, forming a bag. Also *gūga*, but latter rather of a calabash.

[9] *Yāron.* Note the definite article.

[10] *Zannuansu.* Note double consonant *n.* Vide note [14] *sannū* (No. 5, Part II). Found also spelt with one *n*, but better two.

[11] *Rigāye.* Vide note on [15] *rigāyi* (No. 1, Part I).

[12] *Ya che yaa je.* Vide note on the past and future tenses under [13] *yā zō* (No. 1, Part II).

[13] *Rufēwa.* Vide note on [21] *rufēwa* (No. 5, Part II).

[14] *Yā.* Aorist tense.

[15] *Ina-ji(n)-wārin mutun.* Cf. 'Jack and the Bean-stalk' of our own folk-lore.

[16] *Daa.* Note the following words, *daa . . . daa,* in the protasis and apodosis of a conditional sentence. *Da* (short *a*) when and with *dā,* 'a son'.

[17] *Sasabe.* The first clearing of the 'bush' for a garden.

[18] *Fūda.* Of ploughing with a *galma.* *Nōma* used when a *hauya* is employed.

[19] *Takuna.* Error for *tukuna.*

[20] *Kasō.* From *kashe.* Here the idea contained in the verb with the *o* termination is 'kill and bring back'. Vide note on [2] *karbōwa* (No. 1, Part I).

[21] *Hannunsa.* Vide note on [14] *sannū* (No. 5, Part II).

[22] *Dinga ragāwa. Ragāwa,* derivation *rege,* 'to diminish'. Translate 'make light of it', 'do not make a fuss of it'.

[23] *Karfī.* Vide note on [10] *karfī* (No. 9, Part II).

[24] *Kā gani.* Aorist tense. *Ka* would not be correct here.

[25] *Kungurus.* Vide note on [21] *kungurus* (No. 1, Part II).

No. 13

[1] *Gātanan.* Vide note on [3] *gātanan* (No. 1, Part II).

[2] *Ya mutu.* Past tense. Vide note on [13] *yā zō* (No. 1, Part II).

[3] *Taa mutu.* Future tense. Vide note under [13] *yā zō* (No. 1, Part II).

[4] *Kīshīa.* Vide note on [5] *kīshia* (No. 7, Part II).

[5] *Chiutar nan.* Note the definite article. Vide note on [7] *dōkin nan* (No. 1, Part I).

[6] *Yā karbi.* Aorist tense. Vide note on [13] *yā zō* (No. 1, Part II).

[7] *Nā bar.* Vide note above, [6] *yā karbi.*

[8] *Matsāfa.* Cf. *sāfe = tūrū.*

[9] *Kun ka gani.* Should be *kun gani.*

[10] *Karfē.* Vide note on [10] *karfī* (No. 9, Part II).

[11] *Kungurus.* Vide note on [21] *kungurus* (No. 1, Part II).

No. 14

[1] *Gātanan.* Vide note on [3] *gātanan* (No. 1, Part II).

[2] *Ya tāshi, ya kōma.* Past tense. Vide note on [13] *yā zō* (No. 1, Part II).

[3] *Maatansa.* Mistake for *maatarsa.* Vide note on [4] *maatansa* (No. 1, Part II).

[4] *Garin.* Note the definite article. Vide note on [7] *dōkin nan* (No. 1, Part I).

[5] *Naa ba.* Future tense. Vide note on [13] *yā zō* (No. 1, Part II).

[6] *Yaa tafi.* As above, [5] *naa ba.*

[7] *Tafiasa.* For *tafia(r)sa.* Vide note on [24] *tafia tasa* (No. I, Part I).

[8] *Tatara.* Reduplication of *tāra.*

[9] *Kungurus.* Vide note on [21] *kungurus* (No. 1, Part II).

No. 15

[1] *Ya tafi.* Past tense. Vide note on [13] *yā zō* (No. 1, Part II).

[2] *Budurin.* Note the definite article. Vide note on [7] *dōkin nan* (No. 1, Part I).

[3] *Yā fāra.* Aorist. Vide note on [13] *yā zō* (No. 1, Part II).

[4] *Kā chika.* As above.

[5] *Kungurus.* Vide note on [21] *kungurus* (No. 1, Part II).

No. 16

[1] *Gātanan.* Vide note on [3] *gātanan* (No. 1, Part II).

[2] *Ya haifu.* Past tense. Vide note on [13] *yā zō* (No. 1, Part II).

[3] *Ya bi ta kāfar.* Cf. idiom, *shiga ta kōfa nan.* The *ta* perhaps is explained by the word *hainya* being understood before it.

[4] *Gūda.* Note the length of the vowel. *Guda* means the dot below a letter, and number. *Gūda* is a sound made on joyful occasions. It is made by holding the nose and making a shrill cry, *ru! ru! ru! ru!* Cf. the *ntulungwani* of the Mang'anja of Nyassaland, who make this same sound, but by rubbing the lips with the finger.

[5] *Kungurus.* Vide note on [21] *kungurus* (No. 1, Part II).

No. 17

[1] *Daudawa.* Seeds of the *dorawa* tree.

[2] *Gabū.* Onion leaves dried and pounded (?).

[3] *Daudawar batsō.* Pounded seeds of the *yakua* tree.

[4] *Gātanan.* Vide note on [3] *gātanan* (No. 1, Part II).

[5] *Zaa su.* Vide note on future tense under [13] *yā zō* (No. 1, Part II).

[6] *Ta bi.* Past tense. Vide note on [13] *yā zō* (No. 1, Part II).

[7] *Make.* As *labe,* 'to slink', 'sidle past'.

[8] *Kyale.* Spelt *kelē.*

[9] *Nā ji . . . nā ji.* Aorist tense. Vide note on [13]*yā zō* (No. 1, Part II).

[10] *Kudai.* Better *kadai,* singular.

[11] *Kilīshi.* Note the long vowel. *Kilishi* is dried meat.

[12] *Kōran ta.* Vide note on [8] *aka-bōye* (No. 1, Part I)

[13] *Naa dinga.* Vide note on future tense under [13] *yā zō* (No. 1, Part II).

[14] *Kuyanginta.* *Kuyanga,* 'a girl slave', masc. *magudanchi.*

[15] *Kungurus.* Vide note on [21] *kungurus* (No. 1, Part II).

No. 18

[1] *Mūsa.* Hausa for 'Moses'.

[2] *Gātanan.* Vide note on [3] *gātanan* (No. 1, Part II).

[3] *Ya haifi.* Past tense. Vide note on [13]*yā zō* (No. 1, Part II).

[4] *Wāne wai ka zō.* A Hausa will never call her husband by his name nor talk about him by his name. He is usually spoken to and of as *mai-gida.*

[5] *Naa yi.* Future tense. Vide note under [13]*yā zō* (No. 1, Part II).

[6] *Kyale.* Spelt *kelē.*

[7] *Ruan.* Note the definite article. Vide note on [7] *dōkin nan* (No. 1, Part I).

[8] *Gaia.* As *keta,* 'spiteful'.

[9] *Ruan.* As above, definite article, *ruan.*

[10] *Nā ki.* Aorist tense. Vide note on [13]*yā zō* (No. 1, Part II).

[11] *Yaa.* Vide note on future tense under [13]*yā zō* (No. 1, Part II).

[12] *Kungurus.* Vide note on [21] *kungurus* (No. 1, Part II).

No. 19

[1] *Ya yāda.* Past tense. Vide note under [13]*yā zō* (No. 1, Part II).

[2] *Gasa,* 'to roast'. Note the word *gāsa!* an interjection of wonder.

[3] *Nā yas.* Aorist tense. Vide note on [13]*yā zō* (No. 1, Part II).

[4] *Tafia(r)sa.* Vide note on [24] *tafia tasa* (No. 1, Part I).

[5] *Uwar gidansa.* When a man has more than one wife the first one he married is called *uwar gida,* 'mother of the house'.

[6] *Yā zō.* Vide note above, [3] *nā yas.* Here *ya zō* would be quite incorrect.

[7] *Gūda.* Vide note on [4] *gūda* (No. 16, Part II).
[8] *Su-ka-sasāre.* Note reduplication of the verb.
[9] *Kuyangi.* Vide note on [14] *kuyanginta* (No. 17, Part II).
[10] *Naa.* Vide note on future tense under [13] *yā zō* (No. 1, Part II).
[11] *Au . . . au.* Unusual. *Kō . . . kō* generally used, 'either . . . or'.
[12] *Kungurus.* Vide note on [21] *kungurus* (No. 1, Part II).

No. 20

[1] *Ta haifi.* Past tense. Vide note on [13] *yā zō* (No. 1, Part II).
[2] *Yā chainye.* Aorist tense. Vide note on [13] *yā zō* (No. 1, Part II).
[3] *Yā kōmō.* As above, [2] *yā chainye.*
[4] *Zaa ka chi.* Vide note on future tense under [13] *yā zō* (No. 1, Part II).
[5] *Kungurus.* Vide note on [21] *kungurus* (No. 1, Part II).

No. 21

[1] *Lādi.* Perhaps for *lāhadi.* So called because born on a Sunday.
[2] *Mātansa.* Vide note on [4] *maatansa* (No. 1, Part II).
[3] *Tā yi.* Aorist tense. Vide note on [13] *yā zō* (No. 1, Part II).
[4] *Bubuge.* Note the reduplication of the verb.
[5] *Kyale.* Spelt *kelē.*
[6] *Tsugunē.* Present participle. Vide note on [12] *zamnē* (No. 1, Part II).
[7] *Mālam.* Vide note on *mālami* (No. 9, Part II).
[8] *Mālam.* Better *mālami.*
[9] *Nā gaia.* Aorist tense. Vide note on *yā zō* (No. 1, Part II).
[10] *Ashā.* Note different from the word *ashē*, 'indeed', 'truly'.
[11] *Ashē.* Vide above, [10] *ashā.*
[12] *Ina-sonsa.* Vide note on [8] *aka-bōye* (No. 1, Part I).
[13] *Yaa.* Vide note on future tense under [13] *yā zō* (No. 1, Part II).
[14] *Ana-gūda.* Vide note on [4] *gūda* (No. 16, Part II).
[15] *Maatar.* Note the definite article. Vide note on [7] *dōkin nan* (No. 1, Part I).
[16] *Kungurus.* Vide note on [21] *kungurus* (No. 1, Part II).

PART III. ANIMAL STORIES

No. 22

[1] *Gātanan.* Vide note on [3] *gātanan* (No. 1, Part II).

[2] *Ya kashe.* Past tense. Vide note on [13] *yā zo* (No. 1, Part II).

[3] *Ta-na-ganin.* Note verbal noun. Vide note on [8] *aka-bōye* (No. 1, Part I).

[4] *Kyale.* Pronounce thus. Spelt *kelĕ.*

[5] *Tafia tata.* Vide note on [24] *tafia tasa* (No. 1, Part I).

[6] *Kwāshi.* As *sōma, fāra,* 'to begin'.

[7] *Kūra.* Vide note on [4] *kūra* (No. 6, Part II).

[8] *Kungurus.* Vide note on [21] *kungurus* (No. 1, Part II).

No. 23

[1] *Ya yi.* Vide note on [13] *yā zō* (No. 1, Part II).

[2] *Tōshe = Rufe.*

[3] *Kūra.* Vide note on [4] *kūra* (No. 6, Part II).

[4] *Fājimata . . . gīwa gai.* Imitating the hyena's supposed bad accent or lisp. Fātimata was the daughter of Mohammed.

[5] *Nā san ki.* Aorist tense. Vide note on [13] *yā zō* (No. 1, Part II).

[6] *Yāmin bāki,* 'a lisp'.

[7] *Alāgidigūa.* Also *kwatana,* 'waist beads'. Of a man, *gūru.*

[8] *Su-ke-shan.* Verbal noun, *sha.* Vide note on [8] *aka-bōye* (No. 1, Part I).

[9] *Zaa zu.* Vide note on future tense under [13] *yā zō* (No. 1, Part II).

[10] *Yā kafe.* Aorist tense. Vide note on [13] *yā zō* (No. 1, Part II).

[11] *Daa . . . daa.* Vide note on [16] *daa . . . daa* (No. 12, Part II).

[12] *Bulbule.* A pretty example of onomatopoeia.

[13] *Ribibi.* As *wasōso,* 'to scramble'.

[14] *Ta kwāsa.* A curious use of *ta,* the idiom, if one is not known to the writer. Perhaps an error in the Hausa script.

[15] *Gayā.* Vide note on [1] *gayā* (No. 4, Part II).

[16] *Kungurus.* Vide note on [21] *kungurus* (No. 1, Part II).

No. 24

[1] *Gātanan.* Vide note on [3] *gātanan* (No. 1, Part II).

[2] *Maatar.* Vide note on [4] *maatansa* (No. 1, Part II).

[3] *Kūra.* Vide note on [4] *kūra* (No. 6, Part II).

[4] *Ta tafi.* Past tense. Vide note on [13] *yā zō* (No. 1, Part II).

[5] *Nā je nā taras.* Aorist tense. Vide note on [13] *yā zō* (No. 1, Part II).

[6] *Kāshe.* Note long *ā*. *Kashe* is a different word.

[7] *Nā je . . . naa kayar.* Aorist and future tense. Vide note on [13] *yā zō* (No. 1, Part II).

[8] *Adaa* = *Adua.*

[9] *Sabkō.* Note the idea of 'to me', 'for me' in the *o* termination. Vide note on [2] *karbōwa* (No. 1, Part I).

[10] *Gudānō*, 'ran and came here'. Vide above, [9] *sabkō.*

[11] *Maatar.* Note the definite article. Vide note on [7] *dōkin nan* (No. 1, Part I).

[12] *Kungurus.* Vide note on [21] *kungurus* (No. 1, Part II).

No. 25

[1] *Gātanan.* Vide note on [3] *gātanan* (No. 1, Part II).

[2] *Ya je . . . ya . . . ya nōmē.* Past tense. Vide note on [13] *yā zō* (No. 1, Part II).

[3] *Kyale.* Spelt *kelē.*

[4] *Kūra.* Vide note on [4] *kūra* (No. 6, Part II).

[5] *Maatarsa.* Vide note on [4] *maatansa* (No. 1, Part II).

[6] *Gidan.* Vide note on [7] *dōkin nan* (No. 1, Part I).

[7] *Kā sani . . . idan kā je.* Aorist tense. Vide note on [13] *yā zō* (No. 1, Part II).

[8] *Mu giyāra wuri.* Here we have a record of an ancient heathen custom among the Hausas before their conversion to Mohammedanism. A similar custom is found among the Mang'anja of Nyassaland.

[9] *Naa . . . kaa.* Future tense. Vide note on future tense under [13] *yā zō* (No. 1, Part II).

[10] *Kungurus.* Vide note on [21] *kungurus* (No. 1, Part II).

No. 26

[1] *Alkume.* Here also called *būzūzu*, 'the dung beetle'. An onomatopoetic word.

[2] *Gātanan.* Vide note on [3]*gātanan* (No. 1, Part II).

[3] *Ya yi.* Past tense. Vide note on [13]*yā zō* (No. 1, Part II).

[4] *Gayā.* Vide note on [4]*gayā* (No. 4, Part II).

[5] *Muzūrū*, 'a tom cat'. Fem. *kyanwa.* The tom cat is a regular bad character according to the Hausas. Cats are nevertheless rather held in awe by the Hausas. Cf. the status of cats in ancient Egypt.

[6] *Kūra.* Vide note on [4]*kūra* (No. 6, Part II).

[7] *Yā ji.* Aorist tense. Vide note on [13]*yā zō* (No. 1, Part II).

[8] *Kare yā kashe . . . kūra tā.* This story contains excellent examples of the past and aorist tenses all through; note the correctness with which each is used in turn. Vide note on these tenses under [13]*yā zō* (No. 1, Part II).

[9] *Sannū.* Vide note on [14]*sannū* (No. 5, Part II).

[10] *Hata.* Arabic = *har.*

[11] *Alhāli.* Arabic = *kadan.*

[12] *Karfī.* Vide note on [10]*karfī* (No. 9, Part II).

[13] *Kungurus.* Vide note on [21]*kungurus* (No. 1, Part II).

No. 27

[1] *Gizo.* Vide note on [25]*gizō* (No. 6, Part II).

[2] *Sun. Su*, 'to look for anything in the water'. Cf. the Fante root *su*, 'water', but this is probably only a coincidence.

[3] *Ya kāma.* Past tense. Vide note on [13]*yā zō* (No. 1, Part II).

[4] *Banda*, 'to roast over a fire'.

[5] *Makwarwa.* Also *fakara.*

[6] *Naa yi.* Vide note on the future tense under [13]*yā zō* (No. 1, Part II).

[7] *Kyale.* Spelt *kelē.*

[8] *Banke.* As *buga.*

[9] *Karfī.* Vide note on [10]*karfī* (No. 9, Part II).

[10] *Churakai. Churaki*, an iron skewer about 12 in. long, the point slightly bent, used to burn the skins of horses, donkeys, and cattle, to cure them of colds.

[11] *Chuwai.* Supposed to imitate the burning flesh.

[12] *Maatar.* Vide note on [4] *maatansa* (No. 1, Part II).

[13] *Asha.* Not to be confused with *ashē,* 'indeed', 'truly', which is a different word.

[14] *Yā fi.* Aorist tense. Vide note on [13] *yā zō* (No. 1, Part II).

[15] *Nā ji.* As above, [14] *yā fi.*

[16] *Zākin.* Note the definite article. Vide note on [7] *dōkin nan* (No. 1, Part I).

[17] *Kaa gani.* Vide note on the future tense under [13] *yā zō* (No. 1, Part II).

[18] *Kaa ga.* As above, [17] *kaa gani.*

[19] *Kungurus.* Vide note on [21] *kungurus* (No. 1, Part II).

No. 28

[1] *Gizō.* Vide note on [25] *gizō* (No. 6, Part II).

[2] *Ya ji . . . da su-ka-kōmō.* Past tense. Vide note on [13] *yā zō* (No. 1, Part II).

[3] *Zaa shi.* Vide note on future tense under [13] *yā zō* (No. 1, Part II).

[4] *Su-na-chin.* Vide note on [8] *aka-bōye* (No. 1, Part I). Here *chi* is a verbal noun.

[5] *Daa.* Vide note on [16] *daa* (No. 12, Part II). Here the *daa* in conditional sentence is omitted. Or the *daa* here may be for *dā,* 'of old', 'long ago'.

[6] *Shāmu.* For *sāmu.* Imitating the spider's supposed lisp.

[7] *Yāyi,* 'straws', 'refuse'. Possible derivation, *yas,* 'to cast out'.

[8] *Tā yi.* Aorist tense. Vide note on [13] *yā zō* (No. 1, Part II).

[9] *Yā yi.* As [8] *tā yi* above.

[10] *Ayāhu akubai* = *Aluhu akubar.* Cf. [6] *shāmu* above.

[11] *Naa zō.* Vide note on the future tense under [13] *yā zō* (No. 1, Part II).

[12] *Tsugunē.* Present participle. Vide note on [12] *zamnē* (No. 1, Part II).

[13] *La iya'.* For *la ila'.* Vide note on [19] *la ila'* (No. 8, Part II).

[14] *Ku bai* = *Ku bari.* Imitating the spider.

[15] *Nā gani . . ., naa tafi.* *Nā,* aorist, *naa,* future. Vide note on [13] *yā zō* (No. 1, Part II).

[16] *Kungurus.* Vide note on [21] *kungurus* (No. 1, Part II).

No. 29

[1] *Gizō.* Vide note on [25] *gizō* (No. 6, Part II).
[2] *Maata.* Vide note on [4] *maatansa* (No. 1, Part II).
[3] *Wāke,* 'bean'.
[4] *Ta haifi, ta . . . ta . . .* Past tense. Vide note on [13] *yā zō* (No. 1, Part II).
[5] *Dan.* Note the definite article. Vide note on [7] *dōkin nan* (No. 1, Part I).
[6] *Tanbō.* As *kangō.*
[7] *Sāniar nan.* Cf. [13] *dōkin nan* (No. 1, Part I).
[8] *Nā kōmō.* Aorist tense. Vide note on [13] *yā zō* (No. 1, Part II).
[9] *Naa yi.* Future tense. Vide note on [13] *yā zō* (No. 1, Part II).
[10] *Shauki. Sauki.*
[11] *Yayafa. Rarafa.*
[12] *Dadi.* Note *dādi* is a different word, means 'sweet'.
[13] *Banbadāwa.* Followers of a chief who sing his praises.
[14] *Tuntoja. Tujewa,* 'to pluck'.
[15] *Tafia tasa.* Vide note on [24] *tafia tasa* (No. 1, Part I).
[16] *Kungurus.* Vide note on [21] *kungurus* (No. 1, Part II).

No. 30

[1] *Gizō.* Vide note on [25] *gizō* (No. 6, Part II).
[2] *Ya tafi . . . ya che.* Past tense. Vide note on [13] *yā zō* (No. 1, Part II).
[3] *Shaki yuwa, dōyina. Sarkin rua, dōrina,* to imitate the supposed lisp of the spider.
[4] *Tā yi.* Aorist tense. Vide note on [13] *yā zō* (No. 1, Part II).
[5] *Taa ba.* Future tense. Vide note on the future tense under [13] *yā zō* (No. 1, Part II).
[6] *Maatarsa.* Vide note on [4] *maatansa* (No. 1, Part II).
[7] *Gizāma na kōki.* Kōki, 'the praying mantis', said by the Hausas to be the wife of the spider.
[8] *Yanju . . . shaki . . .* Imitating the spider.
[9] *Maatansa.* Better *maatarsa.*
[10] *Bajimsō.* Bajamsu on the Volta river, north of *Kratchi.*
[11] *Dōkin.* Note the definite article. Vide note on [7] *dōkin nan* (No. 1, Part I).
[12] *Tā ba.* Aorist. Vide note on [13] *yā zō* (No. 1, Part II).
[13] *Nā jāwō, nā kāwō.* As above, [12] *tā ba.*
[14] *Kungurus.* Vide note on [21] *kungurus* (No. 1, Part II).

PART IV. CUSTOMS AND ARTS

No. 31

[1] *Bābi.* Arabic, 'gate', 'gateway'. Hence 'entrance', 'beginning'.

[2] *Alaada.* Arabic. Also *ada*, 'custom', 'religious observance'.

[3] *Sūna.* Note long vowel. *Suna* is a different word.

[4] *Nana. Nanga.*

[5] *Kā gani.* Aorist tense. Vide note on [13] *yā zō* (No. 1, Part II).

[6] *Gu. Wuri.*

[7] *Kyale.* Spelt *kelē.*

[8] *Sādu. Gamu.*

[9] *Uban.* Note the definite article. Vide note on [7] *dōkin nan* (No. 1, Part I).

[10] *Kurdi alif.* Equivalent to 6*d.* English currency; 500 cowries = 3*d.*

[11] *Kworia guda.* A standard of currency, 100 kola nuts value 10*s.*

[12] *Mātan.* Vide note on [4] *maatansa* (No. 1, Part II).

[13] *Marmarin.* Plur. *marmaruna*, 'sexual desire'. Used of the female for the male.

[14] *Shāta*, 'slashed white cloth'.

[15] *Lālāta.* Lit. 'worthless', i.e. it is something thrown in as it were.

[16] *Lalē.* A decoction of the leaves of the *Lawsonia inermis.* Henna, used by the Hausas to stain the nails; in the case of a bride the whole feet are stained up to the ankles, the hands to the wrists.

[17] *Jawābi.* Arabic = *magana.*

[18] *Dārō.* As *tasa.*

[19] *Ta zuba.* A drop of the henna is put on the girl, and as soon as this is done the person who has done so sounds the *gūda.* Vide note [4] *gūda* (No. 16, Part II).

[20] *Abuyar amarīa.* Vide note on [23] *abuya* (No. 5, Part II). This custom of having a pretence bride is probably a survival, and was intended to distract the attentions of any evil spirits from the true bride.

[21] *Zaa. Su* understood.

[22] *Gūda.* Vide note on [4] *gūda* (No. 16, Part II).

[23] *Tā je.* Aorist tense. Vide note on [13] *yā zō* (No. 1, Part II).

[24] *Dākin mijinta.* Each wife has a hut of her own, where she sleeps. When the husband wants a particular wife he does not go to her hut but she comes to his sleeping-place, called *turaka.*

[25] *Kari.* As *kyeauta.*

No. 32

[1] *Lalē.* Vide note on [16] *lalē* (No. 31, Part IV). The bridegroom is supposed to have this done without warning. The writer's *mālam* was touched with henna when at prayers.

[2] *Haīla.* Arabic. Hausa idiom, *yin jini, pashe salla.*

[3] *Wa kīla.* Arabic. In Hausa, *wadansu sun fadi.*

[4] *Suna.* Cf. *sūna*, 'a name'.

[5] *Mātansa.* Vide [4] *maatansa* (No. 1, Part II).

No. 33

[1] *Faslun.* Note the definite article in the *rufua bissa bīū.* Vide note on [7] *dōkin nan* (No. 1, Part I).

[2] *Yā ji.* Aorist tense. Vide note on [13] *yā zō* (No. 1, Part II).

[3] *Waliyina.* Arabic, 'guardian' (*wali*). The person who gives the bride away, father, mother, or guardian. The dower, *sadak* (Hausa *sadaki*), is fixed by the guardian, and no marriage can take place unless the woman is so represented. *Wakīli* used in a similar sense.

[4] *Lāmu.* *Yerda.*

[5] *Kurdi alfin.* 2,000 cowries, value 1*s*.

[6] *Gōrō hamsin.* Vide note on [11] *kworia guda* (No. 31, Part IV).

[7] *Abuyar amarīa.* Vide note on [20] *abuyar amarīa* (No. 31, Part IV).

No. 34

[1] *Wakīli.* Vide note on [3] *waliyina* (No. 33, Part IV).

[2] *Tarālia.* *Yerda.*

[3] *Alahuma . . . wasalim.* These lines are Arabic.

[4] *Alahuma . . . amin.* As above.

[5] *Ya wakīlche.* *Ya che.*

[6] *Nakadan.* Arabic.

[7] *Ajalan.* Arabic.

No. 35

[1] *Faslun.* Note the double *rufua bisa* the definite article. Vide note on [7] *dōkin nan* (No. 1, Part I).

[2] *Yā.* Aorist tense. Vide note on [13] *yā zō* (No. 1, Part II).

[3] *Azāna sūna.* Note the idiom for naming a child is *zāna sūna.* *Sūna*, long *ū*. *Suna* is a different word.

No. 36

[1] *Faslun.* Vide note on [1]*faslun* (No. 35, Part IV).

[2] *Alahuma . . . majidun.* Arabic.

[3] *Fātimata kō Hadijatu.* The first a daughter, the second a wife, of Mohammed.

[4] *Wanzāmai.* The infant's head is shaved.

No. 37

[1] *Bābun.* Vide note on [2]*bābi* (No. 1, Part II).

[2] *Sha gaba,* 'to circumcise'; also *kāchia.* As applied to a woman, *makasche.*

[3] *Rāme.* A small hole about half a foot across is dug, and the foreskin is buried in it.

[4] *Aririke.* Reduplicated from *rika.*

[5] *Yā warke.* Aorist tense. Vide note on [13]*yā zō* (No. 1, Part II).

[6] *Wurin.* Note the definite article. Vide note on [7]*dōkin nan* (No. 1, Part I).

No. 38

[1] *Faslun.* Vide note on [1]*faslun* (No. 35, Part IV).

[2] *Kāchiar.* Also *makasche.*

[3] *Māta.* Vide note on [4]*maatansa* (No. 1, Part II).

[4] *Maatar nan.* Definite article. Vide note on [7]*dōkin nan* (No. 1, Part I).

[5] *Kāmō,* 'seize and draw towards', the latter idea expressed in the *o* termination of the verb. Vide note on [2]*karbōwa* (No. 1, Part I).

[6] *Shārō.* As above, [5]*kāmō,* 'cutting towards', *o* termination.

[7] *Sābōni.* Soap made of ashes (wood).

No. 39

[1] *Bābun.* Vide note on [2]*bābi* (No. 1, Part II).

[2] *Alkibla. Gabas.*

[3] *Kabri.* Arabic. Hausa *kushēwa.*

[4] *Wāta fudu da kwāna gōma.* The *idat* period of retreat, enjoined by Mohammedan law. *Idat,* Arabic; in Hausa *takaba.*

No. 40

[1] *Faslun.* Vide note on [1]*faslun* (No. 35, Part IV).

[2] *Agina wata karama chiki.* A ledge is thus formed all round on which the cross-sticks are laid, the idea being of course to keep the earth from falling on the body.

Compare the *mudzi* of the Mananja grave, where an ordinary pit is first dug and then a side niche or room made in which the body is placed.

[3] *Asasāre.* Note the reduplication.

[4] *Karfī.* Vide note on [10] *karfī* (No. 9, Part II).

[5] *Amaida gabansa gabas.* The corpse is laid full length, lying on its right side, the head to south, feet to north. The grave is very narrow, just wide enough to let the body in sideways.

[6] *Yā kāre.* Aorist tense. Vide note on [13] *yā zō* (No. 1, Part II).

No. 41

[1] *Yā kārē.* Aorist tense. Vide note on [13] *yā zō* (No. 1, Part II).

No. 42

[1] *Bābun.* Vide note on [2] *bābi* (No. 1, Part II).

[2] *Chiniki.* Any kind of trade or business.

[3] *Yā halalta.* Vide note on [13] *yā zō* (No. 1, Part II).

[4] *Chin kūra.* Lit. 'the eating of the hyena'. Vide note on [4] *kūra* (No. 6, Part II).

[5] *Kausuwa.* Also *kasua.*

[6] *Sha jiki.* Lit. 'drink the body'. Any second-hand garment is so called.

[7] *Zanbar dari.* 100,000 cowries = 50*s.*

[8] *Nā rage . . . naa saye.* Aorist and future. Vide note on [13] *yā zō* (No. 1, Part II).

[9] *Muu.* Future tense. Vide note on [13] *yā zō* (No. 1, Part II).

[10] *Idānu guda daia.* Vide note on [13] *idānu guda* (No. 6, Part II).

[11] *Murgu.* Work done by a slave who is away from his master for the time being.

No. 43

[1] *Tā game.* Aorist tense. Vide note on [13] *yā zō* (No. 1, Part II).

[2] *Yā fadi.* As above. Aorist tense.

No. 44

[1] *Bismi alāhi alrahmani alrahīmi.* Pronounce *bismi 'lāhi 'rahmani 'rahīmi.* Vide note on [1] *bismi alāhi* (No. 1, Part I).

[2] *Mutun mutumi.* Brass castings; 'Benin' figures.

[3] *Karfē.* Vide note on [10] *karfī* (No. 9, Part II).

[4] *Ashainya rāna shi būshē.* This is the first stage in the process of making. Vide Plate III, Fig. 1 *a*, and Plate II, Fig. 1 *b*.

[5] *Shi-na-walkīa.* Here ends the second stage of the process. Vide Plate III, Fig. 2 *a*, and Plate II, Fig. 2 *b*.

[6] *Zankāyen.* Note the definite article. Vide note on [7] *dōkin nan* (No. 1, Part I).

[7] *Yā kāre.* Aorist. Vide note on [13] *yā zō* (No. 1, Part II).

[8] *Yā gama.* As above, [7] *yā kāre.*

[9] *Mutun mutumin.* Note the definite article. Vide note on [7] *dōkin nan* (No. 1, Part I).

[10] *Saanan aparpashe.* This final stage is illustrated in Plates II and III, Figs. 3 *a* and 3 *b*.

The following notes are from an article by Professor Henry Balfour, which appeared in the *Journal of the Royal Anthropological Institute*, vol. xl, 1910:

'Of the specimens secured by Mr. Rattray, the clay head (Plates II and III, Figs. 1 *a* and 1 *b*), which forms the first stage in the process, is 27 cm. high, and is carefully fashioned to form the core on which the wax model may be built. It is of well-worked clay, and while accurately shaped as regards the general outline of the desired design, is not worked up in detail, and has no suggestion of ears and other surface details. It is merely the base on which the wax may be spread to a more or less uniform thickness. The core is hollow, with a view no doubt of giving it an equal thickness with that of the outer casting-mould so as to admit of a uniform rate of heating and of cooling throughout the mass.

'Figs. 2 *a* and 2 *b* show a similar clay core enveloped in the finished wax model. In this brass model all the details required in the brass casting appear. The wax is of an average thickness of about 3 mm., the ears being much thinner and unsupported by the core.

'In the next stage (Figs. 3 *a* and 3 *b*, also Figs. 4 and 5) the wax model having been first completely encased in clay to a thickness varying from about 1·5 cm. to 3·3 cm., is melted and allowed to escape through the duct (seen in Fig. 3 *a* (at *a*) and in Fig. 5) which is left for the purpose. The molten brass is poured in through the same duct, and if the casting is successful completely fills the space formerly occupied by the wax, the result being an exact *replica* of the wax model in brass.

'Some of Ali's designs in brass are fairly ambitious, as may be seen in the examples shown in Plates I and II. In II is seen a chief on horseback attended by his wives, one with a child on her back, and sundry retainers; at the top a lion surrounded by four cocks.

Fig. 4.

Fig. 5.

'The other piece (Plate I) has a male and female figure each about 50 cm. high, designed to form supporters of a pair of small elephant's tusks. Behind each figure is a dog. The large hollow cast head suspended between the figures is hung from a short flat bar furnished with two rings set at an angle so that they could be slipped over the points of the tusks, from which the head was suspended.

'The links seen hanging below the head are for attaching to the loose links upon two rings fitting round the tusks about halfway down, by which the head was held steady and prevented from swinging. Mr. Rattray tells me that these elaborate designs are probably now purely fanciful, and without any special symbolic meaning or obvious utility.

'Although the products of Ali's foundry fall far short of the finer bronze castings of the old artists of Benin, they are none the less a very creditable production, and betray considerable knowledge of the higher *cire perdue* technique. They are interesting, not only as examples of a slightly degenerate survival of a once flourishing local art, but also as giving an insight into the details of the process whereby the wonderful ancient Benin bronze castings were achieved.'

No. 45

[1] *Bābun.* Vide note on [2] *bābi* (No. 1, Part II).

[2] *Gashin.* Note the definite article. Vide note on [7] *dōkin nan* (No. 1, Part I).

No. 46

[1] *Yā yi.* Aorist. Vide note on [13] *yā zō* (No. 1, Part II).

[2] *Nā chi, nā . . . kā ga bākina.* Note the aorist tense. Vide note above, [1] *yā yi.*

The *mālam* who wrote this understood the book ended here. The proverbs were added later, and are written by a different hand.

PART V. PROVERBS

[1] *Muzūrū.* Vide note on [5] *muzūrū* (No. 26, Part III).

[2] *Baje.* A dance.

[3] *Bunga.* A single mound of earth in which the Indian corn is planted. Cf. *kunya*, 'a long furrow'.

[4] *Agwāgwa.* Only fowls are offered as sacrifices.

[5] *Wa masani . . . sai wāwa?* This is supposed to be said to a man who is remonstrating with another because he is lavish in what he gives his relations.

[6] *Kā kōre.* Aorist tense. Vide note on [13] *yā zō* (No. 1, Part II).

[7] *Kinwa.* Pronounce *kyanwa.* Vide note on [5] *muzūrū* (No. 26, Part III).

[8] *Akwia . . . kunne.* If a goat is troublesome and is always going into a hut and upsetting things it is caught and its ears are slit.

[9] *Gātari ga nāma . . . wuta.* Said to two persons who have been vowing vengeance against each other by a third person who sees them meet, to egg them on.

[10] *Gidansu.* Note only the head of the household will say *gidana,*

'my house'; any other member of the family will say *gidamu*, so *gidansa* would only be used when speaking of the owner. Here the son is spoken of, hence *gidansu*, not *gidansa*.

[11] *Adāwa*. Arabic. Hausa, *kiyaya*.

[12] *Dan karamin tsugunī*. An expression used to denote a small settlement.

[13] *Lalē*. Vide note on [16] *lalē* (No. 31, Part IV).

[14] *Idānun*. Note the definite article. Vide note on [7] *dōkin nan* (No. 1, Part I). Note the singular pronoun *ya*.

[15] *Māra*. Vide note on [13] *māra* (No. 5, Part II).

[16] *Gudin*. Probably *gwodin*. *Gwoda*, 'to show'.

[17] *Wīar nika . . . tā kāre*. Grain is ground (between two flat stones). The first grinding (*pashe*) is gathered up and re-ground; this second grinding is called *tushi*.

[18] *Dākin*. P. 276, Proverb No. 128. *Dākin kasa da kasa*. An all mud house, called *sōro*.

[19] *Māku*. Chief of Bida in the Nupe country.

[20] *Tamat*. Arabic. Hausa, *yā kāre*, 'it is finished'.